WEST VALLEY COLLEGE LIBRARY

3 1216 00193 8591

Praise for Seeing White

"Introducing students to the concept of racial privilege is fundamental to teaching about racism, yet hard to do. *Seeing White* is a great resource for those who undertake this important work, providing an excellent primer for classroom discussion." —**Beverly Daniel Tatum**, president, Spelman College; author of *Why Are All the Black Kids Sitting Together in the Cafeteria?*

"*Seeing White* engage... **DATE DUE** ...e needing to be investigated in all its human... great interdisciplinary reach of the authors opens up, for students and all of us, the changing ways in which race has been made over a long history and how it is remade and contested today." —**David Roediger**, University of Illinois; author of *How Race Survived U.S. History*

"This book is a rare gem. There are lots of books on race, and some on privilege, but none brings it all together in one place in such an illuminating and thoughtful way. None so ably connects psychology, identity politics, economics, and policy to explain the origins of race and how it is socially modified over time. The content is both enlightening and challenging, and the examples and stories used in this book will help students really understand the complicated issues of how race affects all of our lives." —**Nyla R. Branscombe**, University of Kansas

"With remarkable clarity, the authors have made the often invisible workings of culture both visible and comprehensible. Focusing on one of the most knotty of problems—entrenched assumptions about racial difference and inequality—this important book will offer students the opportunity to see the familiar in unfamiliar ways, and to challenge the mental baggage that so many carry inside their heads and hearts. The book's goal is to lay the groundwork for a better historical understanding of ideas that too often remain unexamined." —**Stuart Ewen**, Hunter College, CUNY

"This book will challenge students, and it is guaranteed to stimulate discussion and debate. If you seek a stepping stone to debate, discussion, and engaged learning, *Seeing White* is an excellent choice." —**Chris Crandall**, University of Kansas

D0253482

"Now when some would describe our times as post-race, *Seeing White* offers its readers an opportunity to rethink race and power from an interdisciplinary perspective drawing on sociology, economics, and psychology. The great accomplishment of the book is its appeal to readers to reflect on their own view of race as well as their relationship to the privilege of whiteness. *Seeing White* is a must read for all of us." — **Patricia Ticineto Clough**, The Graduate Center, CUNY.

Seeing White

WEST VALLEY COLLEGE LIBRARY

Seeing White

An Introduction to White Privilege and Race

Jean Halley, Amy Eshleman,
and Ramya Mahadevan Vijaya

ROWMAN & LITTLEFIELD PUBLISHERS, INC.
Lanham • Boulder • New York • Toronto • Plymouth, UK

Published by Rowman & Littlefield Publishers, Inc.
A wholly owned subsidiary of The Rowman & Littlefield Publishing Group, Inc.
4501 Forbes Boulevard, Suite 200, Lanham, Maryland 20706
http://www.rowmanlittlefield.com

Estover Road, Plymouth PL6 7PY, United Kingdom

Copyright © 2011 by Rowman & Littlefield Publishers, Inc.

All rights reserved. No part of this book may be reproduced in any form or by any
electronic or mechanical means, including information storage and retrieval systems,
without written permission from the publisher, except by a reviewer who may quote
passages in a review.

British Library Cataloguing in Publication Information Available

Library of Congress Cataloging-in-Publication Data

Halley, Jean O'Malley, 1967–
  Seeing white : an introduction to white privilege and race / Jean Halley, Amy
Eshleman, and Ramya Mahadevan Vijaya.
    p. cm.
  Includes bibliographical references.
  ISBN 978-1-4422-0307-5 (cloth : alk. paper) — ISBN 978-1-4422-0308-2 (pbk. : alk.
paper) — ISBN 978-1-4422-0309-9 (electronic)
  1. Race awareness. 2. Whites—Race identity. 3. Race discrimination. I. Eshleman,
Amy, 1974– II. Vijaya, Ramya Mahadevan, 1974– III. Title.
√ HT1521.H265 2010 |
  305.809'073—dc22

                                                                        2011004624

∞™ The paper used in this publication meets the minimum requirements of
American National Standard for Information Sciences—Permanence of Paper
for Printed Library Materials, ANSI/NISO Z39.48-1992.

Printed in the United States of America

HT
1521
.H265
2011

For our mentors, Patricia Ticineto Clough, Christian S. Crandall,
Jane R. Dickie, and Kathleen O'Malley, who helped us to see more clearly,

and to our students, may they live in a more just world.

27.95

8/2012

Contents

Acknowledgments

To borrow from Sir Isaac Newton's famous quote, we "stand on the shoulders of giants." In writing this book, indeed in living and shaping our own lives, we three are deeply indebted to innumerable scholars, activists, and writers. Jean Halley and Amy Eshleman are well aware that our whiteness has benefited us in countless ways, including in no small part providing us this opportunity to write this textbook on race with Ramya Vijaya. Here we wish to reiterate what Tim Wise notes in his wonderful book about white privilege. "You are not reading this book because [we are] great writer[s] . . . or particularly smart. There are lots of folks, especially persons of color, who know a lot more about racism than [we] do."* For all kinds of reasons to be discussed in the upcoming pages, white privilege, the privilege of Halley and Eshleman being white, helped to open up the possibility that we three would have an easier time being *considered* legitimate ones to write this book on race. Nonetheless, our small contribution rests on the work of many, many other race scholars both of color and white. To all of them, we owe a great debt.

In particular, we are profoundly grateful to the following brilliant and brave thinkers who have inspired us to write this book: Gloria Anzaldúa, César Estrada Chávez, Grace M. Cho, Patricia Ticineto Clough, Jane R. Dickie, W. E. B. Du Bois, Ralph Ellison, Louise Erdrich, Stuart Ewen, Frantz Fanon, bell hooks, Audre Lorde, Cherríe Moraga, Toni Morrison, Rakesh R. Rajani, Beverly Daniel Tatum, Patricia J. Williams, and Malcolm X. To our students and others who have not yet read their works, we hope you, too, will explore and learn from their writings.

Many more people were involved and very helpful in writing our book than we can possibly acknowledge. We hold deep gratitude to so many. Among them, Michael S. Kimmel wrote a textbook on gender that inspired us to emulate it. He was incredibly generous in reviewing an early draft of our book proposal and connecting us to individuals who helped us to find our home at Rowman & Littlefield Publishers, Inc. Alexa S. Dietrich and Celeste Marie Gagnon fed us wonderful anthropological work regarding the nonbiological nature (so to speak) of race and provided invaluable feedback throughout our writing. Nicholas P. Richardson gave us a smart metaphor for uncritical multicultural programs. Laurence J. Nolan provided critical insight on our discussion of cranial capacity. Ron Nerio gave us permission to use his powerful unpublished memoir, and he generously read and offered feedback on drafts of some chapters. Sofia Bautista Pertuz, Jacob Segal, and Janet Spector read and gave us very thoughtful feedback on several chapters as well as interesting discussion questions. Segal read numerous drafts, helped with the research, and assisted us in understanding the guaranteed income.

As always, Donna Toscano helped in innumerable ways, getting things taken care of for us before we even realized something needed to be done. We are so grateful to our research assistants Megan Allen, Sophie Fonner, Tiarra Rogers, and Mary Beth Somich who performed a wide range of tasks that made our lives easier and the book significantly better. Among their many undertakings, they contributed discussion questions, read drafts of pieces of the book, and gave us feedback as well as performed ethnographic fieldwork, studying race on one of our college campuses. We are very thankful to several anonymous reviewers of our proposal and final manuscript for their helpful suggestions. Finally, we owe a deep debt to all of our students who, over the years with great insight and patience, discussed race, class, gender, sexuality, and social power with us.

Each of us would also like to acknowledge our gratitude to our personal networks of support:

Jean Halley: To my very dear family, Kathleen O'Malley, Janet Spector, Lore Segal, Kate Maxfield, Andrew Maxfield, Sharon Saydah, Rakesh Rajani, Maggie Bangser, Beatrice Segal, David Segal, Richard Holland, and most especially, Jacob Segal, Isaiah Halley-Segal, and Kathleen Halley-Segal, I offer my profound gratitude, and so much love. They relentlessly supported me as I struggled through writing a book about a deeply complicated, and at times heartbreaking, subject.

Amy Eshleman: I am deeply grateful to my family for their encouragement. Nick, thank you for listening critically and offering your honest perspective to countless questions. Without the generous support of my parents, David and Lorraine, I cannot imagine who I would be today. Thank you to Jenny, Mark, David, Lindsey, and Madeline for the joy you bring to my life.

Ramya Vijaya: An immeasurable gratitude is due to my parents, Vijaya and Mahadevan, and to Usha, Renuka, and Radhika for their generous support of all my endeavors. Much love and thanks to Bill for his unstinting support and comforting good humor about this, at times, very emotional topic. Thank you to Bidisha for the numerous discussions of all my work and critical feedback whenever I have any doubts.

Note

* Tim Wise, *White Like Me: Reflections on Race from a Privileged Son* (Brooklyn, N.Y.: Soft Skull Press, 2005), 10.

CHAPTER ONE

~

The Invisibility of Whiteness

A white boy who is very close with one of the authors of this text has been raised in a predominantly white, small town in the Midwest. On a family trip to the big city in 2008, the boy, then eight years old, enjoyed playing in an interactive water room at a children's museum. Always a gregarious and friendly child, the white adults who accompanied the boy—including one of the authors of this text—enjoyed watching him play with other children as he enjoyed the activities of the museum. Upon exiting the exhibit, in a crowded hallway filled with a racially diverse collection of individuals, the white boy announced proudly and loudly, "I just made an African American friend!"

The white adults accompanying the white boy were surprised by the boy's exclamation and by their own reactions to it. They wondered why the boy had been so cognizant of the race of his new playmate, questioning what his understanding of race—his own and that of others—might be. They considered where the boy had picked up the term he chose to describe the race of the playmate, pondering how race might be addressed in the boy's school or in media he viewed. They wondered how often they themselves addressed race with the boy and how they might have shaped—or failed to shape—his understanding of race. They were also disquieted by their own sense of embarrassment at the loud announcement by this white boy, especially because the bystanders who were likely to have overheard included many individuals of color. How might the bystanders interpret the boy's words? How did the announcement reflect on the boy and his adult companions? How might the new friend have felt if he had overheard himself being referred to as an "African American friend"?

The boy regularly makes friends whenever the opportunity is available, but he had never before announced that he "just made a white friend." He clearly noticed and categorized this playmate based on race. We will explore what incidents like this reveal about whiteness and about the visibility of race.

How Do We Come to Know Things?

In thinking about race, it is interesting to ask, *how* have we come to know what we know about race? Indeed, how have we come to know *anything* about anything? What does it mean to "know" something? How can we be sure that what we "know" really is true? People in different cultures and times sometimes understand the world in very different ways. Who is wrong and who is right?

People also learn about the world in different ways. Diverse cultures have different authorities that they trust and different processes to access knowledge. Are they all valid?

As an example, we might consider feudal times in Europe. Most people in feudal Europe were very poor (extremely poor by middle-class standards in the United States today). Most people lived as farmers. They farmed land that belonged to someone else, to the aristocracy, the kings, queens, lords, and other nobility that ruled over the various geographic areas of Europe. The Catholic Church existed in close connection with and strongly supportive of the aristocracy. In exchange for being allowed to use the land, peasants paid a tithe (or rent) in the food that they produced to the aristocracy. Historians Stuart Ewen and Elizabeth Ewen note, "There was a vast chasm between the material abundance of the Church and aristocracy and the scarcity experienced by the peasantry, and this system was represented as the immutable order of things."[1]

How did the aristocracy come to own all of that land? Well, today we know that they *took it*, by force. Yet in feudal times, most people believed that the aristocracy owned everything and ruled over everyone because God wanted it that way. People thought that "social inequality was the way of God."[2] They believed God had chosen the aristocracy and that the aristocracy was a distinct group of humans, almost a species. In this thinking, called the "Great Chain of Being," the peasants were also like a distinct species. People accepted as "truth" that humans were born into the group where they belonged according to God's will. Sharply distinct from the pull-yourself-up-by-your-bootstraps and change-your-lot-in-life thinking common in the United States today, people's thinking in feudal times held that one should not, indeed one *could not*, change one's position in life. One was born a peasant much like a cow was born a cow. As far as we know, cows do not dream of being horses someday; and in feudal times, peasants did not dream of being kings and queens.

So how did people in feudal times come to "know" all of these "truths"—that the poor were meant to be poor and the aristocracy was in control because God wanted it that way? How did people come to "know" that this was God's will? Who expressed God's will in feudal times?

As you might guess, the aristocracy and the feudal Catholic Church (supported by the aristocracy) dictated God's will, claiming that God had appointed them to voice His wishes. (During this time period in Europe, the Catholic Church understood God to be decidedly male.) Who benefited from these dictates? The aristocracy and the Church. Ewen and Ewen write about this political and economic system:

> The Bible was the Word of God, the universal law, but its interpretation was kept in the hands of the privileged few who were sanctioned to read it. Biblical interpretation tended to uphold the immense social and political landholding power of the nobility and the Church. . . . Although feudal power was often held and defended by the sword, it was justified by the Word. The monopoly over the Word, over literacy, and over the ability to interpret what was read, was a fundamental aspect of rule.[3]

So in terms of the issue of knowledge and how we come to "know" something, we can see from the example of feudalism that different cultures believe in different authorities. Feudal society believed in the authority of God expressed through the aristocracy and the Church. Today, in many places in the world, including Europe, the United States, and most western[4] industrialized nations, we tend to turn to science for knowledge, instead of religion. Instead of the aristocracy and the Church translating God's wishes for us, scientists using the scientific method work to gain what we understand to be truths about our world and ourselves.

It is interesting to note that, in the above example, someone benefited from the "knowledge," the "truth" that everyone believed in. The way of thinking in feudal Europe worked to reinforce the economic and social power of the aristocracy and the Church. Social psychologists Don Operario and Susan T. Fiske define *power* as "the disproportionate ability of some individuals or groups to control other people's outcomes."[5] *Economic power* entails control over resources such as land or water, or even symbolic resources (like money today). In this book, we use the term *social power* to mean economic power as well as the amorphous capacity of dominant groups—groups who control economic resources—to control cultural production; in other words, to establish their cultures and norms as the dominant ones. In this book, because the term *social power* comes up repeatedly, we use the terms *social power* and *power* interchangeably.

In reading our book, we ask that you keep the story of inequality in feudal Europe in mind. *Ideologies* like the Great Chain of Being—ways of thinking and commonly held beliefs—in feudal Europe benefited some over others. How might our ways of thinking about race in the contemporary United States, and in our history, also benefit some over others?

In this book, we argue that critically examining the common ways of thinking in the United States teaches us more about social power than about "objective facts." (In chapter 2, we question race as an objective fact and challenge you to consider the potential bias in science.)

(In)Visibility of Whiteness

The authors of this text challenge you to consider why the white eight-year-old boy announced that he had made an "African American friend" when the boy had never announced the race of a white friend. Legal scholar Barbara J. Flagg argues that white people are often not conscious of being white.[6] Often whites simply perceive themselves as "normal" or "just human" and fail to notice their own race.[7] While whiteness may be invisible to whites, whites tend to be aware of the races of people of color.[8]

In this text, we seek to challenge readers to consider what it means for a white person to perceive of himself or herself as "normal" while seeing others as having a race. We challenge you to consider the extent to which whiteness is invisible and the implications of this. We invite you to critically examine what it means to perceive oneself as normal. In the social sciences, a *norm* is a social expectation[9]—a description of how one is expected to act or what one is expected to believe within a given social setting.[10] Scholars who study the experience of being white in the United States and the concept of whiteness regularly note that whiteness is often perceived by whites, who as a group hold more social and economic power than people of color, as *normative*—ordinary, typical, what is expected. To be normative is not the same thing as being "right" or "correct." Normative aspects of a society typically reflect the culture and values of the groups in power.

An Indian American woman well known to the authors of this text shared a story that revealed normative assumptions of her white friends.[11] The woman's romantic partner, a white man, delights in eating pickled lime, a common relish in Indian food. The woman has teased her partner about his love of pickle because he eats it with an unusual array of foods. While people in India would commonly eat a little bit of pickle as an accompaniment with some foods, her partner has paired larger than normal servings of pickle with breakfast, lunch, dinner, and snack foods. When this couple was having dinner with another couple, the Indian woman playfully teased her partner about his use of pickle. The white man from the other couple joined the friendly teasing, making an analogy that eating pickle with so many foods was like putting catsup on almost everything. The white woman from the other couple then asked, "How do you use normal pickles in India?" By "normal pickles" the white woman was suggesting that pickled cucumbers are "normal" and that pickled limes are not. In India, "normal pickles" are pickled limes. The comment revealed the white woman's expectation that what is common in the United States is normal; here she reflected normative white U.S. culture.

To perceive whiteness as normative is to see being white as normal.[12] If whiteness is normal, what does that communicate about the experience of other races? Sociologist Ron Nerio, the son of a Mexican American father, details a story that reveals the normativity of whiteness. A white woman who was a friend of Nerio's family once tried to compliment Nerio's father by telling him that she did not perceive him as Mexican, but rather saw him as a Spaniard. For this friend, the concept of Mexican was embroiled with racial and class stereotypes that she did not think applied to her friend, whom she saw as being like a European, like a white person. When Nerio's father rejected her identification of him as like a white man, she assumed he was being humble and continued to insist that he really "seemed white." She thought she was complimenting him and never realized how deeply she had offended him.[13] We invite readers to explore why a white woman would consider "seeming European" to be a compliment for a Mexican American man. What did she reveal about her beliefs about whiteness and about being Mexican? We encourage you to think about why the white woman did not realize that her "compliment" was actually offensive. We argue that her obtuse reaction revealed a lack of critical thinking about whiteness.

Social scientific research suggests that when a person gets to know another individual, one stops seeing that person as a member of a category—such as seeing a person as Mexican American or as male—and starts to see the person as an individual.[14] The white family friend seemed to conflate seeing Nerio's father as an individual with seeing him as white. Rather than basing a compliment on his individual character, she attempted to compliment him based on being similar to her concept of whiteness. This suggests that the woman perceived whiteness as normal, as normative and as *better*, and preferable to being of color.

Historically within the United States those who are considered white rarely have been challenged to think about their own race. College campuses today are places where whites are more likely to be asked to think critically about whiteness. Sociologist Charles A. Gallagher notes that being prompted by college courses to think about whiteness can be disconcerting for whites because whiteness is so often invisible.[15] Throughout this book, we challenge readers to think critically about race, especially whiteness. Making whiteness visible is a critical step in thinking critically about race and addressing systematic inequality in the United States.

This text will reveal that whiteness is a shifting category that has been created by historical, political, social, and economic events. Within the United States, the first people considered white were Anglo-Saxon Protestants (an ethnic group with ties to England) and individuals from northwestern Europe. In chapter 3, we explore specifically how Irish Catholics were once considered non-white and how they became white. The history of Italians and Ashkenazi Jews also reveal whiteness as a changing category. These groups, similar to the Irish, became white based on historical, political, social, and economic shifts.

What Is Race?

Before you continue to read, we invite you to consider this question: What is race? How have you understood race? If asked to define race, how would you put the concept into words?

Using evidence from anthropology and biology, we will explain that human physical traits such as skin color and facial features vary on a continuum—slight gradations from one individual to another—rather than differing in distinctly separate groups. As we explore in chapter 2, from a biological standpoint, one cannot definitively group individuals into distinct races that clearly differ from each other.

If race does not exist as biological category, you might be wondering why we have dedicated an entire book to the subject. Although race is not an aspect of our genes, race is critically important in the United States. *Race exists as a social and political understanding of humans that attempts to* assign individuals into distinct groups in a way that systematically benefits some—whites—while limiting opportunities for others—people of color.

Historian Nell Irvin Painter argues, "Race is an idea, not a fact."[16] Throughout this book, we explore how powerful this idea has been in shaping human lives. Following influential physical anthropologists such as George J. Armelagos and Alan H. Goodman, we argue that while race is not a biological category, the important social implications of race and of racism make this socially constructed concept a vital issue for careful study.[17] Operario and Fiske argue, "Racial categories exist because people and societies believe them to be true; they derive from psychological and societal processes, rather than from biological or evolutionary processes."[18]

Sociologist Eduardo Bonilla-Silva has distinguished race from ethnicity. As we will see in chapter 2, race has traditionally been a category assigned to a group in a way that justifies the subordination of groups of color by the group in power. Alternatively, *ethnicity* is a social and cultural category.[19] Ethnicity tends to be viewed as a subgroup of race; all members of a given ethnicity will be viewed as belonging to the same race. As sociologists Michael Omi and Howard Winant identify, social and cultural aspects of ethnicity encompass "such diverse factors as religion, language, 'customs,' nationality, and political identification."[20] We will explore ethnicities that have been included in whiteness, have moved into whiteness, and have been excluded from whiteness.

The Modern World System

One of the authors of this text, Jean Halley, grew up in rural Wyoming in the 1970s believing that there was something biologically distinct about different racial groups. This was why, it was commonly "known," Black and white people should not intermarry. In her childhood, this was a basic, accepted "truth" that people around Halley believed much like they believed women were naturally better, more loving parents than men; men were naturally more rational than women; and the "Reds," as one of her social science teachers called people living in communist nations, were going to march on the United States at any moment.

Where did this idea about race come from? Why did people believe that different racial groups are actually biologically different from one another? Was this thinking merely because the different groups do seem to look different, at least somewhat different, some of the time?

⁓

For a moment let us move back in time to the period when feudalism slowly came undone and a new system began to replace it. This new system, the "Modern World System," came into being in the mid-fifteenth century as people from different geographic locations increasingly began to encounter one another. Africa, Asia, and the Americas had been "discovered" by Europeans.[21] These "new" worlds held new (to Europeans) resources as well as human beings who looked and behaved in strikingly different ways.

Imagine being one of the first of your racial group to see another racial group. How might you have made sense of the visual differences you witnessed? How might you have explained cultures seemingly completely distinct from your own?

In Europe at this time, the beginnings of a system that we live with today called *capitalism* began taking hold with a new class of people, the merchant class, who traded in increasingly available luxury goods supplied by the new lands, including "gold, silver, precious gems, silk, sugar, coffee, tea, spices, and tobacco."[22] As trade grew, "the merchant class, whose wealth was built on such exchanges, followed the social lead of aristocrats and emerged as a prime consumer of luxury items."[23] In Europe, being a peasant, a priest, or a king were no longer the only options. Slowly, the various parts of the world became interconnected as never before. The story of race is inextricably bound with this newly interconnected world.

In this interconnection, Europe began to develop as a powerful region by making use of the labor and resources of other places. Not all global locations and peoples fared as well as Europe in the Modern World System. Indeed, as sociologist Immanuel Wallerstein notes, the development of this new and global community was deeply and fundamentally unequal. Today, springing from this history, we continue to live in a deeply unequal global system. While some places gained great power and wealth in the Modern World System, others lost power over their land, labor, and other resources. Through brutally imposed structures of slavery and forced labor, some even lost claim to their own persons. Indeed, the development of Western Europe depended on the oppression, labor, and resources of peoples in Africa, Asia, and the Americas. As Ewen and Ewen make clear,

> For West Europe to triumph as a global center of commerce and industry, it was necessary for other regions of the world to be maintained in a subservient position, their economies stunted to serve the needs of others. Even within Europe, for certain sectors to emerge as masters of the universe, it was necessary that others live in varying states of immiseration. For "progress" to come into being, it was also seen as necessary for certain indigenous populations to

be subjugated or extinguished. Others were systematically dislocated, enlisted into slavery, governed by the lash.[24]

Much like in feudal times in Europe, people worked to explain this inequality. Yet now, Europeans had a new "religion" from which they claimed to study, understand, and know the world; that is, science.

A Brief Introduction to Cultural Materialism

This text offers a criticism of science and challenges readers to consider other perspectives as well. *Cultural materialism* is a way of thinking about the world often used by both anthropologists and sociologists.[25] Cultural materialists believe that the ways we think about things—and what we "know" about the world—spring from the ways we produce our lives.[26] What does it mean to produce our lives? Well, it can happen in a variety of ways. We humans need food and shelter and to reproduce, bringing new humans into the world as the older ones die. We can get and do these things in many different ways. Some people in some time periods have lived, and many still do live, by farming. Others live by fishing for their food. Some people build temporary shelters because they live nomadic lives, moving from place to place as seasons change or as the animals they herd need new land to graze. Others build permanent structures that last for hundreds of years. Cultural materialists believe that the way a given people *lives* births, so to speak, the ways that people *think* about the world and themselves. The culture, knowledge, and beliefs these people develop and refer to spring from their ways of producing and reproducing, their ways of surviving, in life.

We have already seen an example of cultural materialism in our brief exploration of feudalism. In feudal times, peasants farmed to make their living, and they gave a portion of their produce to the aristocracy in exchange for being allowed to live on the land. As best we can tell, most people did not explain this as we might today; that is, that a brutal and violent ruling class suppressed the poor majority. Instead, people understood that situation as one desired by God. People believed in the "Great Chain of Being," where the powerful ruled because God wanted it this way.

Cultural materialism helps us to understand our own, more recent history in terms of race. In the United States, our historical thinking about race springs from our ways of living—during slavery and during other important periods in the United States, such as reconstruction after the Civil War, the early twentieth century when enormous numbers of people immigrated from eastern and southern Europe, Jim Crow[27] and legalized segregation, and the civil rights movement. How might our contemporary thinking about race in the United States and Europe spring from the ways we build our lives and survive—our material reality—*today?*

Whiteness and White Privilege

In chapter 3 we investigate the social construction of whiteness. The very concept of whiteness was developed to include people from different ethnic backgrounds in a common category that excluded other ethnicities. As we will see in our exploration of Irish Catholics becoming white in chapter 3, ethnic groups who were accepted into whiteness were granted higher status and privileges. As we examine in chapter 8, U.S. law such as the Immigration Act of 1924 systematically privileged whites. This immigration law specified that only white immigrants were eligible to apply for citizenship. Before the concept of white as a race was created, certain ethnic groups held greater social power than others—the most powerful of these ethnic groups were the first to be perceived as white when the concept of white as a race developed. Teutonic peoples (descendants of Germanic tribes), especially the Anglo-Saxons (composed of two Teutonic tribes who invaded Britain during the Roman Empire and became the English), were the first to be categorized as white. As we explore in chapter 3, working-class and impoverished peoples of European descent joined Anglo-Saxons with strong economic resources and social power. Across socioeconomic class, a common identity as white emerged, creating a powerful *ingroup*—a shared identity with a feeling of belongingness to the group and connection to other members of the group.[28] The concept of whiteness helped to solidify the social power of the economic elite by encouraging poor and working-class people who became white to see themselves as part of an ingroup with the elite, a group that excluded and subordinated people of color.[29]

Education scholar Zeus Leonardo identified that the concept of whiteness "depends on the racial other for its own identity."[30] Whiteness only exists as an ingroup because it is contrasted with *outgroups*—groups with which members of the ingroup do not identify, do not feel a sense of connection, and might classify as "the other."[31]

Often when one thinks in terms of "us" compared to "them," one engages in *binary* thinking—perceiving a matter as having two opposing sides. Whiteness is often perceived in contrast to groups of color, as though people come in one of two distinct forms—white or of color. Whiteness is one side of a false binary. In other words, today in the mainstream United States, we tend to think about white people in contrast to the other position on this

10/15/2013

A LINK+ request has been placed on the following item.

Shelving   West Valley College

Call Number: HT1521 .H265 2011

Volume:

Author: Halley, Jean O'Malley,

Title: Seeing white : an introduction to

Barcode: 31216001938591

Record#:   i13151289

Owning Library: West Valley College Library

14000 Fruitvale Ave

Saratoga, CA 95070

Please pull this item and send it to the patron at the library location listed below

Name: **O'Bryant, Nouvella Inez**

Patron   LINK+ Undergrad

Institution: **966** – Whittier College

Delivery   **966** – Library Service Entrance

Pickup At: **Library Circ Desk**

O'Bryant, Nouvella Inez

Hold Expiration Date: _____

O'Bryant, Nouvella Inez

false binary, people of color. Our book focuses on this binary way of *thinking* about race because it is so powerful in our society, *not* because it is real in any biological sense.

Dualism is another term for a binary—suggesting there are two distinct, and only two, positions on an issue. Historically and today in the United States, being white is juxtaposed with being *not* white. This juxtaposition means that whiteness, as a frame for understanding human beings, dictates and necessitates a dualism, a *false* dualism. As we explain in chapter 2, careful analysis of race reveals that humans cannot be clearly separated into whites or any other distinct group based on race. Human genetic diversity varies on a continuum, not as a binary. Further, while we will use "people of color" throughout this book to reveal the false dualism often used to think about race, we encourage you to think critically about the great diversity among individuals classified as "of color."

We, the authors of this text, do not support the false dualism of race. Indeed, we mean to challenge it as a way of thinking that is both wrongheaded and deeply damaging. However, to some extent in our challenge, we will seek to reveal the binary framework by contrasting whites with people of color because that *is* the racial framework we live with in the mainstream United States today.

Through critical analysis of the false dualism and insight into whiteness as it relates to social power, scholars such as Peggy McIntosh, who was inspired by her work in feminist studies, have identified ways that whites are systematically privileged over people of color. McIntosh notes that some of these white privileges—such as not having to fear that one's race may contribute to one being stopped and frisked by police—are advantages that would be ideal to share across all people. We challenge you to consider how social action might widen the number of people who can share such privileges. Other white privileges—such as assuming that whites are more deserving of admission to colleges and universities than students of color—are unfair and biased against people of color. We further explore college admission as it relates to white privilege in chapter 8.[32]

White antiracist activist Tim Wise argues that being white in the United States means "defining ourselves by a negative, providing ourselves with an identity that [is] rooted in the external—rooted in the relative oppression of others. . . . Inequality and privilege [are] the only real components of whiteness. . . . Without racial privilege there is no whiteness, and without whiteness, there is no racial privilege. Being white only means to be advantaged."[33] Revealing white privilege challenges the *myth of meritocracy*, the belief that people who work hard in the United States will succeed and that success is the result of hard work.[34] Critically examining white privilege exposes unfair advantages that make success easier for whites while disadvantaging people of color.[35] Chapter 7 explores the myth of meritocracy.

Racism

A common misconception equates racism with individual acts of intentional bigotry.[36] As we further discuss in chapter 5, racism can be perpetuated by white individuals who fail to realize that they are acting in racially biased ways. Moreover, as we discuss throughout the text, institutional racism is often propagated by social systems such as the criminal courts (see chapters 4 and 7) and immigration law (see chapter 8). Institutional, or systemic, racism consists of policies and practices that systematically favor powerful racial groups—usually whites in the United States—while discriminating against others—groups of color.[37] For example, in chapter 6 we further explore institutional racism in public schools, including unequal funding for education in different neighborhoods and biased expectations that may influence which students are tested for gifted and talented programs.

Sociologists Joe R. Feagin, Hernán Vera, and Pinar Batur note, "Being white in this society almost by definition means rarely having to think about it. Whites must make a special effort to become deeply aware of their own and others' racism."[38] Critical examinations of racism often lead people to move from perceiving racism as a matter of intentional, individual acts to seeing racism in the United States as including subtle and potentially unintentional behaviors by individuals as well as systemic issues.[39] Well-meaning white people may inadvertently support racism by failing to challenge a racist system.[40]

Psychologist Raphael S. Ezekiel argues that it is essential for all whites in America to examine race and racism:

> If you visited South Africa and spoke with older White South Africans, you would expect to find their minds affected by having grown up in a society that was intensely racist. White Americans grow up in a society in which race has been and is profoundly important.
>
> . . . If I am White and grow up in a society in which race matters, I inhale racism, and racism becomes part of my mind and spirit. . . . There will always be layers of myself that harbor racist thoughts and racist attitudes. This is not to say that those must remain the dominant parts of my mind and spirit. It is to say that it is mistaken to presume that I have no traces of racism in me.
>
> The task is to get acquainted with those layers of oneself—to learn to recognize them and not be frightened by them. It is not a disgrace to have absorbed some racism. It is a disgrace not to know it and to let those parts of ourselves go unchecked.[41]

To better understand racism, one must critically examine the relationships of race, especially whiteness, with social, economic, and political power.[42] *Prejudice* is a matter of favoring one's ingroup over outgroups,[43] of disliking groups or individuals based on group membership.[44] Social theorist Oliver Cromwell Cox identified that not all forms of racial prejudice carry the same potential to "subjugate a people"; the racial prejudice of whites is potentially more damaging because of social and political power.[45] In 1970, Patricia Bidol, then school superintendent in Baldwin, Michigan, worked to raise awareness of the special role of whiteness in racism. Because whites hold important power in the United States, she argued that only whites can be racist.[46] Consistent with Cox and Bidol, clinical psychologist Beverly Daniel Tatum argues that racial bigotry is open to everyone but that the term *racism* should be reserved for "prejudice plus power." Because of the disproportionate power held by whites in the United States, we follow Tatum in arguing that anyone can be a racial bigot but that only whites can be racist.[47]

We consider it important for readers to understand how we conceptualize racism—as systemic as well as individual, sometimes unintentional, racial prejudice coupled with power. Like Tatum, we invite readers to develop their own understanding of racism based on critical reflection.

While it may be an interesting intellectual exercise to think of specific situations in which whites are less likely to have power than people of color, we challenge you to consider how frequently whites have greater power than people of color. Journalist Robert Jensen expresses a concern that individuals who focus on the few situations in which whites have less power than people of color may be trying to end a critical discussion of race before the discussion can truly happen.[48]

Similarly, when white racism is raised, some individuals try to change the subject to focus on how certain groups of color are prejudiced against other groups of color. Such discussions have their place, but we encourage you to have them only if you truly want to understand the social problems involved, not if you are simply trying to avoid focusing on whiteness and white privilege.

We invite you to consider how having an African American president of the United States may influence understandings of race and racism. We are heartened that many more opportunities are open to people of color today than historically, but we continue to see strong evidence that whites remain much more powerful as a group than any other.

～

In an occasional misconception of racism we have observed in our teaching, some students have confused having a critical discussion regarding race with being racist. While we invite disagreement about how to define racism, this particular misunderstanding of the concept perplexes us. We have wondered whether strong discomfort regarding the discussion of race could lead some individuals to have avoided thinking critically about race or racism, so much so that they have equated discussions of race with racism.

Perspectives

We three authors of this text have been trained in distinctly different disciplines within the social sciences—sociology, psychology, and economics. Throughout this text, we draw on the theories and evidence within our respective fields while also critiquing these fields. We use theories and evidence from biology, history, and anthropology. (We assume readers have a working knowledge of biology and history but may be less familiar with anthropology, a social science that examines the impact of culture, biology, and evolution on human groups.[49] Anthropology has been an important field in challenging racist ideologies.)

Drawing on her expertise in sociology, Jean Halley infuses this text with a critical examination of social history and cultural studies. As famously noted by C. Wright Mills, *sociology* is the study of both social institutions and of the embeddedness of individual lives in such institutions. Mills called on sociologists to explore the connections between seemingly "private troubles" and "public issues."[50] Race is clearly a matter of both. In studying race, sociologists commonly use theories to be discussed at length in this book, such as that of cultural materialism (defined above) and the social construction of race (to be discussed in chapter 3).

Amy Eshleman contributes her empirical approach to *psychology*, "the scientific study of behavior and mental processes."[51] As a social psychologist, Eshleman focuses on how individuals are influenced by their perceptions of social expectations. Social psychologists seek to understand racism by carefully examining factors that seem to reduce or exacerbate this social problem. We explore the empirical method in chapter 2 and applications of social psychological work in educational settings in chapters 6 and 9.

Ramya Vijaya brings an expertise on economics to this text. Through economic analysis, we explore the vast inequalities related to race and caused by racism. Chapters 5 through 8 provide critical economic concepts and evidence that serve as a foundation for our argument.

When Eshleman communicated to a recent college graduate that she was writing a textbook, she was dismayed when this strong alumna admitted that she had never considered that real people write textbooks. Although the student had read many textbooks throughout her undergraduate career, she treated textbooks as truth rather than as a perspective created by humans. While we authors have been careful to present information as clearly and accurately as possible, we acknowledge that our work—like that of all thinkers—will be influenced by our cultural understandings and ideologies. Political scientist Michael Freeden defines *ideology* as "thought-patterns of individuals and groups in a society which relate to the way they comprehend and shape their political worlds."[52]

Ideologies tend to be taken-for-granted beliefs that both come from and work to reinforce systems of social power. Because they are social, rather than individual, we share ideological ways of thinking with others in our culture, and we usually assume these ways of thinking to be correct without questioning them. In other words, we are born into our ideological frameworks as we are born into communities. We tend to take on the ideological frameworks of our communities, like the air we breathe, without questioning or even thinking consciously about it.

Ideologies play an important role in the production and reproduction of social power. These are ways of thinking that justify social realities; we do not merely take for granted the thinking, we take for granted the system it supports. The now-known-to-be-false belief that race is a biological reality has been at the core of our shared ideologies of race. Much like the ideological framework of the Great Chain of Being underlying feudalism, race as biology is a way of thinking that is more than incorrect. This way of thinking supports and reproduces social power, the power of white people over people of color.

Ideology influences all academic endeavors. Throughout the textbook, we authors refer to our perspective and to how our personal experiences have helped us to see whiteness. We invite you to critically reflect as you read and to formulate any disagreements you have. As you will see in chapter 2, research is advanced by scholars challenging each other's ideas and evidence.

Like all authors of textbooks (or writing of any form), we present a particular perspective and have selected specific issues on which to focus. For example, this text briefly explores intersectionality—how important social categories such as race, gender, socioeconomic class, and sexuality intersect and interact with each other in ways that influence human experiences (see chapter 4). We then invest chapter 5 in exploring how race and socioeconomic class intersect. To keep our focus on how sociology, psychology, and economics can be used to think critically about whiteness, we have chosen not to explore gender and sexuality as deeply as we might have explored these important intersections. We encourage readers to seek further examples of how gender and sexuality interact with race, socioeconomic class, and other important social categories.

Because of our focus on interdisciplinary perspectives on whiteness, we elected not to cover the excellent work of Janet E. Helms on racial identity development.[53] We encourage readers with a particular interest in psychological approaches to studying individual experiences of race to read Helms as well as Beverly Daniel Tatum's review of Helms's theory.[54]

As a genre, textbooks have a tendency to present material as though it is simple, objective fact. We take issue with this tendency. Indeed, we argue there is no way out of opinion in argument. Everyone's arguments, ideas, and claims—including ours in this book—are just that, arguments. We work to offer you the clearest argument possible with strong evidence to back it up as we seek to *problematize* issues of race and racism, particularly whiteness. Our goal is to challenge readers to consider how issues that might have seemed straightforward are actually quite complex when one examines them critically. Given that these issues are complex, we acknowledge that your perspective may differ from ours. We invite you to carefully consider our perspective and to use this material to inform your own perspective. We recognize that some will disagree with us, and we look forward to an ongoing conversation.

What Is in a Name?

Throughout our writing, we have carefully selected the terms we use to identify racial groups, down to the details of capitalization and hyphenation. Here we highlight just a few of our choices, which are driven by respect for these racial groups and their expressed preferences regarding appropriate terms to identify them. We follow convention in capitalizing names for racial and ethnic groups of color such as Latino, Asian, African American, and Native American. Even if these terms were not routinely capitalized, we would have chosen to capitalize them as a way of offering respect to these groups that have been traditionally underrepresented in positions of power. In this line of thinking, we capitalize "Blacks." While other authors who critically reflect on whiteness may choose to capitalize both "Whites" and "Blacks," our intentional choice not to capitalize "whites" is a conscious decision to distinguish the critical examination of whiteness in this text from how white supremacists may refer to whites.

The terms *African American*, *Black*, and *Black American* are currently preferred terms for a wide range of individuals who have lived in the United States for generations or emigrated from places as diverse as the many countries of Africa and areas of the Caribbean. While we recognize that individuals classified within this group may have strong preferences for one of these labels, we use these terms interchangeably with the goal of esteeming all individuals who may be classified by these terms.

When referring to individuals with cultural or family heritage ties to Puerto Rico, Cuba, the Dominican Republic, Mexico, and the countries of Central America and South America, we choose to use *Latina* or *Latino*. The term *Hispanic* was created for the 1970 U.S. Census to classify individuals with ethnic ties to Spanish-speaking cultures. Our preference for *Latina/o* over *Hispanic* is based on the connection of *Hispanic* "to internalized colonization because it is strongly supported by politically conservative groups who regard their European ancestry as superior to the conquered indigenous peoples of the Americas."[55] Further, "Many millions of Spanish-speaking people—such as Native Americans—are not of true Spanish descent, and millions of Latin Americans do not speak Spanish or claim Spanish heritage (e.g., Brazilians), therefore, they are not Hispanics."[56] *Latina/o* is perceived by many, including the authors of this text, as a more inclusive term that does not glorify or require European ancestry. For clarity, we use *Hispanic* only when referring to research and public policy that has used that term to classify individuals.[57]

We caution readers to think critically about the power of words that have been used to derogate racial and ethnic groups. While there are multiple powerful epithets on which we might focus, we briefly explore *nigger* because we believe it can be one of the most powerful words spoken in the United States. Legal scholar Randall Kennedy shares the history and complexity of this slur in *Nigger: The Strange Career of a Troublesome Word*. As a Black man, Kennedy notes that his own relationship with the slur is complicated and nuanced but that it was important to him to communicate clearly to whites that the word is "ugly, evil, irredeemable."[58] Scholars of African American studies have explored the multiple ways the word has been used in the Black community, and influential leaders have disagreed regarding the possible utility of reclaiming the term in certain contexts within the community. While we encourage all readers to learn more about social history and contemporary debates about the power of words, we challenge non-Black readers to focus on the likelihood that use of the word outside the Black community conveys "racial hatred or contempt for all blacks."[59] We acknowledge that some readers from outside the Black community may be confused by the many uses of this word within the Black community. Like Kennedy, we encourage readers to consider the words of former Supreme Court Justice Oliver Wendell Holmes Jr.: "A word is not a crystal, transparent and unchanged; it is the skin of a living thought and may vary greatly in color and content according to the circumstances and time in which it is used." We argue that there are no circumstances or times in which whites can use this word in an inoffensive manner. While we encourage all readers to delve into explorations of matters of race, we doubt that individuals who would not be targeted with this slur will ever fully understand it (including the authors of this text). Therefore, we argue that people who are not Black cannot use this powerful word from within a place of understanding or connection to it.

Did you notice our use of "non-Black" in the previous paragraph? If so, did you have any reaction when reading it? Journalist Robert Jensen has chosen to use the term *non-white* because he wants to make whiteness visible in discussions about race.[60] While many scholars prefer the term *people of color*, Jensen argues that what makes a group "of color" is that the group has been excluded from the category of whiteness. Alternatively, one may argue that *people of color* is a more respectful label than to focus on what a group is not. Choosing either option consciously can be a political decision that conveys information about one's thoughts on race, especially if one notes why that choice has been made. (While *person of color* and *people of color* are commonly used today as respectful terms, these terms are distinct from the outdated use of describing a person as *colored*. While the outdated term was once considered respectful, use of it today to refer to a person or groups of people reveals a lack of sensitivity to language.)

We invite you to pay attention to the terms used to describe racial groups and to consider what information is conveyed by these choices. In quotes used throughout the text, you will see different ways that scholars have presented group names. We also encourage you to note the choices made by media, peers, family members, and others. Consider what terms and form of capitalization you want to use.

Throughout this text (including earlier in this chapter), we note key vocabulary terms from the social sciences in italics. We invite you to reflect on these terms and to try to use them in your discussions and writing about whiteness.

Discussion Questions

1. Did reading chapter 1 arouse any emotions for you? Common emotions during critical explorations of race include anger, frustration, guilt,

discomfort, and confusion. If you had a strong emotional response to a certain aspect of the chapter, identify the part of the chapter, describe the emotion that was aroused, and evaluate this experience. If you did not have any emotional responses to any material in the chapter, explore that.

2. Describe several issues considered to be "truths" in feudal times and in the 1970s that are now understood to be false. Explore possible "truths" today that you predict will be demonstrated to be false in the future.

3. What are social and economic power? Who held power in feudal Europe, and how did they hold on to that power? Who holds power in the United States today, and how do those in power hold on to that power? What is meant by the terms *norm* and *normative*? What has been a common relationship between whiteness and these terms? How might this relate to power?

4. What does it mean to claim that whiteness tends to be invisible to whites? When have you been aware of whiteness? What might that reveal about whiteness?

5. Describe cultural materialism. How does it relate to race, particularly whiteness? Evaluate Tim Wise's argument (quoted within the chapter) that inequality and privilege are essential aspects of whiteness.

6. What are ingroups and outgroups? What is the relationship of these terms to inclusion and exclusion? Who is part of the white ingroup? Who is excluded from this group?

7. Have you ever had an experience when you were keenly aware of yourself as privileged? If so, how did this awareness affect you? How did the privilege affect how others treated you? If you have never been aware of privilege, reflect on why that might be.

8. Racism is described in this chapter as ranging from unintentional individual behavior by whites to policies at an institutional level. It is also argued that racism is "prejudice plus power," such that only whites can be racist. How would you have defined racism before reading this chapter? What are your reactions to the definition of racism in this chapter?

9. What do you think has been the effect of having a president of the United States who is African American? Has this changed understandings of race or racism in the United States? If so, how? If not, why not?

10. What is ideology? How does ideology shape understanding of important issues such as race? Do individuals tend to be conscious of the influence of ideology?

11. Do you consider words, such as racial slurs, to be powerful? Why or why not?

Notes

1. Stuart Ewen and Elizabeth Ewen, *Typecasting: On the Arts and Sciences of Human Inequality* (New York: Seven Stories Press, 2006), 19.

2. Ewen and Ewen, *Typecasting*, 19.

3. Ewen and Ewen, *Typecasting*, 19.

4. We follow intellectuals such as Audre Lorde (*Sister Outsider: Essays and Speeches*, Freedom, Calif.: The Crossing Press, 1984) in consciously choosing not to capitalize "western."

5. Don Operario and Susan T. Fiske, "Racism Equals Power Plus Prejudice: A Social Psychological Equation for Racial Oppression," in *Confronting Racism: The Problem and the Response*, eds. Jennifer Lynn Eberhardt and Susan T. Fiske (Thousand Oaks, Calif.: Sage Publications, Inc., 1998): 49.

6. Barbara J. Flagg, "'Was Blind But Now I See': White Race Consciousness and the Requirement of Discriminatory Intent," *Michigan Law Review* 91 (March 1993): 953.

7. Jessica T. Decuir-Gunby, "'Proving Your Skin Is White, You Can Have Everything': Race, Racial Identity, and Property Rights in Whiteness in the Supreme Court Case of Josephine DeCuir," in *Critical Race Theory in Education: All God's Children Got a Song*, eds. Adrienne D. Dixson and Celia K. Rousseau (New York: Routledge, 2006), 89–111, 93–94.

8. Tanya Kateri Hernandez, "'Multiracial' Discourse: Racial Classifications in an Era of Color-Blind Jurisprudence," *Maryland Law Review* 57 (1998): 97.

9. See Thomas F. Pettigrew, "Normative Theory in Intergroup Relations: Explaining Both Harmony and Conflict," *Psychology & Developing Societies* 3, no. 1 (March 1991): 3–16.

10. Robert B. Cialdini, "Crafting Normative Messages to Protect the Environment," *Current Directions in Psychological Science* 12, no. 4 (August 2003): 105–9.

11. Indian American refers to people with ancestry connected to the country of India. We distinguish this term from American Indian, which refers to Native Americans.

12. Catherine Myser, "Differences from Somewhere: The Normativity of Whiteness in Bioethics in the United States," *American Journal of Bioethics* 3, no. 2 (Spring 2003): 1–11.

13. Ron Nerio, unpublished memoir, 2009.

14. Ziva Kunda, Paul G. Davies, Barbara D. Adams, and Steven J. Spencer, "The Dynamic Time Course of Stereotype Activation: Activation, Dissipation, and Resurrection," *Journal of Personality and Social Psychology* 82, no. 3 (March 2002): 283–99.

15. Charles A. Gallagher, "White Reconstruction in the University," in *Privilege: A Reader*, eds. Michael S. Kimmel and Abby L. Ferber (Boulder, Colo.: Westview Press, 2003), 299–318.

16. Nell Irvin Painter, *The History of White People* (New York: W. W. Norton & Company, 2010), ix.

17. George J. Armelagos and Alan H. Goodman, "Race, Racism, and Anthropology," in *Building a New Biocultural Synthesis: Political-Economic Perspectives on Human Biology*, eds. Alan H. Goodman and Thomas L. Leatherman (Ann Arbor: The University of Michigan Press, 1998), 371.

18. Operario and Fiske, "Racism Equals Power Plus Prejudice," 35.

19. Eduardo Bonilla-Silva, "Rethinking Racism: Toward a Structural Interpretation," *American Sociological Review* 62, no. 3 (June 1997): 465–80.

20. Michael Omi and Howard Winant, *Racial Formation in the United States: From the 1960s to the 1990s*, 2nd ed. (New York: Routledge, 1994), 15.

21. Immanuel Maurice Wallerstein, *The Modern World-System: Capitalist Agriculture and the Origins of the European World-Economy in the Sixteenth Century* (New York: Academic Press, 1974).

22. Ewen and Ewen, *Typecasting*, 12–13.

23. Ewen and Ewen, *Typecasting*, 13.

24. Ewen and Ewen, *Typecasting*, 16–17.

25. Drawing from Karl Marx, Raymond Williams is commonly credited with developing the idea of cultural materialism. For further information on cultural materialism, please do see Williams's seminal book, *Marxism and Literature* (Oxford: Oxford University Press, 1977).

26. Maxine L. Margolis, *True to Her Nature: Changing Advice to American Women* (Prospect Heights, Ill.: Waveland Press, Inc., 2000).

27. "Beginning in the late 19th century, southern states codify a system of laws and practices to subordinate African Americans to whites. The 'new' social order, reinforced through violence and intimidation, affects schools, public transportation, jobs, housing, private life and voting rights. Cutting across class boundaries, Jim Crow unites poor and wealthy whites, while denying African Americans equality in the courts, freedom of assembly and movement, and full participation as citizens. The federal government adopts segregation under President Wilson in 1913, and is not integrated until the 1960s." Public Broadcasting Corporation, "1887: Jim Crow Segregation Begins," *Race: The Power of an Illusion* 2003, www.pbs.org/race/003_RaceTimeline/003_01-timeline.htm (June 30, 2010).

28. William Graham Sumner, *Folkways* (New York: Ginn, 1906).

29. See Nyla R. Branscombe, Michael T. Schmitt, and Kristin Schiffhauer, "Racial Attitudes in Response to Thoughts of White Privilege," *European Journal of Social Psychology* 37, no. 2 (March–April 2007): 203–15.

30. Zeus Leonardo, "The Color of Supremacy: Beyond the Discourse of 'White Privilege,'" in *Foundations of Critical Race Theory in Education*, eds. Edward Taylor, David Gillborn, and Gloria Ladson-Billings (New York: Routledge, 2009), 261–76.

31. Erving Goffman, *Stigma: Notes on the Management of Spoiled Identity* (Engle-wood Cliffs, N.J.: Prentice-Hall, Inc., 1963).

32. Peggy McIntosh, "White Privilege: Unpacking the Invisible Knapsack," in *Race, Class, & Gender: An Anthology*, 6th ed., eds. Margaret L. Andersen and Patricia Hill Collins (Belmont, Calif.: Wadsworth, 2007), 98–102.

33. Tim Wise, *White Like Me: Reflections on Race from a Privileged Son* (Brooklyn, N.Y.: Soft Skull Press, 2005), 170.

34. Laurie T. O'Brien, Alison Blodorn, AnGelica Alsbrooks, Reesa Dube, Glenn Adams, and Jessica C. Nelson, "Understanding White Americans' Perceptions of Racism in Hurricane Katrina-Related Events," *Group Processes & Intergroup Relations* 12, no. 4 (July 2009): 431–44.

35. McIntosh, "White Privilege."

36. Laurie T. O'Brien, Christian S. Crandall, April Horstman-Reser, Ruth War-ner, AnGelica Alsbrooks, and Alison Blodorn, "But I'm No Bigot: How Prejudiced White Americans Maintain Unprejudiced Self-Images," *Journal of Applied Social Psychology* 40, no. 4 (April 2010): 917–46.

37. O'Brien et al., "Understanding White."

38. Joe R. Feagin, Hernán Vera, and Pinar Batur, *White Racism*, 2nd ed. (New York: Routledge, 2001), 238.

39. Eduardo Bonilla-Silva, "Rethinking Racism."

40. Glenn Adams, Laurie T. O'Brien, and Jessica C. Nelson, "Perceptions of Racism in Hurricane Katrina: A Liberation Psychology Analysis," *Analyses of Social Issues and Public Policy* 6, no. 1 (December 2006): 215–35.

41. Raphael S. Ezekiel, "An Ethnographer Looks at Neo-Nazi and Klan Groups," *American Behavioral Scientist* 46, no. 1 (September 2002): 51–71.

42. Jane Dickie, "The Unconscious Devil Within," *Church Herald: The Magazine of the Reformed Church in America* 46, no. 3 (March 1989): 12–15, 51.

43. Operario and Fiske, "Racism Equals Power Plus Prejudice," 49.

44. Christian S. Crandall and Amy Eshleman, "A Justification-Suppression Model of the Expression and Experience of Prejudice," *Psychological Bulletin* 129, no. 3 (May 2003), 414–46.

45. Oliver Cromwell Cox, *Caste, Class, and Race: A Study in Social Dynamics* (New York: Monthly Review Press, 1948), 531.

46. Pat A. Bidol and Richard C. Weber, *Developing New Perspectives on Race: An Innovative Multi-Media Social Studies Curriculum in Race Relations for the Secondary Level* (Detroit, Mich.: New Detroit, 1970).

47. Beverly Daniel Tatum, *"Why Are All the Black Kids Sitting Together in the Cafeteria?": And Other Conversations about Race* (New York: Basic, 2003).

48. Robert Jensen, *The Heart of Whiteness: Confronting Race, Racism, and White Privilege* (San Francisco, Calif.: City Lights, 2005), 9–10.

49. George J. Armelagos and Alan H. Goodman, "Race, Racism, and Anthropol-ogy," in *Building a New Biocultural Synthesis: Political-Economic Perspectives on Human*

Biology, ed. Alan H. Goodman and Thomas L. Leatherman (Ann Arbor: The University of Michigan Press, 1998), 359–77, 372.

50. C. Wright Mills, The Sociological Imagination (Oxford: Oxford University Press, 1959).

51. Douglas A. Bernstein, Louis A. Penner, Alison Clarke-Stewart, and Edward J. Roy, Psychology, 6th ed. (Stamford, Conn.: Cengage, 2008).

52. Michael Freeden, "Is Nationalism a Distinct Ideology?," Political Studies 46, no. 4 (September 1998): 748–65.

53. See Janet E. Helms, "An Update of Helms's White and People of Color Racial Identity Models," in Handbook of Multicultural Counseling, eds. Joseph G. Ponterotto, J. Manuel Casas, Lisa A. Suzuki, and Charlene M. Alexander (Thousand Oaks, Calif.: Sage Publications, Inc., 1995): 181–98; and also Janet E. Helms, "Racial Identity and Racial Socialization as Aspects of Adolescents' Identity Development," in Handbook of Applied Developmental Science: Promoting Positive Child, Adolescent, and Family Development through Research, Policies, and Programs, Volume 1, eds. Richard M. Lerner, Francine Jacobs, and Donald Wertlieb (Thousand Oaks, Calif.: Sage Publications, Inc., 2003): 143–63.

54. Tatum, "Why Are All the Black Kids Sitting Together in the Cafeteria?"

55. Lillian Comas-Díaz, "Hispanics, Latinos, or Americanos: The Evolution of Identity," Cultural Diversity and Ethnic Minority Psychology 7, no. 2 (May 2001): 115–20.

56. Comas-Díaz, "Hispanics, Latinos, or Americanos," 116.

57. The term Hispanic was created in 1977 as a U.S. Census category. "In response to civil rights legislation, the federal Office of Management and Budget issues Directive 15, creating standard government race and ethnic categories for the first time. The categories are meant to aid agencies, but they are arbitrary, inconsistent, and based on varying assumptions. . . . 'Hispanic' reflects Spanish colonization and excludes non-Spanish parts of Central and South America. . . ." Public Broadcasting Corporation, "1977: Government Defines Race/Ethnic Categories," Race: The Power of an Illusion, 2003, www.pbs.org/race/003_RaceTimeline/003_01-timeline.htm (June 30, 2010).

58. Randall Kennedy, Nigger: The Strange Career of a Troublesome Word (New York: Vintage Books, 2003), xv.

59. Kennedy, Nigger, xiii.

60. Robert Jensen, The Heart of Whiteness: Confronting Race, Racism, and White Privilege (San Francisco, Calif.: City Lights, 2005), 2–4.

CHAPTER TWO

~

Scientific Endeavors to Study Race

Race Is Not Rooted in Biology

Early research on race often focused on the shape of human skulls in an attempt to scientifically classify distinct races. In 1775, anatomist Johann Friedrich Blumenbach published the first work distinguishing races of human beings based on physical features. While he focused on the shape of the skull, he also analyzed shades of skin color and facial features, such as the shape of the lips. He classified humans into five races: "Mongoloids, Malays, Ethiopians (Africans), American Indians, and Caucasoids."[1]

Today most researchers who study race argue that distinct racial categories such as those created by Blumenbach do not adequately explain how humans vary from each other. Rather than distinguishing separate groups, human variation is seen as a continuum.[2]

Blumenbach sought to apply scientific principles to his study of race, but his interest in grouping humans into separate races was influenced by the prevailing ideologies of his culture and his historical time that perceived humans from different continents as distinct from each other.[3] Another bias inherent in Blumenbach's work was his association of Europeans as the most beautiful of humans. The Public Broadcasting Corporation's *Race: The Power of an Illusion* notes: "Although [Blumenbach] opposes slavery, he maps a hierarchical pyramid of five human types, placing 'Caucasians' at the top because he believes a skull found in the Caucasus Mountains is the 'most beautiful form . . . from which . . . the others diverge.' This model is widely embraced, and Blumenbach inadvertently paves the way for scientific claims about white superiority."[4]

More than a century of racially biased research succeeded Blumenbach's racial classifications before the first scientific publication directly challenged racist ideology in 1912. Franz Boas, a founder of anthropology in the United States, used measurements of the skull to challenge racism based on biased research. In the early 1900s in the United States, prejudice existed against immigrants from eastern and southern Europe as well as from Ireland. These immigrants were assumed to be inferior to individuals from northwestern Europe. (In chapter 3, we will discuss the complex racial experiences of Irish Catholic immigrants.) Immigration laws in the United States favored individuals from northwestern Europe. Researchers claimed evidence of inferiority of eastern and southern Europeans in the shapes of their skulls. Based on the work of Blumenbach and others, certain shapes of the skull were seen as ideal, while other shapes were devalued.[5]

Boas and his students studied how the environment influences the shape of human skulls. While the prevailing view focused on the heredity of the shape of the skull, aspects of the environment such as nutrition and exposure to illness also influence the formation and shape of the skull. Using scientific methodology, Boas and colleagues focused on families who had immigrated to the United States. The researchers could predict differences in skull shape between individuals who immigrated to the United States and their siblings who had been born in the United States. This information that cranial shape differed within families was "revolutionary" at a time when differences in skull shape were assumed to be stable and distinct across races.[6]

The study of the interplay between heredity and the environment can also be discussed in terms of nature and nurture. Using this terminology, *nature* focuses on genetic variations, heredity, and how genes predict differences across individuals, such as differences in skull shape, intelligence, or likelihood of disease. Genetic differences between individuals—differences based on nature—will be consistent across those individuals' lives and may be passed on to future generations. *Nurture* looks to the environment to predict differences across individuals. Nurture includes all environmental influences from the conception of a person and throughout one's life. Nurture consists of every influence of physical and social experience, including nutrition, exposure to toxins and pathogens, the safety of one's environment, and all social interactions. Throughout this chapter, we will explore how nature and nurture have been used to explain differences between racial groups, focusing particularly on intelligence and disease.

Prior to the work of Boas, in the 1800s, there were two competing nature-based theories about race. While the *monogenists* believed that all human races were parts of the same species,[7] the *polygenists* argued that different races were actually different species. The polygenist perspective suggests that white people are human while other races are not truly human. From the polygenist perspective, any discussion of human equality or human rights applies only to whites. Such beliefs were normative in a political setting, such as that of the United States, during a time of slavery and of savage mistreatment of indigenous populations.[8]

In 1849, Samuel George Morton, a physician and the leading proponent of the polygenist perspective, sought to objectively analyze racial differences. Harvard University science professor Stephen Jay Gould's critical reanalysis in 1977 of Morton's research reveals that ideology unwittingly, but distinctly, biased the decisions Morton made regarding whom to select for inclusion in his research and how to conduct the research. Although Morton believed he had found definitive evidence of important physical differences between races, Gould's reanalysis reveals that Morton's prejudiced approach accounts for the differences Morton thought he found. In fact, using the same *data*—pieces of evidence—as Morton, Gould found no racial differences.[9]

Starting from the biased perspective that only whites were fully human, Morton sought to objectively measure differences between races. He collected skulls of whites, Blacks, Asians, and Native Americans. He attempted to carefully measure the cranial capacity of the skulls, which would yield an accurate measure of the size of the brain that once inhabited the skull. He tried filling each skull with mustard seeds to then measure the cubic inches of space when the seeds were transferred to another container, but he found that the measure lacked reliability. When retesting a given skull, the volume of seeds could be notably different from one attempt at measurement to another. He later settled on using lead shot, specifically the size known as BBs. These small spheres were consistently one-eighth of an inch in diameter and yielded higher reliability when retesting a given skull. Based on his clear communication of his research decisions, Morton seemed to believe he was engaging in a carefully conducted scientific endeavor.

Gould's reanalysis of Morton's work reveals, ". . . a series of unconscious yet systematic errors in the way Morton collected skulls and analyzed their cranial volumes."[10] Morton published enough detail regarding his data that Gould was able to detect the errors. If Morton had been aware of his errors, it is difficult to believe that he would have provided others with the details that would expose them.

Gould revealed multiple ways Morton biased his data to fit his ideology. Morton's decisions regarding which skulls to include in his study were inconsistent, especially in that he failed to account for the relationship between body size and brain size. While a rhinoceros has a larger brain than a human, the rhinoceros is not considered more intelligent. Humans with larger bodies have larger cranial capacities without this predicting greater intelligence. Because of average differences in body size, women tend to have smaller brains than men. For races of color, Morton included a greater number of smaller skulls, such as skulls of women and individuals from ethnic groups who tend to have smaller bodies. For example, when measuring skulls of Native Americans, Morton included a larger number of skulls from Inca Peruvians, who tend to have smaller brains, and a smaller number of skulls from Iroquois, who tend to have larger brains. When measuring the cranial capacity of Caucasians, Morton revealed his choice to exclude data from a number of available skulls of Northern Indian Hindus, who tend to have smaller brains than other Caucasian groups. (Hindus have been classified as Caucasian in only some contexts. When researching for this book, author Vijaya was fascinated to learn that according to some, like Morton, she is Caucasian. She has certainly never been treated as white. As described in chapter 8, in the 1930s the Supreme Court denied citizenship to Hindus on the confusing basis that they were Caucasian, but not white.)

Gould uncovered errors Morton made in calculating the average cranial capacity for each group. These errors helped Morton to rank the groups consistently with prevailing racist beliefs. Ethnically biased beliefs about Caucasians during the time of Morton's work would rank Teutons (Germanic whites) and Anglo-Saxons (English whites)[11] above Ashkenazi Jews, who would be ranked above Hindus. Morton believed he found evidence of cranial differences to support this ranking.[12] Across races, Morton claimed to have found that Caucasians had larger brains than Asians, whose brains were larger than Native Americans, whose brains were larger than Blacks. Morton's research was lauded in its day as objective evidence of group differences, but Gould's work reveals that the groups actually do not differ. Gould challenges readers to consider how unconscious bias may influence many areas of science: "For if scientists can be honestly self-deluded to Morton's extent, then prior prejudice may be found anywhere, even in the basics of measuring bones and toting sums."[13]

We challenge you to read all research critically, exploring the possibility of bias, and to consider who might benefit from the ways of thinking reflected in the research. Much like Blumenbach's work predating Morton and discussed above, Morton's research reflected common ways of thinking in mainstream Europe and the United States. Cultural materialism provides a strong perspective by which we can critique both of these researchers. As defined in chapter 1, cultural materialism reveals how the way individuals within a culture live and meet their needs influences how they understand the world, including how they conceive of race. The racist beliefs proposed by Blumenbach, Morton, and other European and European American scientists sprang from a global context of *imperialism* by Europe and the United States. Imperialism refers to foreign policies where one nation or area of the world acts aggressively to take over and control the resources of other areas. In this case, the western areas of the globe in Europe—and eventually England's former colony, the United States—colonized and controlled, enslaved, or killed the people of those areas. (Please do see the brief discussion of colonization in chapter 3.) Cultural materialism illuminates the racist ways of thinking born from an imperialist economic order.

The Empirical Perspective

One of the authors of this textbook, Eshleman, strongly identifies with empiricism. Like all three of the authors of this book, she is curious and engaged with ideas. The *empirical method* for seeking answers to her questions provides a systematic set of rules and strategies based on principles she deeply respects. To approach a research question empirically is to follow a set of guidelines known as the scientific method. An empirical test of a research question requires one to carefully observe evidence. One must be open-minded to ideas that are contradictory to one's own perspective while maintaining a healthy skepticism about one's own expectations.[14]

Within the empirical method, scholars carefully describe their decisions regarding how to conduct research. To illustrate the empirical approach, we will use evolutionary biologist R. C. Lewontin's classic 1972 study on human genetic diversity.[15] The first step in an empirical project is to frame one's research question. A *hypothesis*—a testable prediction—should be proposed such that the data—evidence—collected in a study will clearly support or refute the hypothesis. While we do not believe it is possible for humans to approach any issue with true objectivity, the empirical approach challenges researchers to share their approach with other scholars. Ideally, different scholars will approach the same issue with distinct perspectives, testing similar hypotheses in different ways. Disagreements between researchers about how to study a research topic can enhance scholarship.

Lewontin sought to study genetic variation in humans. Specifically, he wanted to compare variation *between* human groups to variation *within* groups. In other words, to explore the extent of genetic difference between groups perceived as Asian and groups perceived as European compared to the extent of genetic difference within Asians and within Europeans. He acknowledges that scientific work on this issue has been influenced by ideology, noting that changes in perspectives within evolutionary research on human groups ". . . have been in part a reflection on the uncovering of new biological facts, but only in part. They have also reflected general sociopolitical biases derived from human social experience and carried over into 'scientific' realms."[16] While researchers will not be able to identify all the ways they might be biased, awareness of the potential for bias may lead researchers to communicate their methodological decisions clearly so that another researcher, with a different set of biases, might be able to identify flaws in a study.

To study genetic diversity across humanity, Lewontin selected samples from different populations of humans. By carefully describing the choices he made, he allows other researchers to critique his decisions or to *replicate* his work—repeating his procedures to check whether similar results would be found.[17] Lewontin clearly explains his decisions regarding how to categorize race, noting that classifying humans into races is problematic: "No one would confuse a Papuan aboriginal with any South American Indian, yet no one can give an objective criterion for where a dividing line should be drawn in the continuum from South American Indians through Polynesians, Micronesians, Melanesians, and Papuans."[18] The concept of racial classification suggests that humans can be easily separated into distinct groups, but Lewontin argues that observed physical differences within and across groups of humans suggests a continuum of distinctions, rather than clear and separate groups.

One challenge to drawing lines around groups of humans and calling them different races is that some groups are particularly difficult to classify. For example, Lewontin notes that the Sami people[19] of northern Europe, a nomadic group, are hard to assign to a race because a focus on language suggests they should be classified as Asian, while a focus on physical appearance is ambiguous because they share features with Asians and Europeans, and a focus on genetic traits suggests consistency with Asians on some traits and with Europeans on other traits.[20]

Lewontin carefully describes his decision to adhere to "classical racial grouping with a few switches based on obvious total genetic divergence."[21] This results in seven "races," but Lewontin acknowledges that he might have drawn the lines between racial categories differently. Do you agree with Lewontin's classification of Belgians, Dutch, English, French, Germans, Italians, Russians, and Welsh as "Caucasians"? What do you think of his classification of Arabs, Egyptians, Hindi-speaking Indians, Irani, and Urdu-speaking Pakistani as "Caucasians"? His category of "Black Africans" includes Gambians, Ghanaians, Kenyans, and Liberians. It also includes Black Americans and Iraqi. We invite your perspective on each of these "classic" categories of race. Lewontin uses the term "Mongoloids" to include groups such as Chinese, Japanese, and Koreans. After acknowledging the challenge of classifying the Sami people, they are classified in the "Mongoloid" group, along with Turks. The remaining "races" in the study were "South Asian Aborigines"; "Amerinds," including among others Apache, Chippewa, Eskimo, Maya, Pueblo, and Seminole; "Oceanians," including among others Easter Islanders, Fijians, Hawaiians, Papuans, and Tongans; and "Australian Aborigines" (the only category without any subgroups).[22] If you were asked to separate humans into racial groups, how would you do so? Where would you fit Latina/os who are genetically related to both the Spanish and Native American groups?

Focusing on seventeen genes (ABO blood proteins, Rh factor, and others), Lewontin clearly explains how he used statistical techniques to seek an answer to the question, "How much of human diversity between populations is accounted for by more or less conventional racial classifications?"[23] He tested whether classic racial categories are genetically different from each other and found that only 6.3 percent of genetic variation between humans is accounted for by race. Within a given group, such as the English, 85.4 percent of the diversity among humans occurs. The greatest amount of genetic variability occurs within each of the groups. The remaining 8.3 percent of variation occurred between groups that were classified together into races.[24] Lewontin concludes:

> It is clear that our perception of relatively large differences between human races and subgroups, as compared to the variation within these groups, is indeed a biased perception and that . . . human races and populations are remarkably similar to each other, with the largest part by far of human variation being accounted for by the differences between individuals.[25]

The opening paragraph of the American Anthropological Association's "Statement on 'Race'" emphasizes this finding that there is greater genetic variation within human groups than across human groups. Based on empirical evidence produced by Lewontin and by researchers who conducted replications inspired by Lewontin's research, the American Anthropological Association has rejected race as a biological category.

Lewontin's work provides a strong example of the empirical process. He carefully frames his research question and transparently communicates his decisions regarding from whom and how to collect, analyze, and interpret information. This is all communicated in a way that invites criticism and replication of his work. Indeed, Lewontin's work has been replicated multiple times, yielding similar results across different researchers who have modified the procedure to test for alternative explanations for Lewontin's results. Across eight replications from researchers working independently from Lewontin and testing different genetic markers, the results repeatedly demonstrate that the greatest genetic differences are between individuals within populations, with smaller differences occurring between groups that are classified within the same race and between racial groups. The finding of greater diversity within races than between races is upheld both when classical racial distinctions are used and when researchers begin with genetic distinctions to try to classify distinct racial groups. After reviewing Lewontin's work and the replications of it, physical anthropologists Ryan A. Brown and George J. Armelagos conclude, ". . . the amount of human genetic diversity that is attributable to race is only about 5% to 10%."[26]

Lewontin's work has been highly influential in modern scholarship on race. Unfortunately, biased research such as Morton's flawed work on cranial capacity was also highly influential in its time. All empiricists should be aware that the empirical method does not clearly reveal what is true or what is false. Good empiricism requires that one keep the example of flawed research in mind. One's own work could also be revealed to have been foolish or even applied in horrifyingly harmful ways.

Ideally, incorrect ideas will be ruled out: "Because scientists subject their propositions to confirmation or disproof through empirical testing, science has the potential to be self-correcting. It is assumed that the gradual accumulation of evidence from empirical research will lead to the rejection of inaccurate conceptions and theories and to the construction and refinement of better ones."[27] Anthropologist Alice Littlefield and colleagues note that this ideal in empiricism is rare. Current culture, historical movements, and personal bias—all of which often function outside of conscious awareness—affect empiricists' choices of topic, approach to asking questions, and readiness to accept others' empirical work. For physical anthropology, the termination of the concept of race as a biological category coincided with the civil rights movement in the United States; the political movement prepared researchers to accept ongoing scientific work that revealed that race was not viable as a biological category.

Empirical work, no matter how carefully designed, may be flawed because humans choose what research questions to study and how to study them, including from whom to collect information. Humans are influenced by pervasive ideologies in their culture that may lead to faulty assumptions serving as the foundation for research.[28]

But Isn't Race Clearly Rooted in Biology?

Why Do I Perceive Differences between
Europeans, Asians, and Africans?

In 2001, Eshleman—a white woman—traveled in Europe with a good friend who is a Black American woman and the friend's first cousin, also a Black American woman. Eshleman's close friend has an appearance that one could argue is easily classified as being of African descent, based on her deep brown skin tone and her choice to wear her hair in natural curls, while her cousin may be difficult to quickly classify in terms of race based on her relatively light skin tone and long, straight hair.

On a train traveling through Germany, a young, white German man from a small town approached Eshleman's friend and said words to the effect of "We have a Black woman in my town." He even shared the name of that woman. Eshleman's friend responded politely but was clearly surprised by this man's declaration. Did he think that all Black people across the world were socially connected to one another to the point of knowing all the other members of the group by name? Her cousin was also disturbed by this exchange, but for a different reason. She wondered why he had not addressed his statements to her as well as to her cousin, questioning why he did not recognize them as the same race.

Shade of skin color, profile of nose, structure of eyes, shape of lips, texture and amount of hair have been used to classify individuals in terms of race. Interestingly, these are the same traits that are used to differentiate one person from another.[29] These two women look distinctly different from each other, yet they are considered to be the same race.

Clinical psychologist Marvin Zuckerman argues, "The answer to the question 'What is race?' seems simple to the layperson who makes judgments from prototypical images derived from caricatures found in art, literature, and the media."[30] The man on the train focused his attention on one Black woman who was prototypical of his concept of Black but ignored another Black woman. Zuckerman challenges the concept of race as a biological category, noting that some groups classified as Caucasian have darker skin than those classified as Black Africans.[31] For example, persons from India may have darker skin than individuals from Iraq. Historian Nell Irvin Painter provides further evidence of the difficulty of defining race by physical features: "We usually assume definitions of race as color to be straightforward, as though 'black' Americans were always dark-skinned." Painter argues, "race as color and actual color of skin" are not equivalent.[32]

People in the United States tend to perceive skin color as indicating distinct racial categories, but an objective analysis of skin pigmentation reveals a continuum from pale to dark, rather than distinct groups distinguished by color.[33] Individuals tend to perceive different skin shades for whites, Asians, or Blacks even when pigmentation is identical. Other indicators of race such as shape of eyes and hair texture influence how skin color is perceived. Skin tone distinctions between races can often be less distinct than the great diversity within a race. Two white people may have remarkably different skin tones from each other, as may two African American people.

Evolutionary biologist and African American studies scholar Joseph L. Graves Jr. notes, "None of the physical features by which we have historically defined human races—skin color, hair type, body stature, blood groups, disease prevalence—unambiguously corresponds to the racial groups that we have constructed."[34] Within biology, "The term 'race' implies the existence of some nontrivial underlying hereditary features shared by a group of people and not present in other groups."[35] While such a biological definition of race has often been mistakenly applied to humans, ". . . if race is defined as a population that has achieved the subspecies level of genetic differentiation, no such divergence currently exists in our species."[36]

In chapter 1, we explored different classes in feudal Europe being treated almost like different species—the ruling class as one species while the peasant class would be a distinct species. Given the biological definition of race, the different classes would have been perceived as different races. Why would you or would you not perceive a king in England as a different race than an English peasant who worked on the land owned by the king?

While there are certainly hereditary differences that occur in shades of skin tone, shapes of facial features, hair texture and quantity, body shapes and sizes, and resistance or susceptibility to disease, these hereditary differences are greater within groups classified as races than across races. If we focus on all people who are Asian American, we will find great diversity within the group on lightness to darkness of skin shade, shapes of noses or eyes, body proportions, and health on many different variables.

Empirical work by anthropologists and biologists has convinced many researchers to reject the concept of race as a biological category for humans. Indeed, today most researchers in anthropology, biology, and sociology agree that race is not a biological category. Anthropologists Littlefield and colleagues detailed the following major challenges to the concept of race as biological.[37]

1. If race existed as a biological category, researchers should be able to clearly group humans into distinct races based on biological criteria

alone. Researchers should be able to use a combination of dimensions to distinguish one race from another. Yet no such combination—of shade of skin, hair texture, shape of eyes, body size, genetic blood markers, or disease susceptibility—have clearly been able to distinguish races from each other as distinctly different biological groups.[38]

2. Researchers may try to separate people into racial groups based on one hereditary dimension (such as any of those listed above). If they then check to see if those groups are also distinct on another dimension, the groups created with one biological marker do not coincide with groups created from another biological marker. As Brown and Armelagos explain, "A single trait such as skin color will result in a classification system that is easily determined. Add another trait and classification becomes a more difficult task, and there usually are groups that cannot be classified. As you increase the number of traits, the problems in racial classification become insurmountable."[39]

3. There are many human beings that do not fit into classic racial categories. Human groups have shared genetic material by having children together for so many generations over the last 100,000 years that there are many people who cannot be classified according to race.[40]

4. Rather than distinct categories (e.g., white or Native American), human variation exists on a continuum. Influential physical anthropologist Alan H. Goodman identifies, "Therefore, there is no clear place to designate where one race begins and another ends."[41]

We anticipate that challenging the concept of race as a biological category will be disconcerting for some readers while it will comfortably fit the perspective of other readers.

Goodman recollects his first exposure to evidence that race is not a biological category, in 1973 in an anthropology course taught by physical anthropologist, George J. Armelagos.

> I recollect that it made almost instant sense to me that human races are social constructions. . . . I had grown up in a working-class family in a town composed mostly of second-generation immigrants from Italy and Ireland, and as a boy I was aware of being perceived as Jewish and different from my Irish and Italian friends in some fundamental way. Yet when I began attending a more diverse university, something striking happened: I became "White." I was no longer perceived as very distinct from other students of European descent.[42]

We invite you to reflect on how your personal experiences with race might influence your reactions to the material in this chapter and throughout this text.

Using Cultural Materialism to
Critique Eugenics and the Question of Intelligence

As discussed in chapter 1, religion was once used to uphold the status quo. Science also has been inappropriately used to "explain" why some people are on top and others deserve their place at the bottom.

Cultural materialism offers a critical perspective by which we can evaluate eugenics, a social and scientific movement in the United States and Europe popular in the late 1800s and early 1900s. The eugenics movement was founded and supported by white elites and by scientists and scientific research.[43] (At that time, people considered white were primarily those whose families came from England and northwest Europe.) Much like how the production of "knowledge" and "truth" in feudal times was monopolized by aristocracy and the Church, European and American elites monopolized the production and dissemination of scientific "knowledge" in the nineteenth and early twentieth centuries. And the knowledge they produced benefited some—them—and harmed many, many others.

Elites used the "science" of eugenics to expose what they believed to be the inherent genetic differences between different races. In other words, scientists in Europe and the United States used eugenics to show that people inherited the supposed "characteristics" of their race and social class. If one was a genius, one came from geniuses. If one was a criminal, one came from criminals. And in this framework, geniuses were inevitably British, criminals and "simpletons" always poor or of color. The eugenicists already "knew"— they *believed* they knew—how things were in terms of race. They merely used the "science" of eugenics to "prove" their—wrongheaded—thinking correct.

Francis Galton, cousin of Charles Darwin, invented the term *eugenics* in his 1883 book, *Inquiries into Human Faculty and Its Development*. By eugenics, Galton meant, "to describe the application of scientific knowledge to stem the tide of racial deterioration and bring about the perfection" of the British race.[44] Galton, like many British and British American (also called Anglo American) elites, believed that people understood to be of other racial groups—including Jews, the Irish, Italians, and people from Africa, Asia, and the Americas—presented a threat to the best, purest, smartest, strongest, and most civilized races—primarily themselves, the British. Galton argued, "Human breeding could be systematically managed to ensure the improvement of the British race, as well as other civilized peoples."[45]

Galton believed objective scientists such as he could numerically measure differences between races. And with this information, breeding policies could be implemented to support the proliferation of the pure peoples (people like

Galton) and to stem the growing populations of impure peoples (people coming from backgrounds different from that of Galton and other elites).

In a variety of venues, Galton managed to measure up a storm. He collected data on physical characteristics such as height and weight. He gathered information on people's medical histories, and he even attempted to measure *mental processes*—"internal, subjective experiences . . . sensations, perceptions, dreams, thoughts, beliefs, and feelings."[46] Using the immense amount of data he gathered, Galton leapt to interpret it in ways that fit his own racist and classist philosophy. The logic was circular. Poor people were poor because they were less fit than the middle and upper classes rather than because of a lack of economic and other opportunities. And Black people were servile because they came from a race that is genetically prone to slavery and servitude rather than because of a history of colonization, slavery, and brutal oppression. After a trip to South Africa, Galton wrote, "These savages court slavery. . . . They seem to be made for slavery, and naturally fall into its ways."[47] Graves exposes Galton's thinking on enslaved African Americans, noting, "In his zeal to classify Africans as an inferior type, Galton failed to note or understand that most of the literature on American slave intelligence was written by slaveholders."[48]

Galton maintained a complete ignorance as to the actual lives, histories, and experiences of the supposedly "unfit" that he studied. In other words, he was not interested in the ways environment—nurture—influences people and their development, individually and culturally. He never examined the brutality of colonization or slavery. Much like the nobility in feudal Europe saw the situation of peasants as the will of God, Galton and other eugenicists argued that the poor and non-Anglo lived as they did because of their own genetic makeup, or biological nature. And the eugenicists called their thinking "scientific."

Galton's eugenics became a profoundly popular, international "scientific" movement, one that reverberates through our society even today. In particular, we still struggle with the heritage of the eugenic approach to intelligence. In 1905, a psychologist named Alfred Binet published an article about his work on intelligence levels. From this work, a scale was developed on which individuals could be ranked from "subnormal" to "very superior."[49] Binet did not argue that intelligence was hereditary. Yet the eugenicists did. They jumped on his ideas and used them for their own ends. For the eugenicists, intelligence was clearly an inherited characteristic.

Much like intelligence tests today, the early intelligence tests were highly problematic. For one, they were deeply biased. Stuart Ewen and Elizabeth Ewen note that in a time when many people, particularly poor people and marginalized groups like those of color and new immigrants, had no electricity and thus knew very little about it, the test asked multiple-choice questions like "The watt is used in measuring wind power, rainfall, water power, [or] electricity?"[50]

The eugenicists categorized those who fell in the subnormal category as "feeble-minded." And they fine-tuned this category into "idiots," "imbeciles," and "morons." Morons were the high end, the smartest, of the feebleminded. They presented a special threat as "people who were capable of entering into and functioning in mainstream society, often undetected, but whose genetic flaws endangered the long-term vitality of the race."[51]

Eugenicists recommended that supposedly feebleminded people be sterilized or isolated so that they could not reproduce. Based on their (now understood to be completely bogus) scientific studies, between "1907 and 1968, an estimated sixty thousand forced sterilizations would take place in the United States."[52] Further, Ewen and Ewen note, "Eugenic sterilization practices would also be exported to America's new colonial holdings, most notably Puerto Rico, where one-third of the female population was sterilized between 1920 and 1965."[53] And in Germany, the Nazis revered the work of eugenicists. In 1934, they used it to justify the Third Reich's Sterilization Law and forced 350,000 unwilling people "under the surgeon's knife."[54]

In the United States and other places today, eugenicist ideas about intelligence grip and influence us still. For example, in The Bell Curve, Harvard University psychologist Richard J. Herrnstein and well-known conservative thinker and political scientist Charles Murray argued in 1994 that intelligence is something we are born with (or without); it can be as measured through intelligence tests like Binet's; and it fundamentally shapes people's lives. About this, Halley argues that like the earlier eugenicists, "Herrnstein and Murray reify 'intelligence' by assuming that it can be measured via intelligence tests."[55] This thinking "overlooks the fact that intelligence tests are themselves a socially constructed artifact, not handed to us by God or nature, but by psychometricians" such as Herrnstein and Murray.[56] In this circular thinking, "intelligence is that which is measured by . . . intelligence tests."[57] Yet in reality, as in the example question above, instead of "intelligence," intelligence tests might only measure things such as how much access people have to resources like electricity.

Since The Bell Curve came out, innumerable studies have shown the book's many mistakes in and misuse of statistical data.[58] There is, however, a deeper problem, one we examine again and again in our book. As cultural materialists argue, the reason ideas such as those proposed by eugenicists and later by Herrnstein and Murray keep deeply influencing our society is because they justify and reinforce an extremely unequal and unfair material reality.

Much like the earlier eugenicists, completely ignoring historical and social evidence to the contrary in addition to misreading and misusing statistical data, Herrnstein and Murray argued that inequality happens in society due to a "fair process that sorts people out according to how intelligent they are."[59] Like the earlier eugenicists, Herrnstein and Murray link their claims to race (and in their case to gender). They argue that African Americans and Latina/os are "by nature not as intelligent as whites; that is why they [do] less well economically, and that is why little can or should be done about racial inequality."[60] Herrnstein and Murray base their claims on the same old idea as the eugenicists, one born out of and supporting an economic reality that greatly advantages some and deeply disadvantages others. According to this thinking, people are rich (and white people are more likely to be rich) because they, the rich, are naturally smarter than others, and people are poor (and they are more likely to be Black and Latina/o) because they, the poor, are naturally dumber. In other words, this idea proposes that the economic reality of inequality in our society is the way it is because it is natural.

In sharp contrast to the nature perspective on intelligence, including that of the eugenicists and Herrnstein and Murray, innumerable studies indicate that nurture (or environment) shapes intelligence. People's intelligence varies based on the educational and nutritional resources they have access to starting at a very young age. Studies even suggest that something as simple as breast-feeding predicts intelligence and that breast-fed infants score better on intelligence tests than formula-fed infants. Indeed, a Danish study concluded that the "longer infants are breast-fed the higher they are likely to score on intelligence tests as adults."[61]

In their important book on inequality, Claude S. Fischer and five other sociologists from the University of California at Berkeley show that "even if intelligence exists, it is not a single, unitary and fixed trait" as Herrnstein and Murray and the eugenicists assumed.[62] Fischer and colleagues illustrate that IQ or intelligence test scores "can, and have, historically changed over time. Fischer et al. point to eastern and southern European immigrants whose test scores were below average when first arriving" in the United States around 1900.[63] Many saw this as a sign that the new immigrants were less fit than the Anglo American middle and upper class. "Yet a couple of generations later, the test scores of the new groups had risen dramatically, matching or exceeding those of earlier-arriving white Americans."[64] A couple of generations of this group living in the United States and gaining access to greater resources, nutrition, and education and becoming insiders to the mainstream culture meant a significantly higher level of intelligence, as measured by IQ tests. If intelligence truly were hereditary, these groups' intelligence would have remained essentially the same over time.

The test scores of African Americans and Latina/os have also risen with access to greater resources, but continued inequality continues to predict lower scores for these groups. African Americans and Latina/os today "tend to score lower than do whites on standardized tests."[65] Unlike the European immigrants whose scores increased from below average to reach the level of mainstream white Americans over two or three generations, Black and Latina/o scores have not risen at the same pace. Inequality explains this discrepancy. While European immigrants have gained equality within a few generations of arriving in the United States, Black and Latina/o immigrants have been largely excluded in our society. As Fischer and colleagues argue, "A racial or ethnic group's position in society determines its measured intelligence rather than vice versa."[66] In other words, a group's average IQ scores measure the extent to which that group has gained equality in the United States rather than the group's actual level of intellectual ability.

Historically and today, this phenomenon can be seen in innumerable societies. As discussed above, Jews, Irish, and Italians in the United States became white and gained equality, and their scores rose. And Koreans in Japan,

> who are of the same "racial" stock as Japanese and who in the United States do about as well academically as Americans of Japanese origin (that is, above average), are distinctively "dumb" in Japan. The explanation cannot be racial, nor even cultural in any simple way. The explanation is that Koreans, whose nation was a colony of Japan for about a half-century, have formed a lower-caste group in Japan.[67]

In particular, Fischer and colleagues argue that groups in an inferior position because of "conquest or capture (e.g., the Irish in Great Britain, Maori in New Zealand, Africans, Mexicans, and Indians in the United States) . . . suffer the most drastic and lasting effects of subordination."[68] Fischer and colleagues claim that these subordinate groups face socioeconomic deprivation (to be discussed further in chapters 5 and 7), segregation (to be discussed further in chapters 5, 6, and 7), and a stigma of inferiority (to be discussed further in chapter 6). As groups overcome these effects of subordination, their standardized (intelligence) test scores rise.[69]

The fact that "in the early part of the twentieth century northern *blacks* did better in school than did most white immigrant groups"[70] exemplifies how the position of a group in society determines the group's test scores. In the early twentieth century, when African Americans living in the northern United States experienced a similar level of equality compared to new European immigrants, Black students performed better than the new immigrants in school. And today Black test scores are rising as African Americans overcome the effects of subordination (in spite of ongoing and profound racism and discrimination, as will be discussed in later chapters). Indeed, in his research on standardized test scores, Jonathan Crane found that observed underperformance of Black students in comparison to white students in math and reading can be accounted for by equality-based variables such as income of the child's family and the wealth of the mother's peers when she was in school. When Crane compared Black and white students whose family lives were very similar, he found that their test scores were similar.

Interpreting Empirical Evidence

In addition to the risk of bias seeping into research based on the way data are collected, the interpretation of results can introduce bias. When eugenicist Charles Benedict Davenport found evidence that Black Americans outperformed whites on a test of numerical calculations, he perceived this as evidence of the intellectual inferiority of Blacks, downplaying the skill with which Blacks performed better than whites. One may wonder what conclusion Davenport would have made if the data were in the opposite direction, if whites had performed better than Blacks on the same test. If one would interpret *any* finding as fitting one's preconceived notions, the interpretation becomes meaningless.[71]

Information can be interpreted in drastically divergent ways by different researchers. For example, Elisha Harris, a white physician working in the late 1800s, was deeply concerned about environmental conditions connected to poverty and crime. Harris appointed Richard Louis Dugdale, who shared an interest in sociology, to study a white family from Ulster County, New York. The family, given the pseudonym "the Jukes," was believed to have an unusual number of persons convicted of crime, of impoverished individuals seeking social services, and of people engaging in behavior that was considered sexually promiscuous by the standards of the time. Geneticist Elof Axel Carlson describes Dugdale's 1875 publication, in which Dugdale interpreted the information he collected as evidence of "a bad environment" for the members of the Juke family, interpreting the data in terms of nurture.[72] He argued that the experiences of this family, including a lack of appropriate social support systems, was responsible for their troubles. Further, he argued that the state of New York should invest in higher-quality housing and enhanced education, suggesting that failure to provide adequate resources was costly in terms of funding court fees and prisons when problems later arose.

Interestingly, others dramatically reinterpreted the problems of the Juke family in terms of nature. In 1916, eugenicist Arthur H. Estabrook claimed that the pattern of criminal conviction, poverty, and expression of sexuality within the Juke family provided evidence of a hereditary flaw inherited through genes.[73] From the perspective of eugenics, investing more in social support would be worthless if problems are caused by genes rather than the environment. (Eugenicists would prefer government spending to focus on sterilization of the downtrodden and special opportunities for elites.) Notably, subsequent analyses of the Juke family have revealed a number of upstanding citizens within the family, calling the data themselves—not just the opposing interpretations—into question.[74]

Correlation Does Not Reveal Causation
Focusing on the original data that the members of the extended Juke family were found to be more likely to have social problems, we cannot conclude from these data that the cause is clearly an aspect of nurture or that it is clearly nature. Setting aside for a moment that the data themselves may have been flawed, these data are correlational. A *correlation* is a relationship between one dimension of interest (one variable) and a second dimension of interest (a second variable) that allows us to make predictions.

Turning to an example previously used in this chapter, Galton argued that Black people were servile because their race was genetically prone to servitude. Here Galton claimed to have observed a correlation between race and level of servitude. Galton might have described the variable of race as having several classifications, including Black, white, Asian, and American Indian. He might have ranked servitude from high levels to low levels.

While correlational data allow prediction, one cannot determine cause or effect from correlational data. *Correlation does not reveal causation.* In Galton's time, he would have been able to predict with some consistency how servile someone would act toward him based on his assumptions about the person's race. If he interacted with an enslaved Black person in the United States, Galton would be likely to observe a high level of servitude. If he interacted with a free white person, he would be likely to observe less servitude. In this example, our modern perspective helps us to see the bias in Galton's claim that Blacks were naturally more servile. Galton clearly failed to account for the variables of slavery (and how it was confounded with race) and of oppression (and how it was confounded with slavery).

Social psychologists Bernard E. Whitley and Mary E. Kite identify why correlation is insufficient to reveal causation.[75] While three criteria must be present to claim that one variable has caused a change in another variable, correlation always fails to meet the third required criterion. The first criterion necessary to claim causation is covariation—differences in the first variable must be accompanied by changes in the second variable. Correlation meets the criterion of covariation. In our example, covariation would mean that races would be observed to have different levels of servitude.

The second criterion for causation is that the cause must occur prior to the effect. While this can sometimes be determined for correlational data, it is often difficult to determine because many correlational studies measure both variables at the same time. In our example, Galton observed races as he understood them at the same time as observing level of servitude. Because Galton did not examine evidence of levels of servitude among races prior to colonization or systems of slavery, he cannot conclude which variable might have preceded the other.

The third criterion for causation is that one must be able to rule out other possible causes of the relationship between the two variables of interest. In correlational research, the researcher simply measures the variables of interest without controlling how one variable may influence another. Therefore, other possible causes cannot be eliminated with correlational research. The experimental method is the only technique that allows a researcher to control one variable—an independent variable—to see the effect it may have on a second variable—a dependent variable.

We are dumbfounded that Galton failed to consider the brutal oppression that accompanied colonization and slavery. Focusing on oppression could explain why there appeared to Galton to be differences in servitude related to race. Correlational data can never rule out all the possible alternative causes that could explain the relationship between two variables because the researchers lack the control that is necessary to eliminate other explanations. This is why correlation does not reveal causation.[76]

All data used by eugenicists will be correlational because researchers will not be able to ethically or realistically control heredity for human groups. An experimental design that would allow a test of genes as a causal variable could only occur in a horrifying scenario in which humans were bred for specific genes. (Although breeding plans of elites with elites were a goal of the eugenics movement, it is unconscionable to imagine conducting a human experiment based on selective breeding.) Alternatively, researchers can ethically study certain nurture-based hypotheses, studying how controlled changes to specific elements of the environment affect behavior. Returning to the example of the Juke family, Dugdale called for prison reform so that individuals convicted of crime would be rehabilitated and less likely to engage in further crime. One can imagine an ethical nurture-based hypothesis in which some prison inmates would be given access to vocational education while others would be given access to literacy-based education. In a true experiment, rather than a correlational study, researchers could examine the impact of the type of educational opportunity on *recidivism*, the likelihood of inmates returning to criminal activity.

Science is often treated like proven fact. Scientists are humans who are influenced by cultural understandings, personal experiences, and social ideology. They seek to provide objective evidence, but they may unintentionally engage in biased evaluation of data. No matter how carefully one tries to frame a research question objectively, one might act in biased ways.[77] We challenge you to think critically about how and by whom research questions are framed, how information is collected, from whom information is collected, and how information is interpreted.

Although some scientific work has promoted racism, science also has been valuable in critiquing racism and promoting greater social justice across races. Through empirical work, modern researchers have been able to explain that race is a social and cultural concept, not a biological category.

Studying Racial Health Disparities: How the Social Construct of Race Influences Biology

In the United States today, a racial disparity exists in rates of multiple health problems, including cardiovascular disease, specific cancers, and diabetes.[78] (See box 2.1 at the end of the chapter for a description of sickle cell disease as a historical case of biased racial thinking.) Whites are less likely to experience each of these health problems than are Black Americans. Given that there is greater genetic diversity among whites and among Blacks than there is genetic difference between these groups, nature fails to provide a strong explanation for the health disparity. Alternatively, if one focuses on nurture when seeking an explanation, one may look at environmental variables that tend to differ by racial groups, such as likelihood of experiencing poverty,[79] exposure to environmental toxins,[80] nutrition based on the quality of produce in grocery stores located within neighborhoods,[81] and availability of park spaces perceived as safe places for exercise.[82] Socioeconomic class better predicts disease than does race.[83]

Sociologist Michael S. Kimmel argues that a perspective focusing on nurture will explore how different environmental experiences create unequal situations. His criticism of the nurture perspective is that it does not focus appropriately on inequality as the cause of the differences between groups.[84] The unfair advantages that whites as a group experience in the United States in comparison to Black Americans create different economic opportunities, safer environments, better access to quality nutrition, and more opportunities for healthy physical activity. While the nurture perspective will simply list the disparities, in the following chapter we will further explore the theory of *social construction*, which focuses on how inequality creates difference. Rather than simply cataloguing disparities, focusing on injustice is more likely to lead to appropriate calls for social action.[85]

Anthropologist Clarence C. Gravlee advocates for a focus on social inequalities. While emphasizing that race is not a genetic category, Gravlee challenges readers to consider ". . . how racial inequality becomes embodied—literally—in the biological well-being of racialized groups and individuals."[86] There are biological consequences to the unequal treatment of groups that are socially understood as races in the United States. Individual experiences of discrimination[87] and institutionalized racism predict greater health problems.[88] For example, institutionalized racism predicts the greater likelihood of landfills and other toxic spaces being located closer to neighborhoods traditionally inhabited by African Americans than by whites.[89] Larger historical and political events also predict health disparities. For example, epidemiology scholar Diane S. Lauderdale found that women in California with Arabic names (but not other women) were more likely to experience health problems when giving birth in the six months following September 11, 2001, compared to the six months that preceded the attack.[90] We invite you to consider other major events that could predict differential health outcomes based on discrimination.

Race is not a biological category, yet the impact of political, historical, cultural, and environmental events that target specific populations do influence biology. For example, Ashkenazi Jewish women who have a specific mutation on a gene thought to suppress tumors are more likely to develop breast cancer. In a 1999 study, a comparison sample of British women with the same mutation who were not Ashkenazi Jews were no more likely to develop breast cancer than women without the mutation. If we recognize that race is not biological, we will seek an explanation based on how culture, history, or environment may have affected this gene's relationship with disease in different groups. Graves argues that the Holocaust limited genetic diversity among Ashkenazi Jewish people. This mutation may predict breast cancer similarly in any group exposed to such genetic trauma.[91]

When comparing Ashkenazi Jews to a group that has not experienced a catastrophe such as the Holocaust, we may be viewing the effects of horrifying political decisions that eliminated over 60 percent of the people in a genetic pool (in 1933, an estimated 9.5 million Jews were living in Europe;[92] 5,721,000 of these individuals were murdered in the Holocaust).[93] Graves notes, "The problem is that many biomedical researchers and clinicians are still working under the yoke of the biological race concept. Hence, they see all biological differences between and within populations as potentially due to racial genetic composition."[94] If research begins with an incorrect assumption that race is genetic, researchers may fail to seek cultural, historical, political, or environmental explanations that could lead to a better understanding of how disease affects all humans.

Conclusion

Contrary to much past and present popular thinking, we now understand that race is not biological. Further we see that "western attempts to [examine, measure, and quantify human biological diversity] have historically been both motivated by racist social agendas and infused throughout with racist ideology."[95] Yet this does not mean there is no such thing as race. Indeed, *race exists and profoundly shapes our lives*. As Goodman claims, race "is not biologically based; rather, it is social with biological consequences."[96] Race is, as we argue in the following chapter, socially constructed. And because of its powerful influence, it is deeply important that we recognize race and understand its impact on us as individuals and as a society.

Box 2.1

Sickle Cell Disease: Biased Assumptions about Race

Imagine that you were a researcher in the 1920s in the United States studying sickle cell disease, a hereditary blood disorder in which a double-recessive pairing of a section of one gene causes the shape of red blood cells to obstruct the flow of blood, leading to injuries of the lungs, liver, spleen, kidneys, and eyes.[1] The initial cases of sickle cell disease were observed in African Americans. You, like other researchers at the time, perceived race as a clear and important biological category and therefore followed the lead of other researchers in understanding sickle cell disease as linked to this biological concept of race, as a disease that affects people from Africa. Then you were confused when people of Greek descent were also diagnosed with the disease—surely these individuals must have some African heritage if they are found to have a racial disease that affects Africans.[2]

The initial, and highly influential, claim that sickle cell disease was a racial disease was based on only four observed cases of the disease. The researchers at the time believed race was biological—after all, they might argue they could clearly perceive racial differences between whites and Blacks and Asians. They perceived evidence of a newly discovered disease with cases in only four Black Americans as sufficient evidence that the disease was racial. (By common standards in medical research today, grounding such a claim on only four cases would be considered ludicrous.)[3]

In the late 1940s Anthony Allison, a British student in his twenties, was studying the sciences before beginning his medical training. Allison had grown up in Kenya and sought to become a physician and return to the land of his childhood. In 1949, he traveled with a team to Kenya to research genetic traits related to malaria—a potentially lethal parasitic disease carried by mosquitoes. The researchers discovered that in regions affected by malaria, 20 percent to 30 percent of individuals carried the gene for sickle cell disease. Interestingly, in other areas of Kenya that were not affected by malaria, not even 1 percent of individuals carried the gene.[4]

Today researchers understand sickle cell disease to be related to malaria resistance. Individuals who inherit the gene that produces the sickle cell protein from one parent, but not the other, are resistant to malaria without experiencing sickle cell disease.[5] When individuals inherit the gene that produces the sickle cell protein from both parents, they are also resistant to malaria but suffer from sickle cell disease.

Physical anthropologist Frank B. Livingstone's research on sickle cell disease and malaria helped to develop a theory that sickle cell disease was not linked to race but to natural selection within environments where malaria was a threat. Livingstone studied land in equatorial Africa where tropical forests had been cleared for agriculture. The human alterations of the land created areas where water pooled and mosquitoes flourished. Individuals who were resistant to malaria because they were heterozygous for the sickle cell gene had an advantage of being resistant to the potentially deadly parasitic disease while not suffering from sickle cell disease. Given that such individuals were more likely to survive, they were also more likely to have children and to pass on the sickle cell gene.[6] Modern research reveals that the sickle cell gene is more common in places where the risk of malaria is high, including areas of southern Europe, the Middle East, and southern Asia.[7]

Notes

1. American Anthropological Association, "Race: Are We So Different?" www.understandingrace.org/humvar/sickle_02.html (June 17, 2010).
2. Melbourne Tapper, *In the Blood: Sickle Cell Anemia and the Politics of Race* (Philadelphia: University of Pennsylvania Press, 1998).
3. Graves, *The Emperor's New Clothes*, 142–43.
4. Larsen, *Our Origins*, 85–86.
5. Graves, *The Emperor's New Clothes*, 143.
6. Larsen, *Our Origins*, 103–6.
7. American Anthropological Association, "Race: Are We So Different?"

Discussion Questions

1. List and evaluate multiple explanations for why race is not a biological category. Explore how your personal experiences with race may have influenced your reaction to the evidence that race is not based on genes.
2. How did Franz Boas's research on the skulls of immigrants and their children challenge racism?
3. Define nature and nurture. How have nature and nurture been used to interpret evidence about intelligence of different racial groups? What biases have occurred in attempts to scientifically study intelligence?
4. What biases were present in Morton's analysis of cranial capacity? Explore the possible role of ideology in Morton's work. How did Gould expose Morton's bias?
5. What did Lewontin's research reveal about human genetic variation and race?
6. How has science been used to justify social inequality? Describe the eugenics movement. What were the goals of the movement? What social policies did the movement promote? How was the movement connected to racism?
7. Why does correlation not reveal causation? Choose an example of correlational research from this chapter. Explore how nature or nurture could be used to suggest a causal explanation for the evidence in the study. How do competing explanations relate to the inability to conclude causation from correlational research?
8. If race is not genetic, how can race become embodied? Explore Gravlee's argument and connect it to the evidence on sickle cell disease.

9. The website for the Public Broadcasting Corporation's (PBS's) Race: The Power of an Illusion includes a number of activities that challenge the concept of human races as biological. The website can be found at www.pbs.org/race/000_General/000_00-Home.htm. One exercise invites participants to sort twenty people into racial categories: www.pbs.org/race/002_SortingPeople/002_00-home.htm. After doing the activity, reflect on the extent to which the activity confirmed or disconfirmed the arguments and evidence in this chapter.

10. Read the American Anthropological Association Statement on "Race" www.aaanet.org/stmts/racepp.htm. Respond to the way the statement (a) describes research such as that of Lewontin, (b) explains the ambiguity of racial groups, (c) describes the role of inequality in attempts to understand race as biological, and (d) notes the roles of nature and nurture in descriptions of differences among human groups.

11. Interview someone whose racial interactions in childhood or adolescence were different from your own. If you were raised in a town that was fairly racially homogenous, seek out someone whose high school was more diverse than yours. If you had the experience of being perceived by others as being racially distinct, interview someone whose race did not distinguish him or her.

Notes

1. Clark Spencer Larsen, *Our Origins: Discovering Physical Anthropology* (New York: W. W. Norton & Company, 2008), 121. See also Joseph L. Graves Jr., *The Emperor's New Clothes: Biological Theories of Race at the Millennium* (New Brunswick, N.J.: Rutgers University Press, 2002).

2. Alan H. Goodman, "Why Genes Don't Count (for Racial Differences in Health)," *American Journal of Public Health* 90, no. 11 (November 2000): 1699–700.

3. Graves, *The Emperor's New Clothes*, 40.

4. Public Broadcasting Corporation, "1776: Birth of 'Caucasian,'" *Race: The Power of an Illusion*, 2003, www.pbs.org/race/003_RaceTimeline/003_01-timeline.htm (June 30, 2010).

5. George J. Armelagos and Alan H. Goodman, "Race, Racism, and Anthropology," in *Building a New Biocultural Synthesis: Political-Economic Perspectives on Human Biology*, eds. Alan H. Goodman and Thomas L. Leatherman (Ann Arbor: The University of Michigan Press, 1998), 359–77, 362–63.

6. Clarence C. Gravlee, H. Russell Bernard, and William R. Leonard, "Boas's Changes in Bodily Form: The Immigrant Study, Cranial Plasticity, and Boas's Physical Anthropology," *American Anthropologist* 105, no. 2 (June 2003): 331.

7. In the 1996 statement of the American Association of Physical Anthropologists on "Biological Aspects of Race," the monogenist perspective is clearly stated, see American Association of Physical Anthropologists, "AAPA Statement on Biological Aspects of Race," *American Journal of Physical Anthropology* 101, no. 4 (December 1996): 569–70.

8. Stephen Jay Gould, *The Mismeasure of Man* (New York: W. W. Norton & Company, 1996), 71.

9. Gould, *Mismeasure of Man*.

10. Graves, *The Emperor's New Clothes*, 46.

11. William H. Mace and Edwin P. Tanner, *The Story of Old Europe and Young America* (New York: Rand McNally & Company, 1915), 142–45.

12. Gould, *Mismeasure of Man*, 86.

13. Gould, *Mismeasure of Man*, 88.

14. Paul C. Cozby, *Methods in Behavioral Research*, 10th ed. (New York: McGraw-Hill, 2009), 4–6.

15. R. C. Lewontin, "Apportionment of Human Diversity," *Evolutionary Biology* 6 (1972): 381–98.

16. Lewontin, "The Apportionment," 381.

17. Lewontin, "The Apportionment," 383–85.

18. Lewontin, "The Apportionment," 385.

19. While Lewontin used the now derogatory term "Lapps," we have chosen to describe this group as the Sami people. See the Minnesota State University Mankato electronic museum website for a brief description of the Sami people. www.mnsu.edu/emuseum/cultural/oldworld/europe/lapps.html (June 18, 2010).

20. Lewontin, "The Apportionment," 385.

21. Lewontin, "The Apportionment," 386.

22. Lewontin, "The Apportionment," 387.

23. Lewontin, "The Apportionment," 386.

24. Lewontin, "The Apportionment," 396.

25. Lewontin, "The Apportionment," 397.

26. Ryan A. Brown and George J. Armelagos, "Apportionment of Racial Diversity: A Review," *Evolutionary Anthropology* 10, no. 1 (February 2001): 34–40.

27. Alice Littlefield, Leonard Lieberman, and Larry T. Reynolds, "Redefining Race: The Potential Demise of a Concept in Physical Anthropology," *Current Anthropology* 23, no. 6 (December 1982): 641–55.

28. For a brilliant critique of social scientific methodology, and in particular, ethnography, please do see Patricia Ticineto Clough's *The End(s) of Ethnography: From Realism to Social Criticism* (New York: Peter Lang Publishing, Inc., 1998).

29. Lewontin, "The Apportionment," 382.

30. Marvin Zuckerman, "Some Dubious Premises in Research and Theory on Racial Differences: Scientific, Social, and Ethical Issues," *American Psychologist* 45, no. 12 (December 1990): 1297.

31. Zuckerman, "Some Dubious Premises," 1298.

32. Nell Irvin Painter, *The History of White People* (New York: W. W. Norton & Company, 2010), ix.

33. Graves, *The Emperor's New Clothes*, 29.

34. Graves, *The Emperor's New Clothes*, 5.

35. Graves, *The Emperor's New Clothes*, 5.

36. Graves, *The Emperor's New Clothes*, 6.

37. Littlefield et al., "Redefining Race," 646.

38. See also American Anthropological Association, "American Anthropological Association Statement on 'Race,'" *American Anthropological Association* 1998, www.aaanet.org/stmts/racepp.htm (July 1, 2010).

39. Brown and Armelagos, "Apportionment of Racial Diversity," 34.

40. Race, Ethnicity, and Genetics Working Group, "The Use of Racial, Ethnic, and Ancestral Categories in Human Genetics Research," *American Journal of Human Genetics* 77, no. 4 (October 2005): 519–32.

41. Goodman, "Why Genes Don't Count," 1700.

42. Goodman, "Why Genes Don't Count," 1699.

43. Robert V. Guthrie, *Even the Rat Was White: A Historical View of Psychology*, 2nd ed. (Boston: Pearson, 2004), 43.

44. Stuart Ewen and Elizabeth Ewen, *Typecasting: On the Arts and Sciences of Human Inequality* (New York: Seven Stories Press, 2006), 269.

45. Ewen and Ewen, *Typecasting*, 269.

46. David Myers, *Psychology*, 9th ed. (New York: Worth Publishers, 2010), 6.

47. Francis Galton quoted in Ewen and Ewen, *Typecasting*, 270.

48. Graves, *The Emperor's New Clothes*, 96–97.

49. Ewen and Ewen, *Typecasting*, 285.

50. Ewen and Ewen, *Typecasting*, 303.

51. Ewen and Ewen, *Typecasting*, 285.

52. Ewen and Ewen, *Typecasting*, 299.

53. Ewen and Ewen, *Typecasting*, 299.

54. Ewen and Ewen, *Typecasting*, 299.

55. Jean Halley, "Book Review of *Inequality by Design: Cracking the Bell Curve Myth*" in *Theoretical Criminology* (1998), 136.

56. Halley, "Book Review of *Inequality by Design*," 136.

57. Halley, "Book Review of *Inequality by Design*," 136.

58. Claude S. Fischer, Michael Hout, Martin Sanchez Jankowski, Samuel R. Lucas, Ann Swidler, and Kim Voss, *Inequality by Design: Cracking the Bell Curve Myth* (Princeton, N.J.: Princeton University Press, 1996), 10.

59. For more information on the misuse of statistics and data in Richard J. Herrnstein and Charles Murray, *The Bell Curve: Intelligence and Class Structure in American Life* (New York: Simon & Schuster, 1994), please do see, for example, Fischer et al., *Inequality by Design*.

60. Fischer et al., *Inequality by Design*, 6.

61. Jean Halley, *Boundaries of Touch: Parenting and Adult-Child Intimacy* (Champaign: University of Illinois Press, 2007), 6. For analysis of the complex relationships among race, social class, breast-feeding, and intelligence, please do see Jean Halley's *Boundaries of Touch*.

62. Halley, "Book Review of *Inequality by Design*," 136.

63. Halley, "Book Review of *Inequality by Design*," 136.

64. Fischer et al., *Inequality by Design*, 190.

65. Fischer et al., *Inequality by Design*, 172.

66. Fischer et al., *Inequality by Design*, 173.

67. Fischer et al., *Inequality by Design*, 172.

68. Fischer et al., *Inequality by Design*, 173.

69. Fischer et al., *Inequality by Design*, 172–203.

70. Fischer et al., *Inequality by Design*, 180.

71. Graves, The *Emperor's New Clothes*, 123.

72. Elof Axel Carlson, *The Unfit: A History of a Bad Idea* (Woodbury, N.Y.: Cold Spring Harbor Laboratory Press, 2001), 168.

73. Arthur H. Estabrook, *The Jukes in 1915* (Washington, D.C.: Carnegie Institution of Washington, 1916).

74. Scott Christianson, "Bad Seed or Bad Science: The Story of the Notorious Jukes Family," *New York Times*, February 8, 2003, www.nytimes.com/2003/02/08/arts/08JUKE.html (June 29, 2010).

75. Bernard E. Whitley and Mary E. Kite, *The Psychology of Prejudice and Discrimination*, 2nd ed. (Belmont, Calif.: Wadsworth, 2009), 49–50.

76. Empiricists focus on the experimental method as the only research technique with the potential of revealing cause and effect. We have elected not to delve into research methodology of our three disciplines in this text, but we strongly encourage students to explore the research methodologies used in the fields they study.

77. John Shaughnessy, Eugene Zechmeister, and Jeanne Zechmeister, *Research Methods in Psychology*, 8th ed. (New York: McGraw-Hill, 2008).

78. Clarence C. Gravlee, "How Race Becomes Biology: Embodiment of Social Inequality," *American Journal of Physical Anthropology* 139, no. 1 (February 2009): 47–57.

79. See chapter 5 for evidence supporting this claim.

80. Bunyan I. Bryant and Paul Mohai, *Race and the Incidence of Environmental Hazards: A Time for Discourse* (Boulder, Colo.: Westview Press, 1992).

81. Shannon N. Zenk, Amy J. Schulz, Teretha Hollis-Neely, Richard T. Campbell, Nellie Holmes, Gloria Watkins, Robin Nwankwo, and Angela Odoms-Young, "Fruit and Vegetable Intake in African Americans: Income and Store Characteristics," *American Journal of Preventive Medicine* 29, no. 1 (July 2005): 1–9.

82. Dawn K. Wilson, Karen A. Kirtland, Barbara E. Ainsworth, and Cheryl L. Addy, "Socioeconomic Status and Perceptions of Access and Safety for Physical Activity," *Annals of Behavioral Medicine* 28, no. 1 (August 2004): 20–28.

83. Armelagos and Goodman, "Race, Racism, and Anthropology," 370.

84. Michael S. Kimmel, *The Gendered Society*, 2nd ed. (New York: Oxford University Press, 2004).

85. Kimmel, *The Gendered Society*.

86. Gravlee, "How Race Becomes Biology," 47.

87. See also Louis A. Penner, John F. Dovidio, Donald Edmondson, Rhonda K. Dailey, Tsveti Markova, Terrance L. Albrecht, and Samuel L. Gaertner, "The Experience of Discrimination and Black-White Health Disparities in Medical Care," *Journal of Black Psychology* 35, no. 2 (May 2009): 180–203.

88. Gravlee, "How Race Becomes Biology," 52.

89. Robert D. Bullard, *Dumping in Dixie: Race, Class, and Environmental Quality*, 3rd ed. (Boulder, Colo.: Westview Press, 2000.)

90. Diane S. Lauderdale, "Birth Outcomes for Arabic-Named Women in California Before and After September 11," *Demography* 43, no. 1 (February 2006): 185–201.

91. Graves, *The Emperor's New Clothes*, 186.

92. United States Holocaust Memorial Museum, "Jewish Population of Europe in 1933: Population Data by Country," *Holocaust Encyclopedia* 2010, www.ushmm.org/wlc/en/article.php?ModuleId=10005161#RelatedArticles (June 22, 2010).

93. Graves, *The Emperor's New Clothes*, 139.

94. Graves, *The Emperor's New Clothes*, 174.

95. Graves, *The Emperor's New Clothes*, 8.

96. Goodman, "Why Genes Don't Count," 1699.

~

CHAPTER THREE

Race and the Social Construction of Whiteness

In Gregory Howard Williams's extraordinary memoir, *Life on the Color Line: The True Story of a White Boy Who Discovered He Was Black*, Williams offers a powerful account of race in America. Williams was born in the southern United States and raised until ten years of age as white, the child of a white mother and supposedly white father. Williams grew up thinking his father's "deeply tanned" skin, "heavy lips and dark brown eyes" came from his Italian heritage.[1]

At around nine years of age, Williams's family's fortune took a turn for the worse. They lost their restaurant and with it, their income. At this point, Williams's mother left his alcoholic and physically abusive father. She took the two youngest children with her and abandoned the two older children, Williams and his brother, Mike. Williams and his brother traveled with his father to the northern town of Muncie, Indiana, to live with his father's family, ostensibly until they got on their feet again. As they traveled, Williams's father, James A. "Buster" Williams, stunned his two sons. He confessed to Gregory, nicknamed "Billy," and Mike that he was actually a Black man, and thus, that they were Black, too. "Remember Miss Sallie who used to work for us in the tavern?" Williams's father asked them about a Black woman who had worked with the family in the restaurant and bar they had owned and lost in the early 1950s, the Open House Cafe.[2]

> "It's hard to tell you boys this." He paused, then slowly added, "But she's really my momma. That means she's your grandmother."

"But that can't be, Dad! She's colored!" I whispered, lest I be overheard by the other white passengers on the bus.

"That's right, Billy," he continued. "She's colored. That makes you part colored, too."[3]

Buster Williams tells his sons that they are "part colored," but as Williams finds out when he is suddenly transformed into a Black boy growing up in Muncie, Indiana, there is no "part colored" or, for that matter, part white, at least not in the 1950s in the United States. A person is one or the other, Black or white, and these categories are understood to be opposites. They are opposing sides of a false binary. People of color are on one side, and white people on the other. Each side, our society tells us, has its own characteristics, traits that exist in opposition to the other side of the binary.

Of course, in reality there is no such thing as a human binary. Human beings are human beings, each with the human capacity for myriad abilities, characteristics, and faults. With gender, men are not the opposite of women. Men and women do not each contain one half of all human characteristics, opposing each other. And with race, people of color are not one type of human completely distinct from the other, white type. However, even though our biology does not determine our race, even though our traits are neither fundamentally Black nor white, our cultures and our societies do shape our internal and external realities and the possibilities that exist for us in life.

In other words, if people understand race to be a real, fundamental, and biological fact of human life, the consequences for this thinking about race will shape our lives in multiple, profound, and very real ways. As sociologist W. I. Thomas said, "If people define situations as real, they are real in their consequences."[4] We can see those consequences in, for example, the gap between Black and white earnings[5] (as will be discussed in chapter 7) and the segregation of Black from white communities.

Societies springing from and influenced by western civilizations have long thought about and understood much of life in terms of binaries or dualisms. This either/or framework patterns western individual lives and western societies and cultures. We tend to think of people in either/or terms, Black is one thing, white another, men are one way, women another. Our understandings of race both come from and reproduce these dualisms that exist in our cultures and in our thinking.

What is perhaps most fascinating about Williams's story is that he carries those of us who are white over the "color line" into the "other" group, the other side of the dualism, where most white people will never, ever go. In the first part of the book, we who are white identify with this white boy, as we read his story of growing up with lower-middle-class white parents who have to work too hard to make ends meet. At the beginning, around the edges of his story we encounter other people, Black people, whose lives are not ours. White people, much like the storyteller, watch but rarely enter the lives of people of color. It need not be malicious that most of us—us who are white—will never go to the other side of this racial binary. We have no reason to go there. Many of us do not even realize that there is a "there" to go to. Indeed today, this lack of knowledge is one fundamental piece of what it *means* to be white. We do not know the other side of the color line simply because we do not have to, we do not need to know it. We live our lives and benefit from our privileged position without ever having to recognize that there are other positions, other places on the other side of whiteness.

Halley experienced this privileged lack of knowledge in multiple ways as she read Williams's book. Muncie, Indiana, is a town Halley, like many sociologists, had read quite a bit about. It is the subject of Robert S. Lynd and Helen Merrell Lynd's famous and highly regarded sociological study, *Middletown: A Study in Modern American Culture.*[6] Lynd and Lynd investigated what they considered a typical small American city and the "typical" Americans who lived there. For Lynd and Lynd, as for many Americans, typical means white. In this book there are very few references to the lives of people of color. Indeed, in the index, one finds three pages noted where the book addresses Black people, under the heading "Negroes" (as would be common language of the time). Early in the book, Lynd and Lynd state, "In the main this study confines itself to the white population and more particularly to the native whites, who compose 92 per cent of the population." Lynd and Lynd explain their decision:

> In a difficult study of this sort it seemed a distinct advantage to deal with a homogeneous, native-born population, even though such a population is unusual in an American industrial city. Thus, instead of being forced to handle two major variables, racial change and cultural change, the field staff was enabled to concentrate upon cultural change.[7]

Reading Lynd and Lynd, Halley nearly forgot that a Black community existed in Muncie. As a white person, she forgot about race, and whiteness became invisible to her. Reading Williams pushed Halley to see Black lives in all of their stark contrast from the white "Middletown" reality.

After having been white for ten years, when Gregory Williams finds out that he is Black, he is shocked. "The unsettling image of Miss Sallie flashed before [him] like a neon sign. Colored! Colored! Colored!" In the 1950s,

much of the United States and particularly the South lived in a sharply segregated society. So while Williams never needed to know the Black side of
the color line, he did know that as a white boy, he was on the "right" side, the
side with the power. After his father's disclosure, Williams's brother, Mike,
asked his father, "Daddy, we ain't really colored, are we?" And Williams
answered for his father, "No!" Williams thought fiercely, "I'm not colored,
I'm white! I look white! I've always been white! I go to 'whites only' schools,
'whites only' movie theatres, and 'whites only' swimming pools! I never had
heard anything crazier in my life! How could Dad tell us such a mean lie?"[8]

In the first ten years of Williams's childhood, his father, Buster, "passed"
as a white man. In our society, we use the term *passing* to describe the phenomenon when a person lives with an identity other than the one socially
assigned to her or him. Buster was Black by the standards of his social world.
Because being Black in that racist society limited his life in so many deep
ways, Buster chose to hide his African American heritage and live as a white
man. Being white opened up many life opportunities for Buster and his children. Stigma is a socially constructed phenomenon and tends to involve a
characteristic that is devalued in a specific social setting, including within
a culture at a specific historical time. For Buster, his identity as a "colored"
man was stigmatizing in the United States as he reached adulthood in the
early half of the twentieth century. At that time in the United States,
Buster's opportunities as a Black man were deeply limited. While many never
face the level of oppression faced by Buster, most of us will find ourselves
experiencing stigma of some kind. Stigma exists on a continuum; it might
cause mild discomfort at one end and profound oppression at the other. For
example, this experience can range from a temporary embarrassment (such
as a breakout of acne right before an important social event) to something
more encompassing, like having to carefully manage social situations in
which others' knowledge of a trait one holds might deeply discredit the
individual (such as a lesbian woman who works in a daycare setting where
parents might have misperceptions about how her sexuality may affect her
care for their children).

When an individual has concerns about how a stigma may influence his
or her opportunities or social interactions, it can be very tempting to pass.
The famous sociologist Erving Goffman explores "passing" as a social phenomenon in his book, *Stigma: Notes on the Management of Spoiled Identity*.[9]
Some experiences of stigma are so life-altering that it would be challenging
to choose not to pass, given the potential benefits of others perceiving one
as "normal" rather than as stigmatized. In seeking to understand stigma and
passing, it can be helpful to recognize that, as Goffman argues, most people

pass and hide a stigmatizing aspect of their identity at some point in their lives. Goffman writes that "the problems people face who make a concerted and well-organized effort to pass are problems that a wide range of persons face at some time or other."[10] Even when an aspect of one's identity seems to be *always* apparent, often one finds that there are exceptions. For example, a young woman with disfiguring burn scars, who regularly deals with managing the discomfort of others in face-to-face interactions as casual as approaching a cashier in a store, may choose to create a new, nonstigmatized identity for herself on the Internet by selecting a nonhuman icon for herself and passing as a "normal" person, one who is not disfigured. Passing can be a continuum from something one does occasionally to a fundamental change of life, as in the case of Buster. Buster passed even in his own family such that his mother lived with his family for a period of time and the children never knew she was their grandmother.

Passing can even be unintentional. For example, Goffman points to a child with a physical disability and limited use of one leg. When the child meets new people, they might at first assume that the child was in an accident and that the disability is temporary. Someone who is visually impaired might be thought to see by strangers sitting around her in a dark restaurant. Or Goffman writes, African Americans with dark skin who have never intentionally passed "may nonetheless find themselves, in writing letters or making telephone calls" passing as people with light or even white skin.[11] And of course, people who are gay or lesbian live in a constant process of coming out (or not). They have to decide in each situation—when they apply for a job, get their partner's check cashed, wish to hold hands at the movies, and so on—whether they want to "come out" as gay or lesbian in that moment and place. For a whole variety of reasons, sometimes they might decide to "pass" as heterosexual.

Being able-bodied, having sight, being heterosexual, or having white skin is normative, and not only understood to be "normal" but also valued as better than other possibilities. As Goffman claims, "Because of the great rewards in being considered normal, almost all persons who are in a position to pass will do so on some occasion by intent."[12] Nonetheless, because white people are considered "normal," white people have the profound privilege of not needing to pass in terms of race.

When Buster lost everything and needed to return to his childhood home—home where he could no longer pass as white because people knew him, his family, and his race as Black—he and his children became Black. Williams spent the rest of his childhood growing up in utter poverty in the African American community in Muncie, Indiana. For most of those years, he did not have enough to eat. His clothes were tattered and worn. He lived in tiny, ramshackle housing, sleeping for one period crammed between his grandmother's toilet and the wall in her minuscule house. Deeply impoverished, Williams and his brother lived through their first bitter cold Muncie winter with no heat—the stove did not work—and almost no food.

Williams experienced ongoing discrimination. Williams was harassed and humiliated by white students and white teachers at school and by white members of the Muncie community. In spite of his athletic prowess, he was overlooked for the best positions by football and basketball coaches.

Although he faced profound racism, Williams excelled as a student. Indeed, upon graduating from eighth grade, Williams almost received the honor of being the top student in his class. A well-meaning teacher, who did not understand the way race worked in Muncie, told Williams that he would be recognized as the top student at their school's graduation ceremony. Williams invited his father, who even managed to get some new used clothes for Williams to wear at the graduation ceremony. Williams and his teacher were reminded of the power of race when the school awarded the honor to another—white—student who had performed academically significantly below the level achieved by Williams.

Williams's story begs the question of what it means to be a raced human being. What does it mean to "have" a race? And how do we become this race? Williams's story exemplifies the argument we make in this book. Williams is no more Black or white than his society defines him and his culture shapes him. When he was in the South with his two white parents and three white siblings, he and the world believed him to be white. And so he was. When he lived in Muncie, Indiana, where his father was known to be Black, then Williams became Black. In other words, race most fundamentally is neither fixed in one's biology nor psychology. Ultimately, race is born from and reproduced by the social, or in other words, by the "chaotic cofunctioning of the political, economic and cultural dimensions" of human life.[13] Race has everything to do with power, social power. As discussed in chapter 2, and as historian Noel Ignatiev identifies, race cannot be defined in biological terms. Biology has never

been able to provide a satisfactory definition of "race"—that is, a definition that includes all members of a given race and excludes others. Attempts to give the term a biological foundation lead to absurdities: parents and children of different races, of the well-known phenomenon that a white woman can give birth to a black child, but a black woman cannot give birth to a white child. The only logical conclusion is that people are members of different races because they have been assigned to them.[14]

Whereas the *origins* of race are neither biological nor psychological; nonetheless, in some sense, race becomes both psychological and biological due to the social. The social and those who wield social power mandate social phenomena—like segregation—that result in other phenomena like physical characteristics. Segregation, for instance, limits who interacts with whom in a human community in a particular place. In the United States, through laws, social customs, and sometimes, even outright terrorism (as in the case of organizations like the Ku Klux Klan), white people have perpetrated ongoing and profound racial segregation of Black from white communities for centuries. Thus, for example, African Americans have largely lived only with other African Americans, and largely gone to school, worked, made friends, married, and had children only with other African Americans. To a great extent this segregation exists still today, albeit no longer mandated by law. This social phenomenon, segregation, has meant that the physical characteristics of the Black community have been reproduced and passed on largely just to other members of the Black community.

The social even mandates how we decide who qualifies for the white community and who for the Black. Historically, numerous states defined race by the "one drop of blood" rule, also known as hypodescent.[15] Legal scholar Ian F. Haney López writes, "Under this rule, historically given legal form in numerous state statutes, any known African ancestry renders one Black."[16] In other words, if you had "one drop" of Black blood, someone who was Black in your family ancestry, even someone very remotely related to you, then you were Black. In 1970 Louisiana made this more specific by passing legislation that anyone with 1/32 African ancestry or more was legally Black. If you had less than that 1/32 part, then you were not Black.[17] Being 1/32 part Black means that a person has one great-great-great grandparent of African descent.

In Fannie Flagg's novel, *Welcome to the World, Baby Girl!* her character Marguerite Le Guarde, who has spent years passing as a white woman in order to bestow whiteness and white privilege on her daughter, ends her life delusionally, yet unintentionally, by cutting her wrists and ankles to bleed out that one drop of Black blood. "Where was it, she wondered? Was it on her left side? Where was it lurking? Did it stay in one place or did it travel throughout her body, running and hiding, determined to haunt her year after year? She would just get rid of it once and for all. First the left side, the ankle, then the wrist. She must let it escape. Then the right side. . . . Soon it would be gone. Oh, what a relief to finally get it out. Then she and Dena [her daughter] would be free."[18] Race is, of course, not one drop of somehow distinct blood.[19] Race is socially made; it is socially constructed.

López shows that in U.S. history whiteness was defined only by its negation. In other words, U.S. "courts defined 'white' through a process of . . . systematically identifying who was non-White."[20] Legal scholar Neil Gotanda writes, "The metaphor is one of purity and contamination: White is unblemished and pure, so one drop of ancestral Black blood renders one Black. Black is a contaminant that overwhelms white ancestry."[21]

Social Construction of Race

In this chapter, indeed in this book, much like sociologist Michael S. Kimmel in his work on gender, we intend to unsettle racial categories, to problematize whiteness. In doing this, we use the theory of social construction. Social construction theory builds on the idea that social norms change over time (in history) and place (through culture). Social construction theorists argue that the unequal distribution of economic and social power reinforces (and helps to create) differences between groups and their cultural norms. In turn, the norms shift and change over time and place, again deeply influenced by power.

In his exploration of our "gendered society," Kimmel defines the theory of social construction in terms of how the theory has been applied to gender. His definition is useful to us as we explore race, like gender, as a socially constructed phenomenon. For Kimmel, "Social constructionism builds on the other social and behavioral sciences, adding specific dimensions to the exploration," in our case, of race.[22] Sociology adds to our investigation of race through the sociological analysis of differences between (and among) social groups such as Black and white people. Sociology helps us see the role of social power in action. With sociology we begin to understand the ways that race is not a fixed fact that we are born with but rather a lived experience perpetually changing in the midst of our societies, families, schools, governments, and so on.

Social construction theorists also use disciplines outside of sociology such as anthropology to explore differences between cultures; history to examine changes within cultures over time; and developmental psychology to investigate differences and similarities in individual human beings' lives from younger to older, from one developmental stage to another. Finally, returning to sociology, Kimmel reminds us of variation that occurs within a culture in a particular time. For example, a poor, young, white woman who is home-less probably experiences her race differently than a rich, highly educated, elderly white woman. Definitions and understandings of whiteness "will vary within any one culture at any one time—by . . . class, ethnicity, [gender,] age, sexuality, education, region of the country, etc."[23]

Evidence supporting a social construction explanation of race is revealed by the historical disagreements among scholars when attempting to classify races and by the changes in these classifications within disciplines across time. While evolutionary theorist Charles Darwin argued that there is only one race of humans, he noted in 1871 that others had attempted to identify up to sixty-three distinct races. The fact that scholars could not agree on racial distinctions, creating their own categories of race separate from each other, reveals that race is not an obvious biological fact, but is, instead, socially constructed. Many anthropologists historically classified humans into multiple races, but the majority of modern anthropologists argue, like Darwin, that there is only one race of human beings. This shift in thought about race across time reveals that race is not fixed and apparent for anyone to observe. Race is constructed within historical and cultural contexts, based as much on prevailing ideology as on empirical evidence.[24]

Kimmel identifies a major distinction between a nurture-based perspec-tive and a perspective based on social construction. Someone using nurture to explain racial differences would argue that experiences throughout life create differences between racial groups and that these differences lead to unequal treatment and experiences of inequality. The nurture perspective argues that racial groups truly become different through experiences and that inequality is a response to those true differences. A social construction argument challenges the nurture perspective. Social constructionists would argue that inequality creates differences. Different racial groups are treated in unequal ways because of societal and individual expectations of the groups; in other words, because of stereotypes. That unequal treatment is responsible for many of the differences between the groups. For example, white people are more prone to certain diseases and less prone to others (such as asthma) than Black people. These biological differences spring from inequality. For example, as we note in chapter 2, Black people are more likely to be exposed to toxins in the environment. These toxins predict the development of asthma.

For social constructionists, the key to any understanding of social phe-nomena is power, social power. By way of comparison to another point of view, multiculturalism, like the nurture perspective, offers yet one more way of understanding race and difference in the United States. While social constructionists think about race in terms of power, multiculturalist thinking tends to ignore or even deny the relevance of social power, often portraying every group as *equal* but different. For multiculturalists, the answer to social problems involves respect for each other and the celebration of our differences. In contrast to multiculturalism, social constructionists argue that we *should* be equal (and that all cultures are worthy of celebration); however, when it comes to social power, we are not equal.[25]

When explaining the social construction of gender, Kimmel emphasized the importance of understanding power. Focusing on power is essential to understanding whiteness. Applying Kimmel's argument on social construction to race, we argue that race "is about inequality, about power. . . . [race] is about the power that [white people] as a group have over [people of color] as a group."[26] As noted above, power produces what we observe as distinctions between the groups we consider to be racial groups.

The focus on power is what makes the theory of social construction markedly different from approaches to race that accentuate multicultural celebration. While we fully agree that each ethnicity and culture has significant aspects worth celebrating, we are concerned that the multiculturalist approach fails to create a critical analysis of race because it fails to recognize the power of whiteness over all other groups in the United States. Like Kimmel, we acknowledge that focusing on power is controversial, yet we insist that focusing on power is critical to a fully honest exploration of race. (In chapter 6, we address alternative ways of learning about difference and the importance of curiosity.)

Unfortunately, because the multiculturalist approach fails to focus on power, it often feels safe to white people. Multiculturalism might entail a superficial investigation of the foods, clothing, language, and public customs of different cultures or subcultures. For example, at one such event when Eshleman was a college student, a young Japanese woman, an international student, kneeled before her white peers serving them tea. The event included no critical examination of culture or of power. Students and teachers alike might find an uncritical multiculturalist celebration delightful, but in the absence of an exploration of power, a shallow approach to multiculturalism is unlikely to move individuals to a greater understanding of how social injustice or inequality create many differences, differences considered *racial* differences. Worse yet, a multiculturalist approach can reify the power of whiteness over people of color in a setting purported to be a multicultural celebration. In other words, the presentation of those who are "ethnic" to those who are *understood* to be not ethnic and thus "normal"—white—is also a problem at many such events. These celebratory multicultural events can be eerily similar to visiting a carnival freak show.

In a freak show, a barker encourages others like himself to "Step right up!" and marvel at the curious appearance and behaviors of the "freaks" in the show. The "freaks" have volunteered to be on display because they desire to share their distinctiveness with members of the dominant group. Without a critical inspection of power, a well-meaning, predominantly white institution might appoint one or more whites to work with people of color to create an event in which other whites gawk at the unusual (to mainstream white people) clothing, music, dance, and food of other cultures. If power is not addressed, the event reinforces the power of whiteness as the whites amuse themselves in a position of comfort as people of color work to entertain them.

Outside of multicultural events, yet living still in this framework of white, unrecognized power, white people sometimes feel free to ask the race and ethnicity of people of color, as though there is nothing intrusive or inappropriate about putting another person on center stage regarding his or her cultural background. Not only does the questioner come from and situate herself in a position of power when asking the question, the assumption behind the question for white people is "Because I am white, I am normal. Because you are not white, you are not normal and I, from my privileged position of normalcy, want to know *what* you are."

On a weekend trip that brought together friends of friends, Eshleman overheard a new white acquaintance ask a friend, and the only man of color in the group, "What language do you speak?" The Chinese American friend politely tried to dispel the question: "American." The new white acquaintance seemed frustrated and did not accept that answer, "No, like do you speak Mandarin?" Eshleman wondered why the white woman did not accept the man of color's respectful attempt to discourage her question about his ethnic background. Was this white woman aware of her relative power in this situation? Was she aware of making this man of color feel uncomfortable? Eshleman concluded with some horror that the white woman seemed clueless about her relative social power when Eshleman heard the woman later teasing the friend about eating bok choy.

The incident reminded Eshleman of a family story in which a cousin's young, modern, three-year-old daughter was introduced to three similarly aged Amish girls wearing traditional dress. The young relative asked aloud, "What are these?" We may all have curiosity about others who are distinct within any given situation, but racial awareness requires that we develop beyond a young child's demand for information to be able to quickly categorize.

Halley recently overheard a group of college students sharing their ethnic and religious background during a discussion. One young woman turned to a young man who had not volunteered any information and pointedly asked the Latino man with a light complexion, *"What* are you?" On Eshleman's trip, the acquaintance also, essentially, asked, "What are you?" And in a *Newsweek* article entitled "Please Ask Me Who, Not 'What,' I Am," journalist Jordan Lite writes about her regular experience as a biracial person of being asked, "What are you?" She notes, "Isn't it rude to ask 'what' someone is when you've just met? Common courtesy would suggest so. But many people seem to feel uncomfortable if they can't immediately determine a new person's racial or ethnic background."[27] Indeed, many of us have heard (or asked) some version of the "What are you?" question. What makes each of these individuals feel she has a right to demand to know the race or ethnicity of someone who chooses not to volunteer that information?

While it is much more comfortable for white people to avoid addressing power, such an analysis of race without exploring social power will fail to lead to greater justice in our society. One challenge of addressing power is arousing "white guilt." If such feelings of guilt cause whites to avoid thinking critically about race, then the guilt will be ineffective and unhelpful. Beverly Daniel Tatum offers an important argument related to white guilt. No one is responsible for the actions that occurred within one's group before a person had power to affect those actions. In other words, no one should feel guilt regarding the injustices committed by one's group in the past. But everyone is responsible for addressing the injustice that currently exists in our world. We should feel responsibility to understand the injustice and to act within our spheres of influence to combat it.

Further, Tatum argues that whites have a choice—they can fight against racism or they can be racist. This is another controversial line of reasoning. A white person can be actively antiracist, working within his or her social network and within his or her means to reduce the impact of racism. A white person can be passively racist, doing nothing to address racism. Or a white person can be actively racist. When reading Tatum's options, many white students in Eshleman's classes have responded that they want a passively antiracist option. They do not want to take any action, and they want to be absolved of responsibility. Tatum notes that *doing nothing supports racism.* In a racist society, going with the flow allows racism to continue. To be passive in regard to racism is to be racist.

We acknowledge that some white readers may feel uncomfortable processing this argument. Many whites (including the two white authors of this book!) have been passive at some point in our lives with regard to race.

Tatum acknowledges that being called a racist feels like a slap across the face. Eshleman and Halley admit that they have felt this sting when others have pointed out their own racism. It feels awful. It takes a moment to recover. But Eshleman and Halley would much rather be called on their unintentional racism (even though it smarts!) than to be unaware and inadvertently harming others in ways much more devastating.

Tatum and Kimmel both address the fact that individuals with power are unlikely to recognize the power and may feel uncomfortable when someone tries to reveal it. Because white privilege tends to be invisible, Tatum notes that any given individual white person is unlikely to be aware of racial advantage. Kimmel identifies that white people might not feel *personally* powerful, and that because of this, arguments about power in the theory of social construction might not resonate with them. If the focus is shifted from individuals' feelings of power to an analysis of who tends to hold power as a group, it becomes clear that whites are highly likely to be overrepresented on corporate boards and in legislative bodies. When an important decision is made that affects many others, it is disproportionately more likely to be made by a white person than a person of color. "Power is not the property of individuals—a possession that one has or does not have—but the property of group life, of social life. Power *is*. It can neither be willed away nor ignored. . . . And it is so deeply woven into our lives that it is most invisible to those who are most empowered."[28]

Social constructionists argue that the phenomenon of race springs from social relations that both enact and reproduce social power. White people as a group have power over people of color as a group. As we explore in other chapters, white people make more money and have access to better educations; better housing; more interesting, higher status and professional careers; better health care; and more leisure time and leisure activities. This very real lack of equality between white people and people of color must be addressed for any meaningful social change to happen. Celebrating and respecting each other is, quite simply, not enough.

How the Irish Became White: A Case Study of the Social Construction of Whiteness

Since 1492, every group that has immigrated to the United States (including recent African immigrants) has struggled with the issue of race. Many groups came to the United States with one "race"—Italian, for example—and slowly changed into another, in the case of Italians, white. Such change, such transformation enacts social construction. Society constructs race through particular phenomena like the cultures of groups and the social systems that produce and reproduce the power that some groups have over other groups. In part, white people become white and maintain their whiteness through white and middle-class culture and social power. Assumptions about "normal" manners, child-rearing practices, physical contact, sexuality, and norms around physical space, education and governmental systems, and cultural ideals like that of individualism all play a part in the production of whiteness.

As Ignatiev explains in his seminal book, *How the Irish Became White*, when the Irish first emigrated from Ireland, they were one race, Irish.[29] Over the ensuing century, they shifted from Irish to white. Halley's Irish American family took part in this transformation. Prior to immigrating in the nineteenth century, when Halley's family came to the United States, most Irish in Ireland were Catholic and lived as agrarian peasants. Deeply disempowered in a feudal society, Terry Golway notes that Ireland was "a country of landless peasants and farm laborers who worked fields they did not own and raised crops they could not eat."[30]

Although they grew and raised many things, the Irish Catholic majority themselves ate potatoes. Other crops, crops more desirable to elites, were paid as rent to landlords who were neither poor nor Catholic. Crops such as wheat, oats, and barley, and livestock such as pigs, cows, sheep, and chickens thrived in abundance, even in the worst years of the infamous potato famine. How strange for Halley's Irish ancestors—in the midst of a famine when at least one out of every eight Irish died—to have enough food all around and to have grown this food through their own backbreaking labor, and nonetheless, to starve. No one was prepared for the six years of famine in Ireland from 1845 to 1851. The loss of potato crops was immense, producing only "20 percent of its pre-Famine yield" in 1846.[31] The loss of human lives was, also, vast. The figures vary. Yet most believe that during the six-year famine, Ireland lost one million to immigration and one million to death.

Here it is important to note that most of us know this history, that of the potato famine, because the Irish *did become white*. Groups in power, like white Americans, tend to be the ones most studied in school, written about, researched, celebrated, known, and understood. Indeed, Vijaya learned about the Irish potato famine as a child in school in India. In contrast, growing up in the United States, Halley and Eshleman knew nothing about the Bengal famine of 1770 in which the death toll was so extensive the full population of Ireland would have been killed twice over. In the Bengal famine, approximately fifteen million people died. If the Irish had not become white, their history as a colonized people would probably have remained unknown to most of the world.

The issue with both the Bengal famine and the potato famine was not a lack of food (or of laziness on the part of the Indian or Irish "races"). As with most human catastrophes, the issue in both cases was social power— and powerlessness. Robert Kee, a British historian and journalist, noted the profuse amounts of food shipped out of Ireland for profit by Irish landowners during the potato famine. In the Bengal famine as well, there were plenty of crops being grown. Yet those in power appropriated the food for trading purposes rather than local human consumption. About the situation in Ireland, Irish immigrants to the United States, years later, told their children, "of the sight of food convoys under armed guard making their way past hollow-eyed men, women, and children whose mouths were green from eating grass."[32]

Devastating effects of colonization similar to those documented in Ireland and India have been observed around the world. Evolutionary biologist Joseph L. Graves Jr. notes the "evidence for the negative biological impact of colonialism on the colonized."[33] Under colonization from 1832 to 1872, the Hawaiian Islands lost two-thirds (68 percent) of its population. Like in India and Ireland, colonization in Africa and Latin America forced systems of producing crops for export rather than food for local consumption. "Thus, the contradiction of these colonial agricultural economies was that although their agricultural productivity was high, they produced little food for the indigenous populations."[34] Malnutrition and reductions in population were common results. Near complete elimination of native populations also occurred under colonization, as happened post–Christopher Columbus in large areas of the Americas.

In the seventeenth and eighteenth centuries, Ireland was a colony under England. This meant that England controlled all Irish resources. As in many other colonial situations—many of them British—England did not do the work of being a colonial power on its own. Middlemen were effective tools of colonization. Underneath the British but above Irish Catholics in Ireland were "the Dissenters." These Irish non-Catholic Dissenters, "who were mostly Presbyterian farmers, mechanics, and small tradesmen," helped maintain the oppressive hierarchy imposed by Britain.[35] They saved the English labor and trouble, often receiving relatively little in return. They did gain one important benefit from their social position. Like Irish Catholics, they themselves might live in terrible conditions, but as Protestants, they could at least consider themselves part of the dominant—the better—race. In other words, in terms of their "race," all Protestants benefited from the

British-imposed hierarchy. No matter how poor they might be, Protestants gained a psychic power from being Protestant Irish, not Catholic.[36]

On the other hand, Halley's Irish Catholic ancestors living in Ireland under what were called the Penal Laws were not allowed to: "vote; . . . practice law; hold a post in the military or civil service; teach in a school; . . . attend the university; educate their children abroad; manufacture or sell arms, newspapers, or books; own or carry arms; own a horse worth more than five pounds; take on more than two apprentices (except in the linen trade); be apprentices to Protestants; rent land worth more than thirty shillings a year; lease land for longer than thirty-one years; [or] make a profit from land of more than one-third of the rent paid."[37]

Through the six years of the potato famine, the English—Anglo-Saxons— ruled Ireland. They believed (like many elite conservatives in the United States today) that no one should hinder the supposedly natural movement of "free" trade and the "free" market. In other words, they thought that if people and nations were allowed to trade food and other goods without restrictions imposed by governments, then a natural balance would be found in this "free" global market. They held that this "free" market, unencumbered by laws and restrictions, would be fair, just, and balanced. The reality behind this thinking was that the relatively wealthy landowners in Ireland, as well as the British government, depended on the exporting of crops to maintain their powerful position and wealth. In other words, the ideology of a "free" market supported the reality of elite power (again, not unlike the thinking of global elites today). Ideas about race played an important role in Anglo-Saxon thought. Because Anglo-Saxon elites believed Irish Catholics to be a race, and a less civilized, more animalistic race at that, Anglo-Saxon elites justified their exploitation of Irish Catholics. Anglo-Saxons and Irish Catholics alike *also* considered Anglo-Saxons a race, and an idealized one. In reality, Anglo-Saxons held power over Irish Catholics through colonization and exploitation. The ideology of those in power maintained that Anglo-Saxons held power *because* they were racially superior.[38]

In spite of British greed sitting at the heart of the famine, British ideology held that the real problem sprang from the Irish character. Charles Trevelyan, appointed by the British prime minister to oversee relief operations in Ireland during the potato famine, wrote about the Irish, "The great evil with which we have to contend [is] not the physical evil of famine, but the moral evil of the selfish, perverse and turbulent character of the people."[39]

The Irish, of course, are no more a race than any other group of human beings. As discussed above, race is an idea born out of culture, the manifestation of structures of social power. As described in chapter 2 and by Ignatiev, outside of the cultural labels regarding race "and the racial oppression that accompanies them, the only race is human." Yet the Irish, or more specifically, the Irish Catholics, have been in a variety of positions when it comes to *ideas* about race, and when it comes to oppression. In other words, Irish Catholics have been raced in diverse ways at different times. When Halley's family and other Irish Catholics immigrated to the United States in the mid-1800s, "they were fleeing caste oppression and a system of landlordism that made the material conditions of the Irish peasant comparable to those of an American slave."[40] (The material conditions were the actual, concrete circumstances of their lives.)

Most Irish immigrating to the United States up until the 1830s were Irish Presbyterians who came to be called "Scotch-Irish" or Irish Protestants. This group was originally known in the United States as simply "Irish." However, over time, the Scotch-Irish worked to disassociate themselves from the poorer and Irish-speaking Catholic immigrants who came to the United States just before and during the potato famine. These Irish Catholics who came later were so poor that most could not pay their own ticket for the trip. During the potato famine, for many of the destitute Irish Catholics, their only option was to die of starvation on the land they farmed (but did not own). Yet, the Irish landlords paid the cost of travel for some as a means to get them off the land.

When Irish Catholics arrived in the United States—before becoming white—many lived and worked in and among impoverished and free Black communities. The Moyamensing district in Philadelphia was one such Irish and African American neighborhood. Black and Irish people had children and made families together as well as lived and worked in the same places. The African American and Irish communities also played and worshipped together. For instance, Ignatiev writes that a church "in Philadelphia was presided over after 1837 by an Afro-American minister; baptismal records for the next twenty years suggest that one-third of the members were Irish."[41]

The Anglo-Saxon middle class witnessed Irish and Black intermingling with anxiety and disapproval. For example, a contemporary newspaper article described the multiracial inhabitants of a Philadelphia lodging house in horror:

> The walls were discolored by smoke and filth, the glass was broken from the windows, chinks in the frame work let in the cold air, and every thing was as wretchedly uncomfortable as it is possible to conceive. Yet in every one of these squalid apartments, including the cellar and the loft, men and women—blacks and whites by the dozens—were huddled together . . . keeping

themselves from freezing by covering their bodies with such filthy rags as chance threw in their way.[42]

While the Irish in the 1800s United States were not Black, they were also not white; so such mixing of communities was not seen by the middle class to be as terrible as it would have been for Anglo-Saxon and Black people to live and build families together. About the question of whiteness, Ignatiev writes,

> The first Congress of the United States voted in 1790 that only "white" persons could be naturalized as citizens. Coming as immigrants rather than as captives or hostages undoubtedly affected the potential racial status of the Irish in America, but it did not settle the issue, since it was by no means obvious who was "white." In the early years Irish were frequently referred to as "niggers turned inside out"; the Negroes, for their part, were sometimes called "smoked Irish."[43]

Irish Catholics arrived in the United States as—and understanding themselves as—an exploited and oppressed "race," akin to African Americans. Of course, there is an enormous difference between being a slave and not being a slave. Yet the work, life, and material conditions of these two groups were not so distinct. The new Irish immigrants found a set of diverse work relationships that further complicated the experience of race in the United States.

Prior to the American Revolution, in the eighteenth century "the range of dependent labor relations had blurred the distinction between freedom and slavery. The Revolution led to the decline of apprenticeship, indenture, and imprisonment for debt."[44] The decline in these slavery-like work relations, along with the growth in slavery itself as the foundation of Southern life, "reinforced the tendency to equate freedom with whiteness and slavery with blackness."[45] Because race is a social construction, not a biological reality, people consciously and unconsciously construct racial groups in a particular society, place, and time. And these social constructions change.

The Irish who migrated to the United States went from a preindustrial society to one rapidly industrializing. "In America, where domestic manufacture had grown as a result of the Napoleonic Wars, there was a shortage of wage laborers. The country scooped up the displaced Irish and made them its unskilled labor force."[46] The new industrial work that was available tended to involve brutal, unsafe conditions and long hours. The Irish Catholics and others who took up this industrial work recognized that their lives were in many ways not so different from those who were enslaved. Indeed, early on, factory workers often called their work "wage slavery." Nonetheless, the

Irish moved from being Irish and akin to people of color to being white and understanding themselves as different from, and better than, people of color. They took the "wages of whiteness" instead of the greater bargaining power of organizing together with all working-class people.[47]

As historian David R. Roediger points out, past and present-day white, working-class people and working-class people of color share many interests economically in the United States.[48] Together they could have organized around their shared power as workers, or in other words, as "labor." When workers (labor) join together, they have the power of their numbers to help them make demands on those who hire them (in sociological and economic terms, the owners/employers are also called "capital"). Coming together as a large group, workers have greater bargaining power; with this, they are in a better position to demand higher wages, shorter working hours, better working conditions, and so on. However, in spite of sharing many concerns, historically white working-class people have organized *against* working-class people of color by joining white working-class movements and workplaces. And due to this, the working class in general has been less powerful and more vulnerable.

Why would the white working class shoot itself in the foot, so to speak, by keeping people of color out of white working-class movements? Drawing from the seminal work of the famous African American labor historian W. E. B. Du Bois and his idea about the "psychological wages of whiteness,"[49] Roediger argues that instead of organizing together across racial/ethnic groups to gain greater working-class power, "the white working class [settled] for whiteness."[50] In other words, in their racism, the white working class gained something in exchange for their loss of shared working-class power. They settled for the gains of whiteness, or what Roediger, following Du Bois, calls a "psychic wage"; that is, "status and privileges conferred by race . . . to make up for the alienating and exploitative class relationships" within which they lived and worked. Roediger writes, "White workers could, and did, define and accept their class positions by fashioning identities as 'not slaves' and as 'not Blacks.'"[51] This is perhaps similar to the situation and choices of the Protestant Irish in Ireland. The Protestant Irish, like the white working class in the United States, chose greater psychic power instead of opting for the potential power of greater numbers—bargaining power—had they organized together with the least powerful in their society.

Again drawing from the work of Du Bois, Roediger argues, "White labor does not just receive and resist racist ideas but embraces, adopts and, at times, murderously acts upon those ideas. The problem is not just that the white working class is at critical junctures manipulated into racism, but that it comes to think of itself and its interests as white."[52]

Irish Catholic immigrants like Halley's ancestors took part in a process where they increasingly distanced themselves from African American and other members of color of the working class. Indeed, Roediger argues that "working class formation," the development of an identity as working class, and "the systematic development of a sense of whiteness went hand in hand for the U.S. white working class."[53] As the United States industrialized and a class of people—the working class—developed in and around that industrialization, for those among this group that were white, their new identities as working-class people were inextricably bound with their developing identities as white people.[54]

Karl Marx developed the concept of *false consciousness* to reveal beliefs that are inconsistent with the interests of a group, such as working-class white people preferring to exclude people of color from workers' movements when inclusion may have created greater bargaining power. While false consciousness may be caused by multiple factors such as failing to recognize an unjust situation or resisting social change,[55] social psychologists John T. Jost, Mahzarin R. Banaji, and colleagues have focused on explaining false consciousness.[56] Across fifteen years of research, these scholars have acknowledged three ways that people justify their support for discrimination. *Ego justification* is the first label—extensive evidence reveals that individuals whose self-esteem is threatened are more likely to use stereotypes and act in ways that disadvantage other groups.[57]

Group justification, the second label, is highly relevant for explaining white working-class discrimination against workers of color. Group justification is the term used to identify people who seek to distinguish their own group— their ingroup—from other groups—outgroups.[58] In the case of white workers, they perceived their ingroup as white rather than as being a worker in solidarity with people of color. By identifying as white, people of color became an outgroup.[59] Through group justification, people may seek to separate their ingroup from an outgroup, even at the expense of the ingroup. When one perceives oneself in competition with an outgroup, one may sacrifice the gains of the ingroup for the sake of clearly distinguishing the ingroup from the outgroup. In a classic study by Henri Tajfel, when one faces a choice either to allocate a large amount of reward to one's ingroup along with a nearly-as-large amount of reward to an outgroup or to allocate a moderate amount of reward to one's ingroup along with a small amount of reward to an outgroup, individuals are likely to choose to take less for the ingroup in order to make sure to give the least to the outgroup.[60] Such research may provide insight into situations such as Protestants in Ireland supporting a social system that treated them unfairly while the system treated Irish Catholics even more unfairly.

System justification highlights a third type of justification for discrimination that offers an explanation for some instances of false consciousness. "According to system justification theory, there is a general ideological motive to justify the status quo and bolster the legitimacy of the existing social order. People want to believe that the social system affecting them is fair and legitimate and they are willing to sacrifice personal or group interests to bolster such beliefs."[61] People tend to want to believe that justice is the norm in the world and that people are treated fairly, that "we get what we deserve and deserve what we get."[62] Believing in a just world can create a false sense of security at the expense of failing to acknowledge injustice, even when that injustice targets you. System justification reveals an ideology that validates social systems, encouraging individuals to "accept existing inequality as fair and legitimate."[63]

Social justice movements must first recognize injustice and overcome the tendency to perceive injustice as inevitable. Personal or group needs can become so great that they overwhelm inclinations that favor system justification.[64] Chapter 4 identifies movements that have been inspired by the recognition of injustice. Moving toward social justice can also be sparked by empathy toward an outgroup. In chapter 9, we will explore how a more inclusive ingroup identity could lead to social justice work that is inclusive across race.

Discussion Questions

1. How do we become/get/be a race? And how can one race change into another?

2. Why are individuals sometimes motivated to pass? How is passing related to stigma? Explore the difference between intentionally passing and unintentionally passing. Intentional passing will range from being pointedly dishonest about one's identity to consciously allowing others to make an assumption about one's identity. Do you perceive these different forms of passing as relatively similar or as distinct from each other?

3. Why did only one drop of Black blood make a person Black? Why did the reverse not work? Why did not one drop of white blood make a person white? In this (racist) thinking, is whiteness an exclusive club easily "tainted" by other races? Or is whiteness fragile and Blackness powerful? What is the meaning behind the one-drop rule?

4. Who decides someone else's race? When asked to think of an African American person, what family history do you picture for that person? Who would you include or exclude? What race would you ascribe to a man who was raised primarily by his white mother and white grandparents and whose father was an international student from Kenya, such as Barack Obama? To what extent does Obama share a common social history with other African Americans? To what extent is this true for any race? If author Jane Lazzare claims that because she is a white mother of Black sons, she is no longer merely white, is she?[65] Historically, some people of color have passed and lived as white. Does this mean that they and their descendants today are now white?

5. Is it ever okay to ask someone about his or her racial/ethnic background? Is it okay to be curious about people, about their culture and heritage? Conversely, is not asking or discouraging curiosity similar to doing nothing when it comes to racism? Does asking about someone's racial/ethnic background perpetuate racism? If one is curious about another person's race or ethnicity, what might be a socially sensitive way to inquire?

6. If one feels uncomfortably placed in a spotlight when another person asks, "What are you?" in terms of race or ethnicity, what sort of response would be appropriate from the person in the spotlight? In other words, if one feels that a question was asked in an insensitive way, what would be an apt response?

7. Describe the social construction explanation of race. What evidence supports this explanation of race?

8. Have you ever attended an event intended to celebrate multiculturalism? If so, did it address social power? How might such events move from ones that do not address social power to being ones that do address social power? Argue for or against the importance of addressing social power at multicultural events. What do you think the effects might be of multicultural events that do, and that do not, address social power?

9. Think of a time you or someone you know intentionally *or* unintentionally "passed" as something you/they are not. What were the circumstances? How can you explain or understand why "passing" was important (or even necessary) given current ways of thinking about race, ethnicity, or/and sexuality in our culture? If you were in charge of organizing a major social event that was mixed in terms of race, class, gender, sexuality, and disability, what could you do to reduce or eliminate individuals feeling compelled to "pass"?

10. Suppose a good friend asked you to explain the concept of the "social construction of race" and how the concept is useful for understanding our culture. Using chapter 2, contrast the theory of social construction with the eugenic perspective on race.

11. Suppose you were asked to design a "multicultural" event for your school or some other organization of your choice. How would you avoid doing this in a superficial way? What would you do to take issues of social power into consideration?

Notes

1. Gregory Howard Williams, *Life on the Color Line: The True Story of a White Boy Who Discovered He Was Black* (New York: Plume, 1995), 33.

2. Williams, *Life on the Color Line*, 33.

3. Williams, *Life on the Color Line*, 32–33.

4. W. I. Thomas in Lisa J. McIntyre, *The Practical Skeptic: Core Concepts in Sociology* (Boston: McGraw-Hill, 2008), 3.

5. For example, Margaret L. Andersen and Patricia Hill Collins write that in 2007, the "median income for non-Hispanic white households was $54,920 (meaning half of such households earned more than this and half below); this is the 'middle.' Black households had a median income of $33,916" (*Race, Class and Gender: An Anthology*, Belmont, Calif.: Wadsworth Cengage Learning, 2010, 71).

6. Robert S. Lynd and Helen Merrell Lynd, *Middletown: A Study in Modern American Culture* (Orlando, Fla.: Harcourt Brace Jovanovich, 1929/1957).

7. Lynd and Lynd, *Middletown*, 8–9.

8. Williams, *Life on the Color Line*, 33–34.

9. Erving Goffman, *Stigma: Notes on the Management of Spoiled Identity* (Englewood Cliffs, N.J.: Prentice-Hall, Inc., 1963), 74.

10. Goffman, *Stigma*, 74.

11. Goffman, *Stigma*, 74.

12. Goffman, *Stigma*, 74.

13. Brian Massumi, "Requiem for Our Prospective Dead (Toward a Participatory Critique of Capitalist Power)," in *Deleuze and Guattari: New Mappings in Politics, Philosophy, and Culture*, eds. Eleanor Kaufman and Kevin Jon Heller (Minneapolis: University of Minnesota Press, 1998), 40–64.

14. Noel Ignatiev, *How the Irish Became White* (New York: Routledge, 1995), 1.

15. Joseph L. Graves Jr., *The Emperor's New Clothes: Biological Theories of Race at the Millennium* (New Brunswick, N.J.: Rutgers University Press, 2002).

16. Ian F. Haney López, *White by Law: The Legal Construction of Race* (New York: New York University Press, 1996), 27.

17. David L. Brunsma and Kerry Ann Rockquemore, "What Does 'Black' Mean? Exploring the Epistemological Stranglehold of Racial Categorization," *Critical Sociology* 28, no. 1–2 (2002).

18. Fannie Flagg, *Welcome to the World, Baby Girl!* (New York: Ballantine Books, 1998), 440.

19. Halley's grandfather's brother, her great-uncle, was an avid racist *and* a medical doctor who in the 1960s argued to Halley's mother that Black people's blood was different from white people's blood. Unfortunately, this racist thinking was probably not unusual among white people of his generation, even white health professionals.

20. López, *White by Law*, 27.

21. Neil Gotanda in Ian F. Haney López, *White by Law: The Legal Construction of Race* (New York: New York University Press, 1996), 27.

22. Michael S. Kimmel, *The Gendered Society*, 2nd ed. (New York: Oxford University Press, 2004), 95.

23. Kimmel, *The Gendered Society*, 95.

24. Graves, *The Emperor's New Clothes*.

25. Please do see chapter 6 for a discussion of critical multiculturalism.

26. Kimmel, *The Gendered Society*, 99.

27. Jordan Lite, "Please Ask Me Who, Not 'What,' I Am," *Newsweek* (July 16, 2001), www.newsweek.com/id/78724/page/1.

28. Kimmel, *The Gendered Society*, 100, emphasis in original.

29. Ignatiev, *How the Irish Became White*.

30. Michael Coffey and Terry Golway, *The Irish in America* (New York: Hyperion, 1997), 4.

31. Coffey and Golway, *The Irish in America*, 5.

32. Coffey and Golway, *The Irish in America*, 5.

33. Graves, *The Emperor's New Clothes*, 68.

34. Graves, *The Emperor's New Clothes*, 68.

35. Ignatiev, *How the Irish Became White*, 35.

36. For further exploration, also see David R. Roediger, *The Wages of Whiteness: Race and the Making of the American Working Class*, rev. ed. (London: Verso, 1991).

37. Ignatiev, *How the Irish Became White*, 34.

38. For further explanation of similar ideologies, read about social Darwinism in Graves, *The Emperor's New Clothes*.

39. Charles Trevelyan quoted in Coffey and Golway, *The Irish in America*, 14.

40. Ignatiev, *How the Irish Became White*, 1–2.

41. Ignatiev, *How the Irish Became White*, 41.

42. Quoted in Ignatiev, *How the Irish Became White*, 40–41.

43. Ignatiev, *How the Irish Became White*, 41.

44. Ignatiev, *How the Irish Became White*, 95.

45. Ignatiev, *How the Irish Became White*, 95.

46. Ignatiev, *How the Irish Became White*, 38.

47. Roediger, *The Wages of Whiteness*.

48. Roediger, *The Wages of Whiteness*.

49. W. E. B. Du Bois, *Black Reconstruction in the United States* (New York: Harcourt, Brace and Company, 1935).

50. Roediger, *The Wages of Whiteness*, 6.

51. Roediger, *The Wages of Whiteness*, 13.

52. Roediger, *The Wages of Whiteness*, 12.

53. Roediger, *The Wages of Whiteness*, 6.

54. For an insightful critique of Roediger's *Wages of Whiteness*, please do see Theodore W. Allen, "On Roediger's *Wages of Whiteness*," *Cultural Logic* 4, no. 2 (Spring 2001).

55. John T. Jost, "Negative Illusions: Conceptual Clarification and Psychological Evidence Concerning False Consciousness," *Political Psychology* 16, no. 2 (June 1995): 397–424.

56. John T. Jost and Mahzarin R. Banaji, "The Role of Stereotyping in System-Justification and the Production of False Consciousness," *British Journal of Social Psychology* 33, no. 1 (March 1994): 1–27.

57. For a classic example, see Steven Fein and Steven J. Spencer, "Prejudice as Self-Image Maintenance: Affirming the Self through Derogating Others," *Journal of Personality and Social Psychology* 73, no. 1 (July 1997): 31–44.

58. John T. Jost, Yifat Kivetz, Monica Rubini, Grazia Guermandi, and Cristina Mosso, "System-Justifying Functions of Complementary Regional and Ethnic Stereotypes: Cross-National Evidence," *Social Justice Research* 18, no. 3 (September 2005): 305–33.

59. Classic theory on group justification is presented by Henri Tajfel and John C. Turner, "The Social Identity Theory of Intergroup Behavior," *Psychology of Intergroup Relations* 7 (1986): 7–24.

60. Henri Tajfel, "Experiments in Intergroup Discrimination," *Scientific American* 225, no. 5 (May 1970): 96–102.

61. Jost et al., "System-Justifying," 308.

62. Don H. Hockenbury and Sandra E. Hockenbury, *Psychology* (New York: Worth, 2008), 505.

63. Jost et al., "System-Justifying," 310.

64. John T. Jost, Mahzarin R. Banaji, and Brian A. Nosek, "A Decade of System Justification Theory: Accumulated Evidence of Conscious and Unconscious Bolstering of the Status Quo," *Political Psychology* 25, no. 6 (December 2004): 881–920.

65. Jane Lazzare, *Beyond the Whiteness of Whiteness: Memoir of a White Mother of Black Sons* (Durham, N.C.: Duke University Press, 1996).

CHAPTER FOUR

~

Ways of Seeing Power and Privilege

When Halley was in divinity school, she took a class from a scholar of Native American religions, who was herself Native American. Halley's professor started her lecture on the first day by noting that while there are many Native American Indian groups in the United States, the "Wannabe Indians" are the biggest tribe.[1] Jokingly, Halley's professor was referring to the many ways white Americans have adopted and appropriated pieces of Native American culture. The "Want-to-be Indians" often take the pieces out of context with little understanding of the history and society from which they came. For example, one can visit most New Age religious businesses and find that, while the business caters largely to a white clientele, the products being sold include numerous artifacts understood by the business to be Native American. Some of the white customers go so far as to identify with being Native American, or at least their understanding of what it means to be Native American, taking new names and practicing what they believe to be a Native American religion. Often a piece of the identification romanticizes the "noble savage" as a person who is both in sync with nature and at odds with the modern world.

Not only is the decontextualized appropriation of colonized Native American cultures problematic, this romanticizing dehumanizes indigenous people in that it replicates a dualistic framework common in western thought (as discussed in chapter 3). In this thinking Native Americans are less human, more animalistic, and earthier than other human beings. Further, this romanticization of Native Americans is problematic because of the slippery nature of race in this thinking. Can white Americans simply be Native American when it suits them? Can someone from outside of a culture and a race simply make a choice to switch into that racial group? The Irish immigrants discussed in chapter 3 became white. Like them, can white people become another race, too?

In chapter 3 we established that race is socially constructed. Where do we go from there? How do we understand race, given social construction? In this chapter, we explore different ways of identifying with and understanding one's own and other people's races. We explore three ways social movements have understood and framed race: identity politics, intersectionality, and cultural materialism. We conclude with cultural materialism (introduced in chapter 1) because we believe it to be the most valuable given its potential for empowering people and bringing about a more just society.

Race is socially, not biologically, constructed, and thus fluid. In other words, we are not genetically raced but socially raced. This fluidity does not mean that anyone can switch races, like changing jobs or getting a new hairstyle. Race is not a matter of pure individual choice and whim. That race is socially constructed means that racial groups are themselves embedded in a particular (albeit changing) culture and history. It is the shared culture and history that makes one a member (or not) of a racial group.

One piece of this shared history involves the material resources available to a particular group. Over the past five centuries, as white people colonized more and more of the North American continent, Native American groups were pushed off the land where they lived onto smaller and smaller areas called reservations. Reservations were made up of less desirable land, land on which it was harder for Native people (or anyone) to survive. Due to this history, Native American communities remain among the poorest in the United States and have some of the highest rates of unemployment. Native American unemployment springs largely from the reality that reservations are often in remote places where there are very few job opportunities.

About Native American poverty, journalist Tom Rodgers notes, "According to the U.S. Census Bureau, these Americans earn a median annual income of $33,627. One in every four (25.3 percent) lives in poverty and nearly a third (29.9 percent) are without health insurance coverage." Rodgers writes, "Native American communities have fewer full-time employed individuals than any other high-poverty community. Only 36 percent of males in high-poverty Native American communities have full-time, year-round employment. . . . On the Blackfoot Reservation in Montana, for example, the annual unemployment rate is 69 percent."[2] The Blackfoot today continue to suffer an unemployment rate almost three times that of national unemployment during the Great Depression.

The Blackfoot are a Native American people with a shared history of facing profound racism and oppression, including being forced to survive with extremely limited work, land, money, and other material resources. Without the culture, the history, the community, the religion, and the experiences that the Blackfoot share, as middle-class white people, it would be ridiculous, for example, for Halley or Eshleman to assume that they could simply decide to be Blackfoot.

Race is not simply biological, psychological, or merely a matter of individual choice. As discussed in chapter 3, race is socially constructed. However, social construction does not mean that *individuals* can simply choose a racial identity. Instead, racial and other identities are shaped—in large part outside of the choices or even consciousness of individuals—in the context of societies, cultures, and history. Nonetheless, even using the framework of social construction, the lines around any group are usually not exact, or perfectly clear.

Even the U.S. Census Bureau has struggled to answer the question of what makes someone one race or another. (Please do see box 4.1 at the end of the chapter for further discussion about the Census.) A newspaper journalist, Gregory Rodriguez, notes that defining race, what it means to "be" or "have" a race, to be (or not to be) Black, Latina/o, Asian, or white has always presented a problem for the U.S. Census Bureau. Throughout its history, starting in 1790, the Census has categorized people in racial groups. This of course leads to the question: *Why* did the Census focus on racial groups rather than simply counting human beings?

In large part, the Census categorized people by race because some races counted more than others. Free people, who were also white, counted as full people. Enslaved African Americans each counted as three-fifths. This was a compromise for white elites in the southern and northern United States. The South wanted a greater population in order to gain greater representation in government. The North suggested not counting enslaved people at all. In the U.S. Constitution, one finds the following:

Representatives and direct Taxes shall be apportioned among the several States which may be included within this Union, according to their respective Numbers, which shall be determined by adding to the whole Number of free Persons, including those bound to Service for a Term of Years, and excluding Indians not taxed, three fifths of all other Persons.[3]

An enslaved Black American counted as only three-fifths of a person, while indentured as well as free white people counted as full people. (People who were indentured owed a certain number of years of work to someone in exchange for something, such as the fare to come to the United States from another country. This was one way that the Irish managed to immigrate to the United States from Ireland.) The only people who counted as less than full people were people of color, such as enslaved African Americans and Native Americans. In other words, the Census "reflected and upheld the racial hierarchy that existed in society."[4]

Over time, when new groups immigrated to the United States, Rodriguez notes that they were "obliged to fit themselves into this black/white racial scheme. Not surprisingly, most chose to identify themselves with the group that had full rights." Many immigrant groups went from being a more distinct ethnic group—French or Italian or German—to being white because whiteness was normative. Being white meant having more power in the new society. As discussed in chapter 3, the Irish were among many other immigrant groups that became white after immigrating to the United States.

One common way white people define whiteness is that it is "normal." White people often think of themselves as "just human" and raceless. Michael Kimmel describes his own recognition of this at a seminar he attended in the early 1980s. At the seminar, a Black woman asked a white woman, "When you wake up in the morning and look in the mirror, what do you see?" The white woman responded, "I see a woman." "'That's precisely the problem,' responded the black woman. 'I see a *black* woman. To me, race is visible every day, because race is how I am not privileged in our culture. Race is invisible to you, because it's how you are privileged. It's why there will always be differences in our experience.'" At this point, Kimmel explained about himself prior to this seminar, "When I look in the mirror, I see a human being. I'm universally generalizable. As a middle-class white man, I have no class, no race, no gender. I'm the generic person!" Regarding this seminal moment, Kimmel continued,

> Since then, I've begun to understand that race, class, and gender didn't refer only to other people, who were marginalized by race, class, or gender privilege. Those terms also described me. I enjoyed the privilege of invisibility. . . . What makes us marginal or powerless are the processes we see. Invisibility is a privilege in another sense—as a luxury. Only white people in our society have the luxury not to think about race every minute of their lives.[5]

Identity Politics

During the U.S. 2008 presidential campaign, feminist and founder of *Ms. Magazine*, Gloria Steinem, wrote an article for the *New York Times* called "Women Are Never Front-Runners." In this controversial piece, Steinem argued that women experience more oppression than any other group. She wrote,

> Gender is probably the most restricting force in American life, whether the question is who must be in the kitchen or who could be in the White House. This country is way down the list of countries electing women and, according to one study, it polarizes gender roles more than the average democracy. . . . Black men were given the vote a half-century before women of any race were allowed to mark a ballot, and generally have ascended to positions of power, from the military to the boardroom, before any women (with the possible exception of obedient family members in the latter).[6]

Steinem sparked extensive debate. Is it harder to be a woman than a person of color, or vice versa? Is it worse to be a white woman like then-Senator Hillary Clinton, or a Black man like then-Senator Barack Obama? And what about women of color, do they experience the most oppression of all?

Steinem was engaged in *identity politics*—focusing on one's identity and validating one's sense of belonging to a particular group with a particular history. One of the problems with identity politics is that they can have this kind of fracturing effect. In a time, when all women and all people of color experience profoundly harmful forms of prejudice like sexism and racism, should we focus on worrying about who has it worse? Identity politics can also lose track of the complicated nature of human identity, as in the above example where Steinem writes about "women" without race and Black people as men. We are left to wonder, what happened to women of color in her analysis?

Identity politics are problematic, but not only problematic. Recognizing one's identity and validating one's sense of belonging to a particular group with a particular history are deeply important for those who come from marginalized communities. Through the recognition of one's racial identity, one might understand oneself as part of a larger social system. Thus we appreciate the ways one's group's experiences have been shaped by social systems of power. Depending on who one is, we begin to understand how an individual might benefit from a group status or be harmed by it. (Note that focusing on one's identity is very different from choosing an identity, as in the case of white people deciding to be Native American.)

Here it is significant to note that identity politics focus on the ways one's ingroup has been disadvantaged and on revaluing the group as surviving, and as a group with a rich and valuable culture to offer, in spite of oppression. Yet, while not identity politics, challenging and dismantling racism also requires that white people, like Kimmel above, recognize their whiteness and the privilege they gain through it. Indeed, this is the focus of our book.

In terms of gender, for example, one might argue that identity politics help women identify with other women as a group with particular shared concerns. One such shared concern involves the high rates of gendered violence women face in the United States. A housewife in the 1950s whose husband verbally abused her through accusations of unfaithfulness and worthlessness, who found herself nervously looking over her shoulder when shopping because he might have taken off another afternoon from work to follow her, would have been likely to consider her struggle to be personal and to find herself averting her eyes when a neighbor's black eye was visible from beneath the sunglasses she wore inside the grocery store. With the feminist movements of the 1960s and 1970s, women have increasingly recognized that gendered violence is part of our social system and not simply a problem faced by some private individuals.

Kimberle Crenshaw writes, "Battering and rape, once seen as private (family matters) and aberrational (errant sexual aggression), are now largely recognized as part of a broad-scale system of domination that affects women as a class."[7] Crenshaw argues, "This process of recognizing as social and systemic what was formerly perceived as isolated and individual has also characterized the identity politics of African Americans, other people of color, and gays and lesbians, among others. For all these groups, identity-based politics has been a source of strength, community, and intellectual development."[8]

Identity politics can be an important way to bring people in a marginalized group together. Yet identity politics alone are not enough. After coming together around an identity, we argue for the importance of the marginalized group challenging our society and the ways it advantages, in the case of women, men in general over women. When women organize around their identity and come together as a group, they gain the shared power of their numbers. This second step involves recognition of imbalanced social power and the group in question working together to challenge that imbalance. It also involves a critical analysis of social power.

Without an analysis of social power, identity politics alone offer a limited, and at times, even problematic response. If a group, like early Irish immigrants to the United States, is impoverished, it is crucial that we understand that poverty as born from a larger social context and history. Understanding these immigrants as poor simply because of who they are (understanding the Irish as poor because of something about being Irish) means blaming the victim for their own victimization. Nineteenth-century Irish immigrants were poor because of the social context—including the English colonization of Ireland—from which they came.

A Note about Multiculturalism and the Celebration of Diversity

As in chapters 3 and 6, when we discuss multiculturalism, we mean a way of thinking about race that examines differences between groups with the aim to understand and celebrate these differences—to celebrate diversity. Multiculturalism shares much with the identity politics perspective. Like identity politics, multiculturalism tends to focus on the differences between diverse identities. Margaret L. Andersen and Patricia Hill Collins call this a difference framework. They write, "The language of difference encourages comparative thinking. People think comparatively when they learn about experiences other than their own and begin comparing and contrasting the experiences of different groups."[9] The identity politics/multiculturalism/difference framework can be a good place to start when one begins learning about social phenomena like race, class, and gender. This framework can bring about greater tolerance.

Yet, ultimately tolerance is a weak goal. The difference (or diversity or multiculturalism) framework is deeply limited. As Leslie McCall writes, "The multicultural and identity-politics perspective tends to maintain group boundaries uncritically in order to revalue them."[10] There is nothing inherently wrong with celebrating diverse identities through learning about the cultural traditions of different groups. The problem with the difference or multiculturalism framework is that it often neglects to analyze social power through thinking about the social and historical context of each group's experiences and relationships between and among groups. Multiculturalism tends to focus on decontextualized issues of diversity while material realities such as poverty, access to work and decent education, and freedom from violence remain invisible. In other words, multiculturalism suggests that if only we come to appreciate diversity, race and racism will no longer be a problem, even though the material conditions of peoples' lives remain unchanged.

Intersectionality

The perspective of *intersectionality* offers to solve some of the problems with multiculturalism and identity politics. Intersectionality, or what Andersen and Collins call a matrix of domination, focuses on how different aspects of one's identity interact (or intersect) with each other. While some individuals will have one stigmatized aspect of their identity, others will have multiple stigmatized aspects that intersect with each other, forming a matrix that may be used to dominate, to oppress. Andersen and Collins argue that a focus on multiculturalism simply encourages us to compare different identities by noting differences between individuals' experiences.[11] Comparing differences between one identity and another tends to be unproductive in terms of understanding the roles of social systems in oppression. For example, comparing the experience of being Asian American to the experience of being impoverished will likely fail to recognize how systems of power interact and affect identity across various dimensions of individuals' identities. Alternatively, a focus on intersectionality—on the matrix of domination—encourages us to think relationally in terms of power and domination. Thinking relationally encourages one to consider how social systems influence interlocking aspects of identity.[12]

In an exploration of intersecting identities, Black, feminist, lesbian essayist Audre Lorde offers an example of intersectionality in noting that she faces stigma in ways beyond the struggle against sexism and homophobia that she shares with white feminist scholar, Mary Daly. In "An Open Letter to Mary Daly," Lorde writes, "Within the community of women, racism is a reality force within my life as it is not within yours."[13] Because of her race, the oppression Lorde experiences is more profound in relation to white, lesbian women like Daly who face sexism and homophobia, but not racism. Further, compared to Black men who face racism, Lorde faces racism plus sexism plus homophobia. Even many other Black women, those who are heterosexual and middle or upper class, do not have to face oppression on as many dimensions as does Lorde as a lesbian who grew up in poverty.[14]

Along with oppression, intersectionality addresses the complexity—and the reality of diversity—in individuals' life experiences and in their relationships with others.[15] Much like the white woman and the Black woman that Kimmel describes (in the earlier example of what one sees when looking in the mirror), people who experience multiple oppressions are more likely to perceive their identities in complex ways. Those two women overlap in terms of gender, but not in terms of race. Whereas both women face sexism, the Black woman also faces racism.

In this recognition of multiplicity in human experience, intersectionality tends to frame people's experiences in terms of their social and historical context. In other words, each of us has multiple—diverse—identities in our own particular being. Each of these multiple identities overlaps with some people and is simultaneously different from aspects of others' identities.

Some of our identities carry privilege; others, the weight of oppression. And some of our particular personal identities change over our lifetimes. This might happen, for example, as we grow up from childhood to adulthood to old age, or as we slip from working-class status to poverty in a time of recession. Intersectionality recognizes the complexity of human identities.

In terms of race, sometimes it is hard to know what racial group someone belongs to; indeed, often people belong to more than one racial group. Further, as discussed above, along with race, people have multiple other social identities. These include ethnicity, gender, class, sexuality, age, and ability. To complicate matters even more, people may decide to live in a racial group other than the one they were assigned at birth, as when Gregory Howard Williams's father passed as a white man when Williams was a young boy. Sometimes the group people are assigned in childhood is questioned later in life.

The story of Halley's close friend, sociologist Ron Nerio, exemplifies the complicated nature of race and of identity and of the meanings involved in belonging to a racial group. Nerio's multiple identities offer a rich example of human intersectionality. Yet Nerio's story is somewhat unusual, for instead of passing as white, Nerio struggles with the issue of whether he can legitimately claim to be Latino.

Nerio grew up a working-class, closeted gay boy in Saginaw, Michigan. He did not know his biological father who abandoned him and his mother before Nerio was born. At the age of four, Nerio's mother married the man who would adopt Nerio and raise him as his own son. Nerio writes, "He gave me his surname, and I was not to learn about my former name or the adoption until the entire story came tumbling out in an argument years later."[16]

This man, Nerio's father, was a working-class veteran who believed in traditional, normative manhood. He believed men should be tough, athletic, unemotional, and ready for anything. When Nerio was still very small, his new father focused on making a "real" man out of Nerio, usually by beating manhood into the little boy with his belt.

Nerio's father worked as a General Motors (GM) assembly line worker at a local factory. He had little power over anyone, except his growing family, as Nerio's mother had two more children with him, two girls. His identity was as a working-class man in the United States where nearly everyone, even the poor, identify as middle class.[17] Nerio himself, like most of us, grew up with layered identities, some recognized, others not. He was a boy, although he did not feel like the boys around him seemed to feel. Other children noticed this difference, too, and Nerio was often bullied and teased at school for his way of carrying himself and his lack of interest in sports; in other words, his failure to achieve normative manhood. Nerio was also working class. His family did not have much money, but in those days of unionized factory labor, his father made a decent living working at a factory job. And, Nerio was Mexican American. Or so he thought.

Nerio knew he was the son of a Mexican American man and a white woman. Nerio's skin was like his mother's, white-white with freckles, and he had red hair. His sisters had brown skin like his father. Yet, as a young boy it did not strike him that these differences were anything but happenstance. He was as Mexican as his sisters, a member of a large, extended Mexican American family. "It never occurred to me that I was not his natural son, despite the fact that my skin was nearly translucent white and his was a deep, reddish brown."[18] Nerio regularly spent time with his father's extended family, many of whom lived nearby—aunts, uncles, cousins, a grandmother, and a great-grandmother. "My father's mother's house, [was] just two blocks away from us. . . . Grandma Nerio's little three-bedroom bungalow was the center of Nerio life. Every holiday involved homemade tamales, hand-rolled tortillas, and chicken mole. There would be copious drinking and ribald laughter."[19]

None of the children in Nerio's family learned to speak Spanish because the parents of that generation chose not to pass their first language on to their children. This meant that Nerio and his sisters could not speak with his great-grandmother, who lived right next door and spoke only Spanish. Yet, like his sisters, he took full part in other aspects of his family's cultural heritage on both sides. Although Nerio and his mother were the only white people at his father's family functions, as he understood it, he belonged fully. Indeed, even the Saginaw school system classified Nerio as Latino. For a period of his schooling, he was bussed out of his neighborhood to a white school as a Mexican American child, the only white face on a bus full of African American and Latina/o children as part of a program aimed at integrating white schools.

However, when he was about nine years old, an aunt informed him that he was not Mexican by birth; he was the biological white child of two white parents before being adopted by his Mexican American father. Nerio writes, "When the story was out, the relatives had good fun pointing out our paleness." Nerio notes that he was teased and then accepted:

> "You are a Mexican," my Aunt Yolanda announced one Christmas, for all to hear, "just like us." I appreciated the magnanimity in this proclamation. She, the eldest sister in the clan, was letting everyone know that the adopted white child was to be welcomed and treated as one of them. She was also instructing me to be proud of this heritage, to understand who I was. If I had any doubts,

if I did not know where I belonged, she was giving me permission to claim the label "Mexican" as my own.[20]

Now, however, Nerio struggles to define his own racial and ethnic identity.

When people ask Nerio about his racial and ethnic background, he usually identifies as white. This is not because he is ashamed of his Mexican background. Rather, Nerio worries that perhaps, given that both his biological parents are white and he has white skin, he has no right to identify as Latino. He recognizes that because his skin is white, he often benefits from white privilege; he passes, in a sense, as white even though he does not wish to do so. Nerio has a choice, of sorts, to pass by omission as white. His adoptive father does not have this choice.

In thinking about relationships among groups, about social context and social power, it is important to always bear in mind the many dimensions of individuals' experiences. Humans have multiple dimensions to their identities. Once again, these dimensions include race, ethnicity, class, gender, sexuality, ability, and age, and they also have multiple social relationships based on or grounded in those identities. All of these aspects—the intersectionality of human social life and individual experience—matter. Intersectionality refers to the social relationships among and between diverse people and between diverse aspects of our own experiences. In this way, intersectionality addresses the many dimensions of a person and the diverse ways we are formed as individuals.[21]

About intersectionality, Andersen and Collins write, "Race, class, and gender are *intersecting* categories of experience that affect all aspects of human life; thus, they *simultaneously* structure the experiences of all people in this society."[22] Further, Andersen and Collins make clear, "At any given moment, race, class, or gender may feel more salient or meaningful in a given person's life, but they are overlapping and cumulative in their effects."[23]

In the case of Ron Nerio, his identity includes being white *and* Latino, male, gay *and* working class. All of these pieces of his identity matter. All of them play a role in his day-to-day experiences and in his life opportunities and options. And all of these pieces of identity link Nerio to his social context and history in diverse ways. Seeing Nerio's identity and experience in terms of intersectionality makes more sense than merely thinking about him in terms of one aspect—Latino or white or working class or gay.

Because intersectionality helps us to understand people as located and shaped by diverse experiences, relationships, and connections, it helps us to think beyond individual identity and moves us toward seeing everyone as linked to a social and historical context. However, one more step must be taken to better understand race—and social experience. Ultimately, under-standing the intersectionality of a person's identity *within* the framework of cultural materialism offers the optimal way to understand the phenomenon of race.

Cultural Materialism

Cultural materialism (introduced in chapter 1 and discussed in chapter 2) presents a framework for understanding diverse and intersecting identities as born from social structures embedded in social power.[24] As with the above example from Kimmel of looking in the mirror, cultural materialists claim that social ideas (including the lack of ideas that white people have about whiteness) always come from the ways a particular group lives and survives in a particular time and place. Kimmel understands himself as simply a person, because he comes from the most privileged group. He is powerfully positioned in society, and his ideas and the ideas of others in his group, white men, spring from this position of power. He sees himself as a "normal" person instead of a white man because his social position allows him to see himself this way. It is a privilege that comes with being white to *not* see race when one looks in the mirror.

As discussed in chapter 1, those in a society with the most power have the most access to the production of knowledge or ways of thinking. In the early 1800s, white elites in the southern United States reproduced their elite status via an agricultural society built on slavery. From this political and economic system—slavery (and, as discussed in chapter 3, the colonialism that accompanied it)—came ideas about people of African descent. Racism did not bring about an economic system of exploitation based on race; rather, the economic system was the motor behind a way of thinking that we now recognize as racist.

Cultural materialism argues that a society's ways of thinking about a so-cially constructed phenomenon like race springs from the society's economic structures. Thus, when cultural materialists challenge, for example, a racist way of thinking (such as the idea that Black people are less human and more animalistic than white people), they also always work to challenge the eco-nomic inequity (an economy built on slave labor), which accompanies that way of thinking.

The problem of race, the problem of whiteness, most fundamentally has to do with social power. Simply, being white means always having a kind of power; indeed, what *critical race theorists* call a kind of property in one's whiteness. Because Halley and Eshleman are white, they gain all kinds of benefits and privileges in our society. These benefits might range from access

resources,[25] higher and better educations,[26] and healthier
~ less pollution),[27] to being able to shop without worrying
~lowed around with suspicion in the store, and having oth-
~as individuals rather than representatives of their group.[28]
~ike owning a piece of property; whites own these benefits.
As long ago as 1935, labor historian W. E. B. Du Bois (discussed briefly in
chapter 3) identified this.[29] These benefits are rarely questioned—they are
taken for granted—advantages that simply come like a birthright to those
who are white.

To clarify what this means, civil rights activist and law professor Derrick
Bell explains that at one point, he believed along with most other civil rights
advocates that everyone, people of color and white people in the United
States, wanted to end racism. He has slowly realized this is not so. Bell argues that white people gain power and want to protect the power they gain
through whiteness. And the law supports and reproduces this power.[30]

In contrast to basic liberal thought that all are equal in the eyes of the law,
Bell explores critical race theory, arguing that the law is not neutral. (Critical race theory is a form of cultural materialism that focuses on race and the
law. As we explore in chapter 6, critical race theory has also been applied
to critical reflections on race in education.) Indeed the manifestation of the
law in day-to-day life is racial. For example, drug laws bring harsher penalties for drugs more commonly used in African American communities and
conversely lighter penalties for drugs commonly used in white communities,
even when the drugs themselves are similar. So, the laws for crack cocaine
(more common in Black communities than white) have carried mandatory penalties one hundred times harsher than the laws for powder cocaine
(more common in white communities than Black). Only since March 17,
2010, have these laws finally been challenged. And even so, a vast disparity
remains. The disparity between sentences for powder cocaine versus crack
cocaine has been a hundred to one. In other words, "the current decades-old
sentencing law sets a 100-to-1 ratio, requiring the same five-year mandatory
minimum sentence for the possession of five grams of crack cocaine as it does
for the possession of 500 grams of powder cocaine."[31] As of the writing of this
book, both houses of Congress have approved the Fair Sentencing Act of
2010 that will decrease the sentencing disparity to eighteen to one.[32]

Reflecting Roediger, Bell writes, "In the United States, where property
is a measure of worth, many whites with relatively little or no property of a
traditional kind—money, securities, land—cling to their whiteness as a kind
of property. They are reinforced in this by the law, which recognizes and
protects this property right based on color the same way it recognizes and
protects any other property."[33]

In chapters 5, 6, 7, and 8 we explore examples of cultural material (including critical race theory perspectives), exposing the ways in which socioeconomic class, education, work, and public policy predict and may shape our society's thinking about race and whiteness.

Box 4.1 The Census

The defining of racial categories for the purpose of collecting data on race has historically been a controversial and difficult issue. As we describe in this chapter, the introduction of a racial category in the U.S. Census served a racist purpose. Periodically in the United States, particularly during a Census year such as 2010, one hears arguments against the collection of any kind of data on race. Given its extremely problematic history regarding the definition of racial categories, should the census abandon the collecting of racial data altogether and simply count human beings? We strongly argue no. Indeed, this would be counterproductive. Not counting race does not undo the structure of racial privilege and discrimination that has become entrenched in our society. Racial differences do not go away simply because we do not count them. In fact, if we don't count the differences we have no way of knowing or understanding the extent of the discrimination that exists. Without that understanding, we would lose the ability to address the discrimination. Today, enforcing race neutrality on data would only make the privilege of whiteness even more invisible than it already is.

Other countries have also had controversies around racial data. For example, French law prohibits the French government from collecting any official race-related data.[1] The law is meant to promote the ideal of a color-blind state where each person is only identified as French and therefore completely equal before law. France collects no census or other data on the race or ethnicity of its citizens. However, in recent years, the tremendous material differences between the lives of the richer French citizens of European ancestry and the poorer French citizens of African ancestry has generated a debate about the need for racial statistics to combat racism in France. Without data on race and ethnicity, it has been argued that the government has no way of enforcing antidiscrimination laws and measuring the progress of its citizens of color. Due to this debate, the French government has constituted a commission to examine the issue of collecting race-related statistics.[2]

Notes

1. David B. Oppenheimer, "Why France Needs to Collect Data on Racial Identity—In a French Way," *Hastings International and Comparative Law Review* 31, no. 2 (2008).
2. Chrisafis, Angelique, "French Plan to Break Taboo on Ethnic Data Causes Uproar," *Guardian*, March 23, 2009.

Discussion Questions

1. As you read more, what ways, do you imagine, we can address the problems described in this book?

2. To explore how different countries, including the United States, have asked census questions about race, visit the American Anthropological Association's online project entitled "Race: Are We So Different?" at http://www.understandingrace.org/home.html. Within the activities available under the menu Lived Experience, you can choose the Global Census option to see how race is classified in Australia, Brazil, Bulgaria, South Africa, and other countries (www.understandingrace. org/lived/global_census.html). Which of these ways of classifying race surprised you the most? Which seemed most foreign to how you have understood race? Did you approve of any of these ways of classifying race or ethnicity? Please do explain why or why not.

3. Irish and Italian Americans historically have been blamed for their poverty and other social problems because of their ethnic/racial identity, as though that ethnic/racial identity was the cause of these problems. Please identify another racial/ethnic group that has been blamed for the group's own poverty, crime rates, or other social problems. Evaluate systemic injustice as an explanation for the social problems faced by this group.

4. Based on the description within this chapter, do you perceive Ron Nerio as Mexican American or as white? Explain why you do or do not perceive Nerio's race as Mexican American?

5. Explore the case of a person whose biological parents are identified as different races, such as Nerio's sisters from a white mother and a Mexican American father. Are Nerio's sisters Mexican American or white? Can they be both? Why or why not? Can Nerio be both? Why or why not?

6. Within chapter 3, we asked, "What does it mean to 'have' a race?" Across chapters 3 and 4, we argue that race is social but that it cannot be chosen the way some other social identities may be chosen (such as being an environmentalist). Please do respond to our arguments about what it means to have a race. Address the extent to which you agree with social constructionist arguments about race. Do you agree or disagree that race cannot be chosen? Explain why.

7. If Nerio allows others to assume his racial background is white, is he passing? Please refer to arguments and evidence from chapters 3 and 4 in your response.

8. Critical race theorist Derrick Bell has argued that whites actually do not want to end racism because white people want to protect the power they gain through white privilege. If given the opportunity to have a conversation with Bell, how would you respond to his argument?

9. Do you believe white people might gain power and privilege simply from being white? If so, why might white people want to protect this power? Please explain by responding to arguments and evidence from this chapter.

10. Please discuss whether you see sentencing discrepancies as at least partially racial in basis. Explore the relative dangers of the drug crack compared to powder cocaine, the violence predicted by each, and the racial group most associated with each. Do you believe that penalizing crack cocaine to powder cocaine on a ratio of 100 to 1 is fair? Might this sentencing difference be racial? What about the Fair Sentencing Act proposal of a ratio of 18 to 1?

Notes

1. According to Tom Rodgers, Native Americans today number approximately 4.5 million in the United States ("Native American Poverty: A Challenge Too Often Ignored," *Spotlight on Poverty and Opportunity*, www.spotlightonpoverty.org/ExclusiveCommentary.aspx?id=0fe5c04e-fdbf-4718-980c-0373ba823da7 (June 11, 2010).

2. Rodgers, "Native American Poverty."

3. U.S. Constitution, Article One, Section Two, modified by the Fourteenth Amendment, Section Two, www.usconstitution.net (June 11, 2010); for more information on the Three-fifths Compromise, please do see the following online article at www.usconstitution.net/consttop ccon.html (June 11, 2010).

4. Gregory Rodriguez, "The Dark Side of White," *Los Angeles Times*, December 28, 2009.

5. Michael S. Kimmel, *The Gendered Society*, 2nd ed. (New York: Oxford University Press, 2004), 7.

6. Gloria Steinem, "Women Are Never Front-Runners," *New York Times*, January 8, 2008.

7. Kimberle Crenshaw, "Mapping the Margins: Intersectionality, Identity Politics, and Violence against Women of Color," in *Foundations of Critical Race Theory in Education*, eds. Edward Taylor, David Gillborn, and Gloria Ladson-Billings (New York: Routledge, 2009), 213.

8. Crenshaw, "Mapping the Margins," 213.

9. Margaret L. Andersen and Patricia Hill Collins, *Race, Class and Gender: An Anthology*, 7th ed. (Belmont, Calif.: Wadsworth Cengage Learning, 2010), 8.

10. Leslie McCall, "The Complexity of Intersectionality," *Signs: Journal of Women in Culture and Society* (2005), 1772–1800.

11. Andersen and Collins, *Race, Class and Gender*, 7–8.

12. See Deborah M. LaFond, "What Is the Race, Class, Gender Lens?," *Global Citizenship through a Race, Class, Gender Lens* 2010, www.albany.edu/~dlafonde/Global/whatisrgc.htm (July 13, 2010).

13. Audre Lorde, "An Open Letter to Mary Daly," in *This Bridge Called My Back: Writings by Radical Women of Color*, ed. Cherrie Moraga and Gloria Anzaldua (Latham, N.Y.: Kitchen Table: Women of Color Press, 1981/1983), 94–97.

14. Audre Lorde, "The Master's Tools Will Never Dismantle the Master's House," in *This Bridge Called My Back: Writings by Radical Women of Color*, eds. Cherrie Moraga and Gloria Anzaldua (Latham, N.Y.: Kitchen Table: Women of Color Press, 1981/1983), 99.

15. McCall, "The Complexity of Intersectionality," 1771.

16. Ron Nerio, unpublished memoir, 2009: 2.

17. A related piece of the process described by David R. Roediger (1991) involved growing numbers of the working class, particularly over the mid- to late-twentieth century, identifying not only as white but also as middle class. With this, working people increasingly defined their work as "professional." So, all kinds of work, formerly understood as working class, began to be understood and described as a "profession." One could be a professional hairstylist, professional carpenter, or professional butcher. We argue that this ideology of professionalization, like the thinking that one was always middle class no matter what the work or the pay involved, paid a psychic wage not unlike—nor unrelated to—that paid by whiteness.

18. Nerio, unpublished memoir.

19. Nerio, unpublished memoir, 28.

20. Nerio, unpublished memoir, 28.

21. McCall, "The Complexity of Intersectionality," 1771.

22. Andersen and Collins, *Race, Class and Gender* (italics in original), 6.

23. Andersen and Collins, *Race, Class and Gender*, 6.

24. For further information on cultural materialism, please see Maxine L. Margolis, *True to Her Nature: Changing Advice to American Women* (Prospect Heights, Ill.: Waveland Press, Inc., 2000).

25. Thomas M. Shapiro, "The Hidden Cost of Being African American," in *Race, Class and Gender: An Anthology*, 7th ed., ed. by Margaret L. Andersen and Patricia Hill Collins (Belmont, Calif.: Wadsworth Cengage Learning, 2010), 129–36.

26. Roslyn Arlin Mickelson and Stephen Samuel Smith, "Can Education Eliminate Race, Class, and Gender Inequality?," in *Race, Class and Gender: An Anthology*, 7th ed., ed. by Margaret L. Andersen and Patricia Hill Collins (Belmont, Calif.: Wadsworth Cengage Learning, 2010), 407–15.

27. Benjamin F. Chavis Jr., PhD, Executive Director of the Commission for Racial Justice, *Toxic Wastes and Race in the United States: A National Report on the Racial and Socio-Economic Characteristics of Communities with Hazardous Waste Sites* (New York: The United Church of Christ Commission for Racial Justice, 1987).

28. Jane Lazarre, *Beyond the Whiteness of Whiteness: Memoir of a White Mother of Black Sons* (Durham, N.C.: Duke University Press, 1996).

29. W. E. B. Du Bois, *Black Reconstruction in the United States* (New York: Harcourt, Brace and Company, 1935).

30. Derrick Bell's books include *Race, Racism, and American Law*, 6th ed. (New York: Aspen Publishers, 2008), and *Confronting Authority: Reflections on an Ardent Protester* (Boston: Beacon Press, 1996), among many others.

31. Main Justice: Politics, Policy and the Law, www.mainjustice.com/2010/03/17/senate-passes-crack-cocaine-sentencing-bill (June 30, 2010).

32. The Sentencing Project: Research and Advocacy for Reform, www.sentencingproject.org/template/page.cfm?id=128 (May 30, 2010).

33. Derrick Bell, "Epilogue," in *When Race Becomes Real: Black and White Writers Confront Their Personal Histories*, ed. by Bernestine Singley (Chicago: Lawrence Hill Books, 2002), 327–28.

CHAPTER FIVE

~

Socioeconomic Class
and White Privilege

A story in the *Wall Street Journal*, describing the economic hardships in the state of Michigan, makes the following statement:

> But the spread of financial hardship has been jarring for a region where the manufacturing-based economy once provided for high wages and comfortable middle-class lifestyles.[1]

Commenting on the economic downturn facing the country in 2008, an op-ed columnist in the *New York Times* states:

> This recession will probably have its own social profile. In particular, it's likely to produce a new social group: the formerly middle class. These are people who achieved middle-class status at the tail end of the long boom, and then lost it.[2]

An economic crisis often prompts many inquiries about class. A simple search in any newspaper database will lead you to many more such references about the losses and gains of the "middle" and other classes or the fear of losses and gains due to economic uncertainties. But how fluid is class in the United States? And when we think of class in good times or bad, do we merely understand it as a matter of economics? In fact, can you name an income that you think would qualify someone to enter the "middle class"?

Many of us would have trouble coming up with a set of dollar figures to represent any class. This is for good reason since dollar values are never permanent. Even without understanding the intricacies of economics and inflation we know that what sounded like a lot of money twenty years ago will not seem so today. Similarly, if your household had an annual income of about $46,000 in Mississippi in 2008, you might be middle class since you make about the median income in that state. But in New Jersey, your household would need an annual income of about $85,000 to claim the same status.[3] It is therefore difficult to attach a single and enduring economic definition to class.

Yet we do have a collective understanding of class. In the absence of concrete numbers, as a society we do come to an understanding of certain markers that we recognize as belonging to different classes. Are these markers simply things that money can buy like a house, a car, or a good education? Put differently, is gaining entry into a particular class merely a matter of working hard and earning more money? The controversial case of Harvard professor Henry Louis Gates being arrested at his own house near Harvard University raises some of these issues.

Professor Gates, an African American and a renowned scholar of African American Studies, was arrested in July 2009 when Sergeant James Crowley, a white officer, was investigating a report from a neighbor that someone might have broken into the house. The officer claims that professor Gates became combative and raised issues of racism when he was asked to identify himself. Professor Gates says he was disturbed by the officer's reluctance to be convinced that it was indeed Gates's house despite having produced identification cards. Setting aside the issue of whose version is more credible, let us consider whether the incident would have occurred if professor Gates were not African American. Would a famous white male scholar who owns a house in a clearly "upper-class" neighborhood need to produce much evidence of identity, or would he more readily blend in with his surroundings, making identification redundant?

In chapter 3 we discussed David Roediger's influential work in the field of whiteness studies. Roediger argues that class is as much about whiteness as it is about money. We tend to associate white people with qualities of industriousness and independence; things that indicate "class." Roediger observes that these ideas about class characteristics were shaped in the days after the American Revolution when the political fervor of the revolution, grounded in the ideas of "liberty" and "freedom," clashed with the reality of the working life of many poor and working-class white people. Many of them were traditionally peasants or artisans but were too poor to own any land or unable to sustain an independent living and therefore had to turn to wage labor. Roediger writes that ". . . the gradual transition to wage labor from 1800 to 1860 (and beyond) was an extremely serious matter for labor republicans."[4]

Here the term *labor republican* refers to working-class people who supported the idea of an independent American republic free of British colonial rule.

White workers were faced with the dilemma of whether workers who did not own their own land and depended on wages could really be considered free. Particularly against the backdrop of slavery, the wage dependency presented an uncomfortable idea. Roediger explains, "The existence of slavery gave working Americans both a wretched touchstone against which to measure their fears of unfreedom and a friendly reminder that they were by comparison not so badly off."[5] To overcome this complex fear of comparison between wage labor and slave labor, a class identity emerged where white working-class people identified themselves as hardworking, independent-minded people as opposed to their perception of enslaved Black people as lazy and dependent.

This identity formation is reflected, among other things, in the development of a unique vocabulary in the United States around wage labor that distinguished it from slave labor. For example, around this time the Dutch-derived term *boss* began to replace the commonly used *master* to describe an employer, since *master* was too closely associated with *slave*. Roediger notes that the Oxford English Dictionary describes *boss* as a term derived in the United States to avoid the use of the word *master*. In this thinking, a white worker was independent minded, on equal political and social terms with the boss, unlike the enslaved Blacks, who white people saw as having no mind of their own and were dependent on their masters.

This association of whites with independence of character and a hard-working nature, or in other words "class," remains so strong that successful people like professor Gates who are not white tend to be viewed as the exceptions who need to prove themselves. Even when people of color attain the monetary means of the dominant or prosperous "classes," the "class" characteristics are not as easily acquired. Economist William Darity discusses the example of Asian immigrants who have managed some economic successes being referred to as *model minorities*. The implication being that, contrary to what is normally expected of people of color, this group knows "how to behave themselves" in the "correct (white?)" way.[6] Darity contends that "the fact that their behavior is subject to such intense scrutiny means that the 'true' Americans—the established 'white' Americans—sit in perpetual judgment."[7] It is the white perception that decides who has class and who does not. So even as some groups of color attain the model status, they continue to be outsiders or second-"class" citizens.

Classy and Trashy

Vijaya was traveling in New Mexico when she experienced an all-too-common example of an outsider having to prove herself. At the breakfast buffet in a motel in Albuquerque, she was picking up bagels to bring back to her table when a fellow white guest asked her where the decaffeinated coffee was. Not thinking much of it, she indicated she did not know. But just a moment later she was stopped by another white guest who said, "Miss, where is the toaster?" With the second question Vijaya suddenly realized much to her amusement that the two people had thought that she was the waitress. Later the experience also provided her with some interesting reflection.

Vijaya came to the United States more than a decade ago, completed a PhD, and became a college professor. By most economic criteria she would not be in the same socioeconomic class as a waitress. Vijaya is also from India and so belongs to the so-called model minority of Asian immigrants. But since it is the white perception that decides who is a model minority, the white perception can also undecide. So the notion of a model minority is not a constant. In New Mexico, a state with a large Latino population, she wondered if the white perception did not recognize the model. To them was she just some kind of brown (brown: generally low on the class ladder)? So if you are brown, unless you concretely prove yourself, you might not always be recognized as your class.

Counseling psychologist Derald Wing Sue's scholarship has focused on subtle, often unintentional acts of discrimination, such as the experience of Vijaya at the motel breakfast buffet. "Microaggressions are the brief and commonplace daily verbal, behavioral, and environmental indignities, whether intentional or unintentional, that communicate hostile, derogatory, or negative racial, gender, sexual-orientation, and religious slights and insults to the target person or group."[8] Like the white people who mistook Vijaya for a person in a position of service to them, the perpetrators of *microaggressions* are often unaware of having caused offense. Sue notes that any single microaggression may have a small impact but that regular experiences of microaggressions may build on each other. "Many Whites, for example, fail to realize that people of color from the moment of birth are subjected to multiple racial microaggressions from the media, peers, neighbors, friends, teachers, and even in the educational process and/or curriculum itself. These insults and indignities are so pervasive that they are often unrecognized."[9] The perpetrators of these little aggressions often have meant no harm and sometimes even have good intentions.

To Vijaya the breakfast incident in the motel also recalled other issues about race and class markers that she has pondered since coming to the United States. In most cultures, access to the rarefied world of classical music is a class marker, available to the educated and the privileged. Vijaya grew up listening to classical music in her home in India. But when she came to the United States she realized the raced dimensions of this class marker. In the United States the term *classical music* and all its class associations applied to only one specific kind of classical music—*western* classical music, an art form with origins in and continued strong association with normative white culture. Vijaya grew up listening to Indian classical music, a music tradition with its own long, rich, and profound history. But here in the United States it finds its place in the "world" music section or a multicultural event, not equal to the rarefied world of classical (western) music and certainly not a class marker for her anymore.

But when class is so strongly associated with one race, it is inevitable that the culture of that race will become the normative culture, and class markers will largely be derived from that normative culture. Many of our social and cultural markers of class can be traced to white culture. In fact, when we think about any kind of art, not just music, class association is usually strongest with arts that have a white European lineage. The rest is "world" art, a special category—not the mainstream of high "class" art.

Similarly in more mundane affairs, when we think of a "classy" restaurant, someplace expensive, worth a splurge for a special occasion, the association is often with places that serve foods associated with white European cultures. Restaurants that serve foods from non-white cultures such as Chinese or Mexican are often referred to as "ethnic" restaurants and are generally expected to be inexpensive. So white can be classy, whereas non-white is ethnic. Classy is expensive, ethnic is often cheap. Would you refer to an Italian or a French restaurant as ethnic? We encourage our readers to discuss their own examples of social and cultural markers of class.

The fact that class is defined by whiteness is also evident in the problematic term *white trash*. White trash as we know is the opposite of class; a term used to describe white people without class. But "white trash" carries with it the same kind of out-of-the-norm implications as the term model minorities. It implies that the norm is for white people to *have* class. Deviation from this norm is unusual, and therefore it has its own special term. After all, we do not say Black trash or Brown trash. Since we associate only white with class, white people become immediately visible when they step out of this norm. People of color, on the other hand, are not associated with class. So they do not require a special term to indicate the lack of class. They do, however, require a special mention when they do acquire "class." Then they become the special "models" who are deviations from the norm of classlessness for people of color.

The Ladder of Success:
Measuring Income and Class (Im)Mobility

Some might argue that if more and more immigrants and people of color are able to attain economic success in the land of opportunities, the privileged association of whiteness with class will not matter for long. This argument suggests that it is just a matter of time before class and class markers become more race neutral. To explore whether this is the case we have to verify whether opportunities for economic success are indeed as widespread as some might think. When studying economic issues it is important to remember that many individual success stories do not give a complete picture about what is happening in the entire country. Economists have examined the issue of economic mobility in a more systematic manner, using large amounts of data. Could the success of the so-called model immigrants of color be interpreted as fluidity of class in the United States?

Economists Katherine Bradbury and Jane Katz at the Federal Reserve Bank of Boston used data on about three thousand families from the Panel Study of Income Dynamics (PSID), a very commonly used economic dataset maintained by the University of Michigan.[10] Their study begins by dividing the families into five groups depending on their income levels in 1994— poorest, lower middle, middle, upper middle, and richest. All the groups consist of the same number of people; that is, 20 percent (since there are five groups) of the total number of families. They then looked at changes in the families after ten years.

The study found that after ten years, that is, in 2004, the majority (54 percent) of the families that started out in the poorest group in 1994 remained in the same group in 2004. Only 5 percent of those who started out in the bottom group were able to move up to the richest group. Meanwhile, the majority (53 percent) of those who started out in the richest group remained in the same group through the years. Overall, 40 percent of the families stayed in the same group as they began and only about 22 percent of the families were able to move up or down by more than two groups. This low number is significant since people in the poorest group are so poor that they would definitely need to move up by two or more groups in order to work their way out

of poverty. Given this, the authors conclude that relative economic
or the ability of people to move into a different income group is quite

A report by the Brookings Institute, which is part of a research program
called the Economic Mobility Project, finds a similar pattern in economic
immobility.[11] In this report the researchers used data from the PSID to study
changes in the economic ranking of a group of children from 1968 as they
became adults over the next thirty-four years (up to the year 2002). Once
again this study classified families into five income groups.

They found that as adults in the period 1995–2002, a majority of the
children had more real[12] family income than their parents did in 1968. But
having higher money income than their parents does not necessarily mean
a better standard of living. Among other things, it is largely a reflection
of the fact that with more women taking on paid work, families also work
many more hours than they did in the 1960s. For example, economists Jared
Bernstein and Karen Kornbluh use data from the Bureau of Labor Statistics
to estimate that compared to 1979, average yearly working hours for a family
increased by about 11 percent in 2002 due to increased paid working hours
for women.[13] This adds up to about four hundred extra hours of work for the
year. As paid working hours increase, the expenses of a family also increase.

Picture a traditional family in the 1970s where the woman does not have
a paid job or only has a part-time job. This allows her the time to take care
of the kids, clean the house, and cook meals for the family. Now, with more
women working outside the house that time is not available anymore. So
families often have to pay someone else to provide childcare and spend
money to buy meals that previously they might have cooked at home themselves. As a result more money is being spent by families to take care of the
same kinds of household tasks as before. Therefore, the higher money income
that comes with more working hours does not really tell us much about improvements in families' living standards and economic status.

In order to see if families' economic status has improved we can look at
whether the families were able to move into a different income group. This
is where the Brookings study on mobility finds an important pattern. The
study finds that there was limited relative mobility for children belonging
to the poorest families in 1968. That is, although they have more income
than their parents, their ability to move into a different income group was
still restricted. They still continue to belong to the lowest income group as
adults. The study finds that almost half (42 percent) of the children coming from the poorest families remained in the poorest group as adults. They
are unable to move up the class rankings. Similarly, about 40 percent of the
children coming from the richest families tend to stay in the richest group as

adults. This pattern is called *stickiness* at the ends. That is, children belonging to poor families are stuck being poor and children born to rich families tend to stay rich.

The Brookings report also discusses evidence from a comprehensive analysis of international comparisons in mobility conducted by economist Miles Corak.[14] The study looks at the estimates of the impact of the earnings of fathers on the earnings of sons in the United States, Canada, and eight other Western European countries.[15] The relationship between the earnings of fathers and sons is the strongest in the United States and the United Kingdom. In these two countries, on average, almost 50 percent of the sons' income is predicted by the fathers' earnings. For all the other European countries and Canada, the relationship is much weaker. For example, in Canada, Norway, Finland, and Denmark, the relationship is less than 20 percent. The stronger association between parent and child incomes in the United States suggests that family advantages last longer in the United States and that the lack of such advantage lowers mobility prospects.

In another cross-country mobility study Markus Jäntti, Bernt Bratsberg, Knut Roed, Oddbjörn Raaum, Robin Naylor, Eva Osterbacka, Anders Bjorklund, and Tor Eriksson[16] also look at the income association between fathers and sons. In this study the comparison is among a group of Nordic countries (Denmark, Finland, Norway, and Sweden) and the United States and the United Kingdom. For the United States the data include children born between the years 1957–1964 from the National Longitudinal Survey of Youth. Like Corak's, this study found very similar levels of high association between father and son incomes in the United States and low association in the Nordic countries. More interestingly, this study also specifically compared the mobility rates of children from the lowest income group in the six countries. They found that in the United States twice as many children (40 percent) from the poorest income groups remained in the poorest group as adults. In contrast, in the Nordic countries only 20 percent continued to remain in the poorest group as adults.

We can quote several other studies that indicate similar trends in income mobility in the United States. But if, as these studies indicate, contrary to popular perception of the United States as the land of opportunities that mobility is limited, then what of the "model minorities"? Why are they able to succeed? Darity observes that "model" immigrants bring the tools of their success with them.[17] They frequently belong to the middle class in their country of origin and have some amount of accumulated wealth and high levels of education before they emigrate. So when they move to the United States, it is a lateral move—from being middle class in their own country to the middle class in the United States. It is not a vertical move where they have to work their way into the middle class from a position of poverty. For example, in a study on Asian immigrants, economist Timothy Bates finds that the high rates of successful small business start-ups among Chinese and Korean immigrants can be attributed to the fact that they are able to start their business with higher levels of initial investment.[18] These immigrants bring this initial investment with them as savings when they emigrate. Similarly, the Indian community that Vijaya belongs to also presents a striking example of preexisting class advantage. A majority of the Indian immigrants tend to be much more educated than the average person in the United States. Some 74 percent of adult Indian immigrants in the United States have a bachelor's or a degree higher than a bachelor's. In comparison, only 28 percent of the general population in the United States has a bachelor's or higher degree.[19] Clearly this is a group that brings their class advantage with them.

So the success of groups of middle-class immigrants cannot invalidate the findings of restricted mobility in the United States. In addition to the restricted ability of poor families to move into the richer income groups, another troubling trend is the rise in the gaps among the income groups. According to the U.S. Census Bureau, the richest 20 percent of households in the country got 50 percent of the income generated in the country in 2008. In comparison, the poorest 20 percent of households got less than 4 percent of the total income.[20] In fact, the gap has continued to expand very significantly over the years. In a well-known study, economist Emmanuel Saez used income data from the Internal Revenue Service (IRS) and found that the share of income going to the richest 10 percent of households in the country has been steadily increasing since the 1960s. Since the Census data does not fully report the incomes of the richest households and the data collection method has changed over time, Saez used tax data from the IRS to get a more accurate measure of changes in inequality over time. Saez found that while in the 1960s the richest 10 percent of households made about 33 percent of the total income generated in the country, by 2008 that number had grown to almost 50 percent (48.2 percent).[21] A simple example of splitting a pizza among ten people can help illustrate the extent of this growing gap between the rich and the poor. The richest 10 percent getting 50 percent of the income means that one privileged person among the ten gets half the pizza. The remaining nine (that is 90 percent) have to share the other half. Obviously, half a pizza shared among nine people is very unfair when you consider that the remaining one person is eating the other half of the pie by himself or herself.

The overall picture that emerges, then, is that mobility is constrained in the United States and inequality is persistent. Opportunities exist but only for those who already have the class privilege. And since privilege has a definite race in the United States, the strong association of class with whiteness continues, and class markers continue to be derived from whiteness. Therefore, even those who bring their class capital with them, for example, the so-called model minorities, are judged against the image of class as white.

Economics of Class: Inequality and Individualism

There is a lot of debate among economists about the persistent inequality in the United States. One particular stream of thought within economics has long focused on the notion of the conflict between efficiency and equality. *Efficiency* is generally understood as the ability to get more and more output out of the limited resources we have. Efficiency generates economic growth; that is, we are able to make more and more things and create more material wealth. But in order to make more output the economy needs new and improved ways of doing things. In other words, efficiency demands innovation. People are motivated to innovate when they know that they can get rich from their innovation. But as some people get rich from their innovations, this inevitably increases inequality.

In an often-cited paper from 1975, economist Arthur Okun referred to this particular argument as the "trade-off" between equity (equality) and efficiency.[22] People have an incentive to work harder and innovate if they know that they can keep most of the rewards from their work to themselves. If attempts are made to reduce the inequality, for instance, by taking money from the rich innovators and providing more services to the poor, then the rewards to the innovators will be reduced. This lowers the incentive to work harder and innovate and ultimately lowers economic growth. Along the same lines, this efficiency point of view also argues that if everyone were to make similar incomes irrespective of their work or innovation, then there would be little motivation to work more or create something new.

This efficiency argument is often used to justify the inequality trends in the United States. This argument contends that even though inequality exists, the United States also provides the greatest rewards for innovation, which has built the largest economy in the world. Similarly the argument presents the idea that although there is inequality, because of the growth in the economy each generation is making more income than the previous one. The growth that is possible from efficiency benefits everyone, the poor as well as the rich, even though the gap between the rich and the poor might continue to expand.

Such focus on people's incentives is part of the larger theory of *rational choice* in economics. Within this perspective, hypothetical rational individuals weigh all decisions based on costs and benefits. If the costs of innovation in terms of time and effort involved are not matched by the benefit of riches, then hypothetical rational individuals will choose to work less and not innovate. This calculus of costs does not address the issue of what gives people the ability to innovate. The roots of those abilities are left outside the purview of economic analysis. It assumes that all individuals are capable of making completely independent choices, taking only their own needs and interests into account.

Feminist economists and sociologists have often critiqued this blind spot in economic analysis. Sociologist Paula England writes that the focus on individual incentives is a *separative* model because "it presumes that humans are autonomous, impervious to social influences."[23] Similarly, economist Diana Strassman writes, "Such assumptions indeed may be typical of the perceived experiences of adult, white, male, middle-class American economists, but they fail to capture economic reality for many others."[24]

The economic reality for many others, as discussed before, is that perceived increases in money incomes have not really improved living standards. It has just meant that more members of families are working, and every one is working longer hours. An even starker economic reality for many others, particularly non-white individuals, is that historical patterns of discrimination and privilege have a strong and lasting impact on the ability of people to participate equally in economic life. For example, Darity writes about the big advantage in the intergenerational transfer of wealth for white families. In comparison, Black families have much less wealth to transfer due to "a sustained historical pattern of deprivation of the capacity to accumulate property, particularly land."[25]

Wealth and Inheritance

Many studies have documented the role of the Federal Housing Authority (FHA), established in 1934, in generating a significant advantage to average working-class white families in the accumulation of property. By providing government backing or insurance for private lending to home buyers, the FHA made homeownership more accessible to average citizens. In order to qualify for the insurance, the FHA established loan assessment codes that appraised the condition of the individual property as well as that of the neighborhood. The criterion for what qualified as a suitable or "stable" neighborhood was explicitly racial, as expressed in the following quote from the FHA underwriting manual of 1938:

> If a neighborhood is to retain stability, it is necessary that properties shall continue to be occupied by the same social and racial classes. A change in social or racial occupancy generally contributes to instability and a decline in value.[26]

Along with this explicit language that encouraged racial segregation, the FHA manuals also adopted the use of color-coded maps of neighborhoods in cities across the country that were intended to indicate which neighborhoods were suitable for mortgage lending and which were not. Poor neighborhoods and neighborhoods with mixed white and non-white populations were coded red. Such neighborhoods were considered unsuitable for lending since they did not follow the FHA stability criterion of social and racial homogeneity.[27] This process of *redlining* neighborhoods that were not purely occupied by whites ensured that most of the FHA-backed loans went to white people in exclusively white neighborhoods. On the other hand, the lack of loan availability in non-white neighborhoods, particularly in major cities, meant that resale of homes became difficult because without the loans few people could afford to buy homes outright. With limited resale, property values declined and reinforced a pattern of neighborhood deterioration. Sociologist George Lipsitz notes that until 1962, 98 percent of FHA-backed loans went to white people.[28] Lipsitz adds that this bias in lending provided whites with "trillions of dollars of wealth accumulated through the appreciation of housing assets."[29]

The impact of this historic pattern of discrimination in property accumulation is extremely far-reaching since housing is the single largest component of wealth for households in the United States. According to the Federal Reserve's Survey of Consumer Finance (SCF), the primary source of information about household finances, on an average housing accounted for about 31 percent of total family assets, a higher number than any other single asset.[30]

So the FHA loans provided a considerable jump-start to wealth accumulation by white families. Data from the SCF continues to show the considerable gap between wealth accumulated by white and non-white families. The median wealth for white (non-Hispanic) families was about $170,000 in 2007. For non-white families the median wealth was only about $28,000.

It is important to understand the distinction between income and wealth. *Income* is the money that you earn each year; *wealth* is the accumulation of money and assets over the years. You don't necessarily have to earn the income to accumulate wealth since wealth can also be inherited. Accumulated wealth has long-lasting impacts on people and families. Sociologist Thomas Shapiro summarizes findings about racial differences in wealth inheritance based on data from the PSID for the years 1984–1999. About 28 percent of white families inherited some wealth after the death of a parent. In comparison, only 7.7 percent of Black families inherited any wealth. The contrast is even sharper when we look at the average amounts of inheritance. Among the families who do inherit wealth, the average inheritance for white families amounted to $52,430, whereas for African American families the amount is less than half that at $21,796. Both Black and white families also receive financial support from living relatives. Here again the average white recipient receives a much larger amount ($2,824) compared to the average Black family ($805).[31]

Accumulated wealth has long-lasting impacts on people and families. Sociologists Stephen J. McNamee and Robert K. Miller Jr. enumerate several ways in which wealth accumulation allows parents to give a head start to their children at key points of their lives.[32] For example, these include paying partly or fully for college, helping with the down payment when buying a house, and providing a safety net during personal setbacks such as illness. They compare the impact of inheritance to starting points in a relay race. "For a while, we run alongside our parents as the baton is passed, and then we take off on our own. In this relay race, those born into great wealth start far ahead of those born to poor parents, who have a huge deficit to overcome if they are to catch up."[33]

But just as class is not only about money, the impact of inheritance is not merely monetary either. Groups with more accumulated wealth not only have financial power but also social power. They set the cultural and social norms that define what constitutes "class" and what constitutes "trash." It is then they who are able to pass on this cultural and social capital. As McNamee and Miller explain:

> Everyone possesses culture—bodies of knowledge and information needed to navigate through social space. Full acceptance into the highest social circles, however, requires knowledge of the ways of life of a particular group a kind of "savoir faire" that includes expected demeanor, manners, and comportment associated with the upper class. Those born into these high powered circles are trained from an early age in the cultural ways of the group, which allows them to travel comfortably in these circles and to "fit in." Outsiders who aspire to become part of these high-powered circles must learn these cultural ways of life

from the outside in a more difficult and daunting task that continually carries the risk of being exposed as an imposter or pretender.[34]

With the head start in wealth accumulation that white people in this country gained, the accepted norms of demeanor, manners, and comportment are all derived from the white culture. Even though all white people may not be wealthy or have a monetary inheritance, they still inherit the knowledge of the white "cultural ways of life," which in our society are the right or the "classy" ways of life. For people of color, peering in from the outside, the right cultural knowledge is not automatically inherited. Their food is at best ethnic; their music and art is multicultural entertainment, not "class." In order to gain "class," people of color have to step outside their culture and acquire a new cultural knowledge. Sociologist Shapiro aptly summarizes that passing wealth to future generations "involved passing along class standing as well."[35]

Viewed through the prism of inheritance, inequality is not merely an indication of rewards for innovation. It can also be interpreted as a self-reinforcing cycle where past patterns of privilege and inequality are passed on to current and future generations. The ability to innovate and to make many other crucial "rational" economic decisions like owning a home, owning a business, or getting a higher education (all of which can also contribute to the ability to innovate) are influenced by this cycle. Ignoring these influences and focusing only on individual self-interest as the main influence on economic efficiency provides a tool to disregard and disclaim responsibility for historic backgrounds of privilege. Privilege brings with it an invisibility. Only those who have the privilege are able to ignore their backgrounds since the privilege affords them the tools and the training to continue making independent, rational economic decisions. It is in fact convenient to ignore their privileged backgrounds. But for those who do not inherit the privilege, there is the constant reminder that they may never catch up with those with the head start. Even from the perspective of efficiency, it can be argued that there is a loss of efficiency when large groups of people lack the capacity to participate effectively in economic decision making due to their impoverished backgrounds.

Conclusion

When we look closely at the details we discover that many common perceptions about class in the United States do not conform to the facts. The fact that people are unable to move easily from one income group to another questions the perception that the United States is a land of opportunities. McNamee and Miller point out another misperception: "Despite the widely held perception that America is a 'middle class' society, most of the money is highly concentrated at the top of the system."[36] When we combine the concentration of wealth and lack of mobility with the significant head start that white people have in terms of wealth accumulation, we also see that class is not only a discussion about money. Class and race are deeply intertwined. This intertwining creates a cycle where white privilege continues to be perpetuated. Economic philosophies like rational choice that focus purely on individual efforts and choices, while ignoring the role of background and privilege, in fact support and justify this perpetuation. In the following two chapters we will see examples of this cycle of privilege in schools and in workplaces and explore in greater detail the role of race and class in shaping socioeconomic life in the United States.

Discussion Questions

1. What class would you place yourself in? Discuss why and what markers you use to identify or distinguish your class.
2. Provide four examples of things or behaviors that you think are "classy." Then discuss whether these things or behaviors are linked to money or race.
3. Critically reflect on the term *white trash*. What might this term reveal about the assumptions regarding whiteness? How is this term related to class? What might this term reveal about assumptions regarding groups of color?
4. Microaggressions are often unintentional and unrecognized by the perpetrators. Can common unintentional slights that are invisible to the perpetrators have a harmful impact?
5. Given that money income is greater today than in 1970, why is it not a sufficient indication of whether our living standards are improving or not? Can you think of more examples where earning more money than before does not mean one has gained a richer lifestyle?
6. What is the difference between income and wealth?
7. How does inheritance systematically advantage whites in comparison to people of color in the United States? What was the role of the FHA in this?
8. Discuss how wealth has influenced the racial rigidity of class in the United States.

9. How did redlining by the FHA influence accumulation of wealth by race?

Notes

1. Alex P. Kellogg, "Detroit's Food Banks Strain to Serve Middle Class," *Wall Street Journal*, July 10, 2009.

2. David Brooks, "The Formerly Middle Class," *New York Times*, November 17, 2009.

3. U.S. Census Bureau, *2008 American Community Survey*.

4. David Roediger, *Wages of Whiteness: Race and the Making of the American Working Class*, rev. ed. (London: Verso, 1991), 45.

5. Roediger, *Wages of Whiteness*, 49.

6. William Darity, "Stratification Economics: The Role of Intergroup Inequality," *Journal of Economics and Finance* 29, no. 2 (July 2005): 144–53.

7. Darity, "Stratification Economics," 148.

8. Derald Wing Sue, *Microaggressions in Everyday Life: Race, Gender, and Sexual Orientation* (Hoboken, N.J.: John Wiley & Sons, Inc., 2010), 5.

9. Sue, *Microaggressions*, 7.

10. Katherine Bradbury and Jane Katz, "Trends in U.S. Family Income Mobility 1967–2004," *Federal Reserve Bank of Boston Working Paper Series*, no. 09-7 (2009), www.bos.frb.org/economic/wp/wp2009/wp0907.pdf (September 10, 2009).

11. Ron Haskins, Julia Issacs, and Isabel Sawhill, *Getting Ahead or Losing Ground: Economic Mobility in America* (Washington, D.C.: Brookings Institution Press, 2008).

12. Real income refers to income that has been adjusted for inflation. Since prices change every year, one dollar today does not have the same value as one dollar in the 1930s. Obviously, a dollar in the 1930s bought a lot more than what a single dollar will buy today. To account for this difference, economists often refer to the "real" numbers, such as real income where the dollars have been adjusted for inflation or the changes in prices over the years.

13. Karen Kornbluh and Jared Bernstein, "Running Faster to Stay in Place," Work and Family Program Research Paper, New America Foundation, www.newamerica.net/publications/policy/running_faster_to_stay_in_place (June 2005).

14. Miles Corak, "Do Poor Children Become Poor Adults? Lessons from a Cross Country Comparison of Generational Earnings Mobility," IZA Discussion Paper, no. 1993 (Bonn: Institute for the Study of Labor, 2006).

15. These studies focus on the earnings relationships between fathers and sons since male earnings data are more readily available than female earnings data, particularly for earlier years.

16. Markus Jäntti, Bernt Bratsberg, Knut Roed, Oddbjörn Raaum, Robin Naylor, Eva Osterbacka, Anders Bjorklund, and Tor Eriksson, "American Exceptionalism in a New Light: A Comparison of Intergenerational Earnings Mobility in the Nordic Countries, the United Kingdom and the United States," IZA Discussion Paper, no. 1938 (Bonn: Institute for the Study of Labor, 2006).

17. Darity, "Stratification Economics."

18. Timothy Bates, *Race, Self-Employment, and Upward Mobility: An Illusive American Dream* (Washington, D.C.: Woodrow Wilson Center Press; Baltimore: Johns Hopkins University Press, 1997).

19. U.S. Census Bureau, *2007 American Community Survey*.

20. U.S. Census Bureau, Historical Income Tables, Current Population Survey Table H-2, www.census.gov/hhes/www/income/data/historical/inequality/H02AR_2009.xls (August 1, 2010).

21. Emmanuel Saez, "Striking It Richer: The Evolution of Top Incomes in the United States," http://elsa.berkeley.edu/~saez/saez-UStopincomes-2008.pdf (August 15, 2009).

22. Arthur Okun, *Equality and Efficiency: The Big Trade Off* (Washington, D.C.: The Brookings Institution Press, 1975).

23. Paula England, "Separative and Soluble Selves," in *Feminist Economics Today: Beyond Economic Man*, eds. Marianne A. Ferber and Julie A. Nelson (Chicago: University of Chicago Press, 2003), 35–59.

24. Diana Strassman, "Not a Free Market: The Rhetoric of Disciplinary Authority in Economics," in *Beyond Economic Man: Feminist Theory and Economics*, eds. Marianne A. Ferber and Julie A. Nelson (Chicago: University of Chicago Press, 1993).

25. Darity, "Stratification Economics."

26. *Underwriting Manual* (Washington, D.C.: Federal Housing Administration, 1938).

27. For further exploration see Douglas Massey and Nancy Denton, *American Apartheid: Segregation and the Making of the Underclass* (Cambridge, Mass.: Harvard University Press, 1993).

28. George Lipsitz, *Possessive Investments in Whiteness: How White People Profit from Identity Politics* (Philadelphia: Temple University Press, 2006).

29. Lipsitz, *Possessive Investments*, 139.

30. Brian Bucks, Arthur Kennickell, Traci Mach, and Kevin Moore, "Changes in U.S. Family Finances from 2004 to 2007: Evidence from the Survey of Consumer Finances," *Federal Reserve Bulletin* 95 (February 2009): A1–A56.

31. Thomas Shapiro, *Hidden Cost of Being African American: How Wealth Perpetuates Inequality* (New York: Oxford University Press, 2004).

32. Stephen J. McNamee and Robert K. Miller Jr., "The Meritocracy Myth," *Sociation Today* 2, no. 1 (2004), www.ncsociology.org/sociationtoday/v21/merit.htm (July 15, 2010).

33. McNamee and Miller, "Meritocracy."

34. McNamee and Miller, "Meritocracy."

35. Kellogg, "Detroit's Food Banks Strain to Serve Middle Class."

36. McNamee and Miller, "Meritocracy."

CHAPTER SIX

~

(Not) Teaching Race

Imagine a dedicated, young, white eighth-grade teacher who values the potential positive impact she can have in the public school where she teaches. Although the students at the suburban school are predominantly white, Ms. Jones appreciates the modest diversity the school provides in terms of race, ethnicity, and socioeconomic class. As a white woman from a middle-class family, she is like many who have never critically examined the privilege of being white. She has always simply seen herself as normal, human, having what she wishes all her students could enjoy. While she rarely notices the race of her white students, she is keenly aware of the races of her few students of color. Although this example is fictional, throughout reading this chapter please imagine how Ms. Jones might become a better teacher through a clearer understanding of the role whiteness may play in her classroom.

A true analysis of whiteness in the classroom must address the social power that has been conferred on whiteness, including the ways of thinking that support that power. Cultural materialism helps us to see the unquestioned beliefs that many of us hold about white students being smarter, better students than students of color (including the commonly held belief that white schools are better schools because white students are smarter and better students). These deeply problematic—racist—ideas support and reinforce the greater social power of white people. In this chapter, we review evidence that this greater social power continues to afford white people access to a better education than people of color. And the cycle continues.

A critical analysis of race in the classroom must address how the invisibility of whiteness enhances white social power. Whiteness is invisible for individuals who perceive white people as "normal," "regular," or "just human." In this thinking, everyone has a race except white people who, because they are "just human," have no race. Within this perspective, whiteness—a race like any other socially constructed race—is invisible.

Maureen T. Reddy, a scholar in English and women's studies, identifies that most whites are perceived by other whites as objective observers on issues of race.[1] At the same time, most people of color are seen by most whites as being biased when it comes to race. An example of this occurred on one of our campuses when a faculty member from the history department sought to expand the department by hiring an expert on African history. One student, a young white woman, expressed publicly that she supported expanding the areas of expertise in the department to include an expert on Africa but that she was concerned the department was interested in hiring someone from West Africa. The young white woman worried that a person from West Africa would be biased because a person from Africa would not be able to view Africa objectively. We doubt that the same student would be concerned about a scholar from Europe being hired to teach European history. Similarly, we assume that this student would perceive a white scholar from the United States as able to be unbiased when teaching the history of Africa.

While most people of color are viewed by whites as biased in regards to race, Reddy argues that only two categories of whites are considered racially biased.[2] First are those who are notably racist (such as members of white supremacy groups), and second are whites who have intimate relationships with people of color (such as whites who have family members of color). While overt racists and white people with intimate ties to people of color are seen as biased, most other whites are seen as neutral, fair, and open-minded on issues of race.[3] An analysis of the power of whiteness in the classroom must address how an assumption that most whites are fair and neutral regarding race affects authority, perceptions of justice, distribution of resources, and honest discussion in the classroom.

In 1954 the Supreme Court ruled in the case of *Oliver L. Brown et al. v. the Board of Education of Topeka (KS) et al.* that segregation in public schools violated the Fourteenth Amendment of the U.S. Constitution, which promises equal protection in legal matters to all citizens. While segregation within public schools has been illegal for decades, de facto segregation still abounds. Eshleman attended public schools from kindergarten through high school in predominantly white, relatively economically advantaged suburbs, each within a twenty-minute drive of an economically depressed, predominantly

Black inner city (near Detroit, Michigan, for kindergarten through sixth grade, and near Pontiac, Michigan, beyond). The creation of predominantly white suburbs near inner cities that are populated mainly by people of color has been termed "white flight" by sociologists such as William H. Frey.[4] Although segregation was ruled unconstitutional a quarter of a century before Eshleman entered public school, all of her teachers were white and very few of her peers were of color.

During each of Eshleman's family's moves that placed her within the school districts she attended, her parents faced pressures by peers to choose to live in a "good" (predominantly white) neighborhood with "good" (predominantly white) schools.[5] Many white families face a similar decision. In addition to the decisions families face when moving to a new town, school choice decisions may be prompted because of charter school opportunities and private school options.[6] Families selecting schools often face a false dualism that presents schools as "good" or "bad." Schools are complex; most schools include a mix of strong and weak components, aspects that will enhance education and limit potential. Unfortunately, whites too often use race as the most important criterion to determine whether a school is "good" or "bad." Predominantly white schools might receive better funding because of the investment of parents who believe the school is good. Families with options may flee "bad" schools that are populated by more students of color. What might happen if more parents invested in fighting for equality across schools rather than focusing on supporting the "good" schools?

In a 2004 publication, anthropologist Annegret Staiger analyzes the effectiveness of a magnet program designed to entice gifted students to choose a high school that was predominantly of color.[7] Based on exceptional resources that should entice all gifted students, regardless of race, such magnet programs have been proposed as tools of voluntary desegregation. Unfortunately, Staiger finds that the gifted magnet program she studied reinforced racial separations rather than challenged them. The gifted program served a disproportionately high number of white students while the large numbers of adolescents of color within the greater student body of the school were not afforded the same opportunities. Students of color within the general population of the school commented multiple times that the magnet program was a program for white students. Contrary to the goal of the program, its outcome was increased racial distinctions within the school.

Although one could try to argue that the magnet program led to desegregation because it increased the number of white students attending the school, Staiger's analysis compellingly reveals two distinct programs housed within the same building, each segregated—white students in the gifted program and students of color in the general population, a "good" program physically located within a "bad" school. Staiger questions whether it was appropriate to use a giftedness program to lure white students and their families to choose to attend this school. Staiger argues that whiteness came to be seen as synonymous with giftedness. She concluded, "It is not surprising that the gifted magnet would end up as a tool for preserving white privilege rather than for attaining racial equality."[8]

Students and their families had to take several steps before they could be identified as eligible for the gifted program. First, parents must request that their child be tested for giftedness. White families were disproportionately more likely to do this, and Staiger identifies that white privilege increases white families' awareness of giftedness programs and their trust regarding equitable treatment within the school system. Second, students had to achieve high scores on standardized exams, including an intelligence test. Staiger notes cultural concerns regarding the fairness of intelligence tests (also discussed in chapter 2), and we will discuss later in this chapter how stereotype threat may harm the test performance of highly motivated students of color.[9] Ideally this program would have identified gifted students regardless of race. In practice, white students were much more likely to be labeled as gifted than were students of color.

The magnet program on which Staiger focuses failed to critically analyze assumptions regarding whiteness.[10] Those who developed the program seem to have neglected to consider how white privilege might lead white students to be more likely to pursue the opportunity and to be found eligible. If white privilege had been carefully considered, the program may have been designed to more fairly recruit truly gifted students, both white and of color. The program was intended to encourage integration, but it was constructed in a way that failed to anticipate or correct for how white privilege disproportionately encouraged white students to take advantage of the opportunity.

The *myth of meritocracy* is relevant for understanding why a program intended to increase integration had the effect of upholding segregation. Sociologists Stephen J. McNamee and Robert K. Miller Jr. explain:

> According to the ideology of the American Dream, America is the land of limitless opportunity in which individuals can go as far as their own merit takes them. According to this ideology, you get out of the system what you put into it. Getting ahead is ostensibly based on individual merit, which is generally viewed as a combination of factors including innate abilities, working hard, having the right attitude, and having high moral character and integrity.

McNamee and Miller clearly describe how the myth of meritocracy relates to education and challenge readers to consider how unfair advantages, such as white privilege, create unfair opportunities. "According to the American Dream, education identifies and selects intelligent, talented, and motivated individuals and provides educational training in direct proportion to merit."[11] Yet we have seen through Staiger's analysis of the magnet program that families *seek* educational opportunities. While the myth of meritocracy suggests than some amorphous "education" works to identify students with great potential, families use privilege to obtain limited positions. Students from families who have greater resources, such as time to invest in seeking educational opportunities and connections with individuals who will inform them of options, will have greater access to programs than will students from families with fewer resources, such as families in which both parents work more than one job or families for which language barriers limit their ability to communicate with school administrators. The myth of meritocracy suggests that every student has an equal chance to excel. As we will see later in this chapter in our discussion of Jonathan Kozol's *Savage Inequalities: Children in America's Schools*, critical analyses reveal shocking discrepancies in educational opportunities based on socioeconomic class and race.[12] While the American Dream suggests that the educational system is fair and that students have access to appropriate opportunities, the sad reality is that injustice is the norm across schools in the United States. Individuals may push for racist policies without realizing the inherent racism of their actions.[13]

White Teachers, Students of Color

Because of trends toward more teachers being white while more students of color are entering the educational system, students of color in the United States are increasingly likely to have white teachers.[14] Education scholar Sharon M. Chubbuck identifies that few white teachers would consider themselves racist or see racism in educational policies. Racism is perceived as contradicting cultural ideals of equality of opportunity and is recognized as a form of bias that limits opportunities.[15] Egalitarianism is highly valued in the United States, while racism is seen as violating fairness.[16]

Whites resist seeing racism in themselves or the practices they follow. Yet in a 2004 publication Chubbuck acknowledges racism as a systematic problem within the United States, one that is difficult to escape because of pervasive messages that link whiteness with goodness and because of the invisibility of white privilege. Paradoxically, because whites fear being called racist, they may avoid thinking critically about racism, failing to analyze ways they may be enacting racism. White teachers who refuse to examine systemic racism may enact racism while seeing themselves as racially benign. They may not realize that they explain white students' behavior differently from similar behavior from students of color.[17] Social psychologists Regina D. Langhout and Cecily A. Mitchell provide evidence published in 2008 that teachers may interpret a behavior, such as performing well on an assignment, differently based on race. If a white boy performs well on an assignment, it may be attributed to natural talent, while a similar performance from a Latino boy may be interpreted as indicative of hard work on that particular assignment.[18] Through differential responses to students' behavior, teachers may subtly reinforce messages of whiteness as superior.

Education scholar Nora E. Hyland performed an ethnographic study, published in 2005, focusing on four white teachers working in a school that served a majority of Black American students.[19] Each of these teachers identified herself as nonracist, but Hyland's careful analysis reveals a reinforcement of systemic racism in each teacher's description of what made her a good teacher for Black American students.[20] For example, one white teacher saw herself as saving Black American students and their families from themselves. Her perspective was based on an unexamined belief that whites are superior and that she could do for her students and their families what they could not do for themselves.

In a 2006 publication, education scholar Beverly E. Cross critically examines teacher education programs, identifying inadvertent ways that subtle, nonconscious, but potentially devastating racism in white teachers may be reinforced. For example, white future teachers who believe themselves to be free of racism may be sent to observe in diverse classrooms without being challenged to critically examine race. An assignment to interview a student of color may inadvertently encourage a future teacher to treat the perspective of one person of color as representative of his or her entire race. Such practices may reinforce the power and privilege of whites by failing to address these critical aspects of race in the classroom.[21]

Because of demographic awareness that many white teachers will be teaching in racially diverse classrooms, higher education programs that train future teachers have made efforts to address multiculturalism. Unfortunately, this often has been done in a way that fails to critically examine race.[22] Uncritical multiculturalism programs often address relatively comfortable issues of diversity in shallow ways that do not sufficiently analyze power, racism, white privilege, inequality, or injustice. (As the director of the New Jersey Project on Inclusive Scholarship, Curriculum, and Teaching, Paula Rothenberg's extensive, rich, and insightful work offers clear ways to recognize white privilege and honestly explore race in the classroom.[23]) An uncritical approach potentially maintains "oppression that objectifies, dehumanizes, and marginalizes"[24] people of color through treating people of color as objects to be understood from a white perspective.

Critical race theorists, such as education scholars Gloria Ladson-Billings and William F. Tate IV, expand on Cross's criticism to focus on the ways multiculturalism has been addressed in education. Diverse traditions are often reduced to "trivial examples and artifacts of cultures"—sampling "ethnic or cultural foods, singing songs or dancing, reading folktales."[25] In a 2006 publication, they argue that programs that give only a comfortable nod to multiculturalism will not challenge the injustice of white privilege. Education scholar Julie Kailin similarly argues in favor of a critical antiracism education that focuses on the impact of racism.[26] Race, especially white privilege because of its general invisibility, must be carefully examined in teacher preparation and in school curricula to challenge the status quo that has systematically disadvantaged students of color.[27]

Students of Color in Predominantly White Schools

Beverly Daniel Tatum entitled her work with a question she heard from many white educators, *"Why Are All the Black Kids Sitting Together in the Cafeteria?" And Other Conversations on Race.*[28] At predominantly white middle and high schools, white educators often wonder why the few Black students may seem to choose to segregate themselves, eating lunch together at a table where only Black students sit, apparently seeking each other in the hallways between classes. White educators often find this apparent self-segregation of Black students to be disconcerting. With so many peers with whom they could form friendships, white educators wonder why the Black students seek connection with others of the same race. White educators might fail to notice the number of white students who sit at all-white tables and the number of white students who only seek friendships with other whites.

Many educators are aware of the importance of identity development in adolescence. Ideally this will be a positive identity, but adolescents will prefer a clear and negative identity rather than a weakly defined identity. Tatum notes that while white adolescents in predominantly white environments are rarely challenged to consider whiteness as part of their identity, adolescents of color, especially those in predominantly white environments, encounter cultural racism that prompts them to reflect on race as a component of their identity. When exposed to interracial situations, white adolescents often consciously perceive people of color as having race while not recognizing that being white is also an experience of race.

The authors of this text have used assignments that challenge college students to reflect on their race or culture. We have regularly found support for Tatum's argument that white students in the United States fail to perceive themselves as having a race or culture that affects their interactions with others. White students often ask how they are to respond to the assignment, given that they see themselves as simply "normal." They fail to see their experiences as privileged until challenged to compare their opportunities to those of people of color. They do not see themselves as having race or culture until prodded to recognize how race and culture influence them and their interactions with others.

Tatum explains the function of Black students sitting together at a cafeteria table. In a predominantly white school, such a table provides a safe place to explore personal identity development through trying different identities that seem available to Black students. Another function is that the table provides a supportive place to analyze with sympathetic peers any blatant or subtle acts of racism (or potential racism) students have experienced. Black adolescents likely encounter interpersonal racism from white classmates who do not intend to inflict harm as well as from individuals who use racism as a form of aggression.

While white students may hope to be good friends to peers of color, they are often unprepared to be fully empathic with the social pressures of dealing with cultural and personal experiences of racism. The college-level "living and learning" community developed by social psychologist Claude M. Steele and colleagues (see box 6.1 at the end of the chapter) creates opportunities for such important discussions to occur in a safe interracial setting by applying principles of empathy and awareness of the potential for intergroup anxiety. In contrast, many informal gatherings in high school cafeterias may not feel like safe places to discuss race unless students create a racially homogenous situation.

Tatum's psychological argument about identity development is reflected in President Barack Obama's memoir, *Dreams from My Father: A Story of Race and Inheritance.*[29] Before Obama ventured into politics, he shared memories of his identity development as a Black adolescent. At a private high school with very few Black students, Obama became close friends with another Black student who was two years older. Obama reminisced about exploring his identity as a young Black man. Mirroring an argument by Tatum, Obama explores roles of Black men in popular culture and plays with how he might adapt different images to fit his identity. White adolescents also try different identities available within popular culture. While adolescents of color are likely to be aware of race as a component of their identity, white adolescents are likely to see themselves simply as developing a human identity. Obama notes that few options were considered appropriate for a Black male identity compared to the great number of options available for whites to explore.

Obama reflects, "TV, movies, the radio; those were the places to start. Pop culture was color-coded, after all, an arcade of images from which you could cop a walk, a talk, a step, a style."[30] Obama focused on learning to dance the steps seen in *Soul Train*, a popular dance show featuring Black Americans. He developed an ability to curse like comedian Richard Pryor. And he acquired a passion for playing basketball. These were the images of Black men that Obama explored in developing his own identity. White adolescents have a much broader range of roles in the popular media from which to be inspired as they develop a personal identity.

We invite readers to spend an evening watching television and to note all the roles played by whites, by Black Americans, by Latina/os, by Native Americans, and by Asian Americans. Is race distributed across characters in drama and comedy, across reality programming, and across news and sports reporting similarly to recent Census data for the United States? (Among individuals who did not identify as Hispanic or Latina/o in the 2009 American Community Survey, 64.9 percent of people in the United States reported being white, 12.1 percent African American, 0.6 percent American Indian, and 4.4 percent Asian. Across racial groups, 15.8 percent identified themselves as Hispanic or Latina/o. Individuals with two or more races were 2.4 percent of the respondents.[31]) We anticipate that you will find that whites are overrepresented in a variety of positive roles while images of people of color are underrepresented.[32]

Media representations of Asian Americans have often been even narrower than representations of Black Americans. In 1984, director John Hughes released the film *Sixteen Candles*, in which a minor character, the horrifyingly named Long Duk Dong, an exchange student from an unidentified Asian country, personified culturally insensitive *stereotypes*—beliefs about individuals based on group membership or about groups that are often misapplied. Radio journalist Alison MacAdam notes that this character fueled the verbal arsenal of bullies seeking to torment Asian American peers.[33] Two decades later, *Harold and Kumar Go to White Castle*, released in 2004, openly played with stereotypes of Asian Americans, presenting a Korean American character (Harold) and an Indian American character (Kumar) who focus throughout the film on smoking marijuana and searching for the nearest franchise of their favorite fast-food restaurant. Journalist Arun Rath reports that Harold and Kumar became surprising media heroes for Asian American adults who delighted that the characters challenged the model minority stereotype.[34] When Asian Americans are represented in the media, they are often minor characters—the comic relief, the gang member,[35] or the quiet model minority who remains in the background. Harold and Kumar represent breakthrough roles for Asian Americans. They are fully human with hopes, dreams, and thwarted goals. They defy the typical representation of Asian Americans. Yet few parents would probably want to share Harold or Kumar's interest in drug use with adolescents searching for role models in the media.

While Tatum has often been asked to explain why Black students seek connection with each other, white educators are less likely to question the behavior of white students who choose to sit with other whites in the cafeteria. We invite readers to reflect on any large student cafeteria you have ever observed. We anticipate that many tables consisted of segregated groups of white students. We argue that it is unfair only to ask why Black students sit together, ignoring the issue of segregated white students. If white educators were challenged to examine identities that are common among their white students and to consider how those identities may be a reflection of what it means to be white, what would you predict they would discover among their students?

Prior to being challenged to reflect on whiteness, we predict that many white educators would have rarely been aware of the race of white students, except possibly for a distinct subgroup of students who might make whiteness visible by virtue of not "acting white." White educators may find it disconcerting if they interact with students whose whiteness does not match the popular culture image the students chose to follow. A group of white adolescent males who elect to dress and use slang in ways associated with Black hip-hop culture challenges everyone around them to become aware of whiteness. Given that whiteness is so often invisible to whites, such actions could be jarring in terms of revealing whiteness.

The Hidden Curriculum

Messages about one's place in society are subtly communicated in schools through the actions and reactions of teachers, peers, and school administrators. These behaviors communicate the expectations held for students based on race and the stereotypes that might be held against students. School rules and day-to-day practices inform students about their place in the world in terms of how they are racially identified. Social scientists and education scholars study the *hidden curriculum* to reveal the implied messages about race, class, gender, and sexuality that are communicated based on how students are treated and how they are allowed to interact with each other.[36] Langhout and Mitchell identify that "the hidden curriculum consists of the values, norms and beliefs that are transmitted to students and teachers via the structure of schooling."[37] While the overt curriculum of a school focuses on teaching mathematics, science, and language skills, the hidden curriculum is a series of subtle lessons about one's place in society and the extent to which one belongs in school.

Based on a year spent observing two middle schools with very different demographics, Peggy Orenstein outlines the hidden curriculum's lessons. White, middle-class, heterosexual, male students in well-funded schools are likely to learn from the hidden curriculum that they are expected to succeed and that it is acceptable if they speak out of turn because their voices are important. Orenstein observed one teacher shout at Black and Latina/o students in an underfunded school that they were "animals."[38] While that particular lesson of the hidden curriculum was overt instead of subtle, Orenstein details many additional subtle lessons working-class and impoverished students learn about their place in the world, including that teachers do not care about them, that safety is a luxury that will not be provided in impoverished communities, and that little is expected of them.

Because the hidden curriculum is rarely revealed to students or acknowledged by teachers, students learn the hidden curriculum's lessons about themselves and their peers without critical examination of what they are learning.[39] In a 2008 publication, Langhout and Mitchell argue that the hidden curriculum communicates to students that middle-class and economically advantaged white girls belong in school and are good students while Black and Latino boys are bad students. (While middle-class and economically advantaged white boys fair better than Black and Latino boys, the research evidence reveals that the hidden curriculum promotes white girls as ideal students. The hidden curriculum teaches that girls of color should be invisible.[40])

Economists George A. Akerlof and Rachel E. Kranton note that interactions between teachers and students, between school administrators and students, and among students subtly communicate messages about which individuals do and do not match the ideal of a school. If the hidden curriculum communicates that white students fit in, students of color—especially Black American and Latina/o students—may feel as though their experience will be rejected within the school. Facing a biased hidden curriculum, students may elect not to identify with school and not to invest effort in academic achievement within an unfair environment.[41]

The hidden curriculum creates a false dualism between "good" and "bad" students, between those who fit and those who are outcast. Each student has potential strengths and areas for improvement. Classifying white students as "good" students is a form of white privilege that is often unexamined. When students of color are cast as "bad" students in this false dualism, the effects could be devastating. In an ethnographic analysis of a classroom of low-income white, Black, and Latino/a students, Langhout and Mitchell revealed that students' behavior was interpreted by a white female teacher in ways consistent with cultural stereotypes. For example, a white girl who spoke out of turn might be politely thanked for a comment while a Black American boy engaging in highly similar behavior might be reprimanded. A Latina girl might be ignored when she fails to submit homework while a teacher might send a letter to alert the family of a white boy that he has missed an assignment, encouraging communication so he will not continue to fall behind. The hidden curriculum seemed to affect the teacher's behavior outside of her awareness. The teacher's racially biased behavior discouraged Latino and Black boys from being fully engaged in school, therefore limiting their ability to succeed academically.[42]

Revealing the hidden curriculum challenges teachers and school administrators to become aware of the racism in the status quo. Langhout and Mitchell caution that the hidden curriculum is part of the system of education and therefore should be addressed systematically. While individual teachers may be successful in addressing the hidden curriculum in their own classrooms, it will be much more powerful if school administrators work with all teachers to reveal and address the hidden curriculum.[43]

In addition to bias in the hidden curriculum, James W. Loewen reveals that the overt curriculum—the lessons directly taught to students—are infused with a perspective that promotes white privilege. In *Lies My Teacher Told Me: Everything Your American History Textbook Got Wrong*, Loewen illuminates euphemisms in textbooks commonly assigned in high school courses that conceal horrifying actions by whites who subjugated Native Americans and African Americans. For example, when describing early conflicts between Native Americans and whites, whites are regularly depicted as "settlers" rather than "invaders." Violence committed by whites against Native Americans is often minimized while acts of violence by Native Americans against whites are emphasized. Loewen argues that this way of teaching is not only inaccurate and unjust but also boring. History is full of rich stories with the potential to captivate the attention of adolescents. The complexities of race relations and the reality of white privilege should be directly presented in high school classrooms.[44]

Stereotype Threat

In 2004, a colleague who teaches in the sciences at Eshleman and Halley's campus returned from a conference of prehealth advisors, excited to talk with the social scientists about the potential for removing a major obstacle for Black American and Latina/o students who take the Medical College Admission Test (MCAT). This white professor dedicated much of his time on campus to preparing students for applications to medical school by guiding their coursework, encouraging cocurricular service in medical settings, engaging in mock interviews to prepare them for visits to medical schools, and reviewing the challenging academic material covered on the MCAT.

He had been dismayed that some of his most talented and motivated students of color had failed to perform up to his expectations on the MCAT. He worked closely with these students and knew they were capable of much stronger performances. Even more worrisome, he knew that top medical schools might pass over highly talented students because of overreliance on this standardized exam. The students who underperformed in comparison to the advisor's expectations often complained of test-taking anxiety, but he had not understood why it would be that Black and Latina/o students would be more likely to be harmed by test-taking anxiety than would white students who were equally talented and motivated.

While the perils of the hidden curriculum may discourage many students of color from fully engaging in school, this advisor had the opportunity to work closely with highly skilled and academically engaged students who wanted desperately to achieve and to serve the communities in which they grew up through a career in medicine. At this conference for prehealth advisors, our colleague learned of the work by Claude M. Steele and colleagues that focuses on the challenges faced by the most engaged and talented students who face stereotypes that anticipate underperformance.[45] In an impressive program of research that has sparked hundreds of replicating studies, Steele and collaborators explore the power of stereotypes to affect the performance of highly motivated students. This program of research helps explain the prehealth advisor's observations that there was an achievement gap on the MCAT between white students and equally talented students who face unfair racial stereotypes.

Steele and colleagues note that white students sit down to a challenging academic task, such as the MCAT, with the privilege of knowing that others expect people who look like them to perform well. However, Black and Latina/o students face a stereotype about their group that suggests they will perform poorly. Steele and colleagues have revealed the very real effects of these stereotypes on students' performances.[46]

Motivated students may feel pressure to overcome stereotypes that suggest that members of their racial group are unlikely to succeed. In the case of Black Americans, a bright, motivated student carries the burden of knowing that her racial group is expected to underperform compared to white students. She knows that Black leaders in the civil rights movement endured severe physical pain and remarkable psychological stress in order to achieve rights that would benefit her entire group. Black students with strong academic potential may feel pressure, as though a spotlight shines on them, as though they carry the burden of needing to prove the sacrifices of the civil rights movement were worthwhile. On top of feeling as though one's personal success reflects on one's entire race, students who face racial stereotypes are aware that members of their group are not expected to perform as strongly as white students. For African Americans, the combination of feeling in the spotlight, like one is a representative for her entire race, and concern regarding whether evaluators expect less of one due to a negative stereotype can create palpable pressure when faced with a challenging academic task.[47]

While some individuals may respond to that pressure by deciding not to try very hard, others who face negative stereotypes about their performance will be highly motivated to succeed, will genuinely want to prove others wrong. Feeling the threat of a stereotype that is held against an individual is likely to generate anxiety when one tries one's hardest to succeed. Anxiety makes it difficult to perform up to one's potential on a challenging task.[48]

In Steele and colleagues' work on *stereotype threat*, they acknowledge that young Black men and women carry the pressure of proving that the civil rights movement was worth the incredible sacrifices made. While many explanations have been offered for academic underperformance of Black students (including questions about motivation and a potentially distracting peer culture), Steele and colleagues' work focuses on students who are highly motivated to succeed but who face a stereotype that reveals an expectation that they will not succeed. Awareness of the stereotype creates a feeling of threat, a fear of confirming the stereotype. The pervasiveness of stereotypes generates a feeling of apprehension and harms trust between the targets of the stereotype and the people in positions of power who will judge their performance.[49]

Through a series of ingenious studies, Steele and colleagues convince Black students that the stereotype is not a threat in a given situation and compare their performance to more common situations in which the stereotype functions as a threat. For example, in a now classic study published in 1995, Steele and Joshua Aronson studied 117 Black and white students at Stanford University, who they matched based on relevant intellectual skills. In a carefully controlled laboratory experiment, one group of Black and white students was randomly assigned to a condition in which they were asked to take a challenging test that the researchers claimed was a clear measure of reading and verbal reasoning skills. In this situation that mirrors the common circumstances of taking a challenging test, the Black students performed worse than the white students, despite the fact that the students had been selected based on having similar skills.[50]

A more interesting pattern of results emerged when Steele and Aronson convinced another group of randomly assigned Black and white students from the same pool that this same test was being developed and that it had not yet been demonstrated to be a clear measure of skill. In this situation, the test did not arouse stereotype threat. The Black students did not experience anxiety that they must perform well or risk confirming a negative stereotype about their race's ability to perform on such tasks. When the challenging test was presented in this way, the Black students' scores rose to match those of their white peers. Removing the threat had the effect of increasing performance.[51]

Stereotype threat has harmed motivated Black students on tests of verbal skills and motivated girls and women on tests of mathematic skills. In a clever laboratory study, Aronson, Steele, and colleagues have even induced white males to experience stereotype threat. The researchers created a new stereotype in their laboratory and watched how it affected performance. In this study published in 1999, one group of white men took a mathematics test under a fairly innocuous set of circumstances. Another group was convinced that white men tended to perform poorly on the test they were about to take, compared to Asian men. When threatened with a new stereotype, the white men underperformed compared to their peers who were exposed to the same test under nonthreatening circumstances (a total of twenty-three men participated in the study).[52]

These studies reveal that white males generally assume that they will be tested in a fair way. A white student is unlikely to feel as though his performance will reflect on his entire race, and he can usually feel assured that members of his race are expected to perform well. Steele and colleagues sought to demonstrate that stereotype threat could be created even for white male students, but the researchers had to manipulate the situation to convince white males that a test would not be fair. Being able to typically rely on a fair situation is a privilege that students who face racial stereotypes are often denied. When a motivated and talented student who faces racial stereotypes is tested for giftedness, stereotype threat may harm his or her performance.

Steele and colleagues also studied how to reduce the problem of stereotype threat. The first study to explore how teachers may reduce stereotype threat in interactions with their students was published in 1999. Following social psychology's focus on how small actions can have impressive impact, Cohen, Steele, and Ross reveal that a teacher's style can eliminate stereotype threat in an academic situation. The key is for a teacher to instill a genuine trust in students that the stereotype is not relevant and therefore will not be a threat on a given task. When Black and white students were exposed to a teacher who communicated tough standards, high expectations, and confidence that these students would meet those expectations, trust was established. (Across conditions of the study, each student received feedback on an essay he or she had written. The feedback either did or did not directly state that the teacher held tough standards, had high expectations, and was confident in the student's ability to meet those standards.) If the teacher then communicated specific ways to improve performance, Black students' performance rose to meet that of their white peers (ninety-three students participated in the study).[53]

As teachers, it is profound to us that a few phrases in our written feedback to students could make a difference for students who regularly face stereotypes that suggest that they are not expected to perform well. The act of communicating standards, expectations, and confidence is so simple, but the impact may be powerful. Well-meaning white teachers often fail to address how systemic racism may be at play in their classroom. An extra moment spent writing feedback on students' work could remove the threat of systemic racism within a classroom.

As noted in box 6.1 at the end of the chapter, Steele has even explored how eating together can help combat Black underperformance. In the program he designed with colleagues at the University of Michigan, Black and white incoming students were encouraged over their first semester to talk about their new experiences as college students during sessions in which they shared pizza. Black students who attended these sessions experienced less stereotype threat than did those who were not part of these sessions. Steele suggests, "Perhaps when members of one racial group hear members of another racial group express the same concerns they have, the concerns seem less racial."[54] Multiracial groups sharing a meal were able to dispel fears that stereotypes were a threat in specific situations at the school.

These conversations would also help to reveal instances that truly are racially based. For example, a Latina student may share that she was denied access to a dining hall on campus when she arrived just two minutes after the end of posted hours for a meal, yet she has seen white students walk into the dining hall up to fifteen minutes later. She could express a concern that the person scanning dining cards might be racist. Other students will be able to listen to her concern and provide any evidence they have. It may be that the white woman who works the scanner at the end of the meal on Tuesdays is a stickler for the schedule, denying anyone who is even only a second late, but that the worker on Wednesdays is known for being relaxed about letting people in a bit late. Alternatively, the conversation might reveal that white students have been able to talk their way into the dining hall when other students of color have also been denied. The students might decide to talk directly with the dining hall worker or her supervisor if it seems that the worker is engaging in racial microaggression against students of color.

Literally hundreds of studies on stereotype threat challenge one to consider how making the educational system more fair could help to reduce the achievement gap between white students and students of color. If all students felt as though they could trust how they would be evaluated, stereotype threat would cease to harm motivated students of any race. The burden of overcoming stereotypes should be addressed at the level of the system of education and should not be the responsibility of individual students. Stereotype threat can be addressed as easily as acknowledging that stereotypes create anxiety and assuring students that the system will treat them fairly.[55]

Imagine again our fictional example of a dedicated, white eighth-grade teacher, Ms. Jones. How might knowledge of stereotype threat allow her to transform her classroom to make it a place where all motivated students would feel they had a fair opportunity to succeed?

Stereotype threat is created by racism. Students of color regularly face unfair stereotypes that reveal expectations of mediocre or poor performance. In an unfair system in which students fear that stereotypes might influence how they are perceived, it is a further injustice to ask students who face stereotypes to simply try harder. The students who are most motivated to succeed are the ones whose performance will be most harmed by these stereotypes. When anxiety is aroused by stereotypes, trying harder may lead to poorer performance on challenging tasks.[56] In the classroom, racism can prevent talented, hardworking students from meeting their potential.

Removing stereotype threat by creating a truly fair classroom situation has been demonstrated to allow students of color to perform equal to their potential. Talented and motivated white students continue to thrive when stereotype threat has been removed. If teachers engage in concerted efforts to reduce racism in their classrooms and to reassure all students that they will be evaluated by the same challenging yet fair standards, they could help to change an unfair system. How might a school district address stereotype threat?

Returning to our colleague who advises premedicine students, he uses his awareness of stereotype threat when helping to prepare Black and Latina/o students for the MCAT. He teaches them about stereotype threat and acknowledges that students of color carry an additional burden into the testing situation that is not fair. He emphasizes that medical schools are concerned about stereotype threat because they seek to enroll talented students of color as well as talented white students.

White Schools vs. Schools of Color: A Story of Funding

Behind the stereotype of mediocre or poor performance by students of color are of course very real differences in the opportunities given to students of color to succeed. In his groundbreaking book *Savage Inequalities: Children in America's Schools*, Jonathan Kozol, a former teacher and activist, drew attention to the extreme inequalities in resources between schools in prosperous and mostly white neighborhoods and schools in poor neighborhoods that predominantly serve children of color.[57] Kozol extensively researched the conditions facing poor urban schools in cities such as St. Louis, New York, and Chicago in the 1980s. His work continues to inspire activism and research today. Unfortunately, many of the issues he identified remain relevant. He found some very startling statistics. "Average expenditures per pupil in the city of New York in 1987 were some $5,500. In the highest spending suburbs of New York (Great Neck or Manhasset, for example, on Long Island) funding levels rose above $11,000, with the highest districts in the state at $15,000."[58] Kozol further notes

> There is a certain grim aesthetic in the almost perfect upward scaling of expenditures from poorest of the poor to richest of the rich within the New York City area: $5,590 for the children of the Bronx and Harlem, $6,340 for the non white kids of Roosevelt, $6,400 for the black kids of Mount Vernon, $7,400 for the slightly better-off community of Yonkers, over $11,000 for the very lucky children of Manhasset, Jericho and Great Neck.[59]

The fact that richer and often whiter neighborhoods mostly in the suburbs spent almost twice as much as the poorer schools created a devastating difference between the schooling experiences of the rich and the poor. In the poorer schools, Kozol describes scenes where students were packed into gyms, bathrooms, closets, and hallways since the original buildings were meant to hold only half as many students. These schools also had a revolving door of teachers who sometimes changed every month. Such schools could never offer and are not expected to offer the same education experience as the richer schools; that the students in these schools will not succeed is almost certain. Kozol writes, "The fact of ghetto education as a permanent American reality appeared to be accepted."[60]

This major resource gap is a consequence of the fact that a large portion of school funds come from local funding sources, such as money from local property taxes. Obviously, in richer neighborhoods where properties are worth more, there will be more money available for the local schools. Kozol argued that this reliance on local funding created a pattern where the inequalities between neighborhoods are reinforced. Richer localities have more money to spend on their schools from property and other local taxes, so their schools are better. The fact that the schools are better makes the houses and properties in the neighborhood more attractive and therefore increases their value. This in turn creates more money for the already good schools, a classic *virtuous cycle*. Thus the rich schools continue to do better, and the poorer schools and children continue to be doomed into a cycle of poverty. Kozol explains:

> Few of the children in the schools of Roosevelt or Mount Vernon will, as a result, be likely to compete effectively with kids in Great Neck and Manhasset for admissions to the better local colleges and universities of New York state. Even fewer will compete for more exclusive Ivy League admissions. And few of the graduates or dropouts of those poorer systems, as a consequence, are likely ever to earn enough to buy a home in Great Neck or Manhasset.[61]

So the students from poorer schools can never catch up to their richer counterparts and remain trapped in their neighborhoods for successive generations. We have to view this cycle in the context of the racial history of the Federal Housing Authority (FHA) and homeownership that we discuss in the previous chapter. Due to the head start that whiter neighborhoods received from the availability of FHA loans, these are the very neighborhoods that could sustain and have continued to sustain the better schools. In contrast, the absence of mortgage funding led to declines in property values in neighborhoods of color that greatly diminished their ability to fund and maintain good schools. It is no coincidence then that Kozol's research revealed not just that school funding was unequal but it was unequal on very clearly racial lines; richer schools were mostly white and suburban while poorer schools predominantly served students of color in urban areas.

Kozol's research prompted intense scrutiny of unequal school funding, and some states made attempts to target extra funds toward poorer neighborhoods. However, more recent studies show that the inequalities continue to exist. A study conducted by the Education Trust, an education research and advocacy group, showed that even in 2004 state and local funding for the highest poverty districts nationwide was on an average $825 less per pupil when compared to the local and state funding received by the richest districts. The study also found that the district with the highest concentration of students of color on an average received $908 less per pupil when compared to the districts with the lowest concentration of students of color. The authors of the study help us understand the enormity of this difference by comparing two typical classrooms and schools. If we take two typical classrooms of twenty-five students each, the school in the richest district gets about $20,625 more per classroom than the poorest district.[62]

The study also makes an important point about the need for going beyond the comparison of dollar amounts between the funding for richer and poorer districts. While the poorer districts often only have funds from the local government, the richer districts have local government funds and more. They also have a powerful system of social networks and support from the richer parents who are in a better position to be involved with school activities and fund-raising for various special school projects. Moreover, such districts are also able to attract the best teachers who may want to live there so their own children can benefit from better schools. To overcome this built-in advantage and offer a truly equal experience the schools in the poorer districts would in fact need more money per pupil in comparison to the richer districts.

More recently, the latest Census data indicates that reliance on local funding sources continues. In 2008, nationally almost half (about 44 percent) of the total revenue for public elementary through secondary schooling systems continues to come from local sources.[63]

Critical Examinations of Race in the Classroom

Responding to the inequality delineated by Kozol, Gloria Ladson-Billings and William F. Tate use critical race theory to claim that the "savage inequalities" identified by Kozol "are a logical and predictable result of a racialized society in which discussions of race and racism continue to be muted and marginalized."[64] Education scholar Julie Kailin emphasizes that we must first fully examine the history of racism in schools in the United States before attempting to develop solutions.[65]

Failure to fully understand racial injustice may lead to proposed solutions that will be ineffective or harmful, yet there are obstacles to critically discussing race in the classroom. Among the deterrents, white teachers may be unaware of white privilege and subtle racism as it plays out in their classrooms. Some may perceive racism as a problem in the United States but avoid critically discussing it because of concerns that emotions might run high when addressing a sensitive topic. Because of extensive segregation across schools, teachers may be able to avoid discussing race within homogenous classrooms. When teachers do try to critically address race, they may find that white students resist learning about racism or that white parents complain that lessons about racism are not as important as other curricular content. Indeed, the accomplishments of people of color are often treated as marginal contributions rather than as central to an education. For example, white literature is more likely to be considered classic while highly acclaimed works by Blacks may be marginalized as African American literature and treated as part of a niche genre.

We challenge teachers to be creative in how they address race in the classroom. While we certainly want every student in the United States to know the exceptional accomplishments of Dr. Martin Luther King Jr. and of Harriet Tubman, we are concerned that lessons on race too often focus on a few key figures without acknowledging the substantial contributions of many others to any given social movement. Imagining oneself as Rosa Parks, refusing to give up her seat on the bus, is powerful and important, but we challenge teachers to educate students that the social action of Parks was a calculated choice emerging from her work with the National Association for the Advancement of Colored People (NAACP). "Contrary to the folkloric accounts of her civil rights role, Mrs. Parks was not too tired to move. Rather, she had been a knowledgeable NAACP stalwart for many years and gave the organization the incident it needed to move against segregation in the unreconstructed heart of the Confederacy, Montgomery, AL."[66] Rather than presenting Parks as an individual acting on her own, we encourage teachers to ask students to consider how individuals can come together in social movements to effect change. Such lessons would recognize that each individual could play a part in a social movement while acknowledging that the iconic figures of influential movements worked with many others to advance a cause.

Scholars in education and educational psychology have been working on a critical multiculturalism that carefully addresses racial bias, overcoming the problems that might occur when education programs only explore multiculturalism in a comfortable way that reinforces white privilege.[67] Impressive programs for teacher preparation and professional development of teachers work to make whiteness visible in the classroom.[68] Peggy McIntosh's work on revealing white privilege (described in chapter 1) is used in many innovative programs to help teachers see whiteness. Such programs are designed to challenge the status quo and may be met by resistance from people who have historically benefited from white privilege and perhaps unwittingly enjoyed the invisibility of that privilege.[69] Yet initial resistance often gives way to acceptance and passion for social action when teachers are challenged to see whiteness.

Such passion for social action has been applied in exemplary innovative programs. Halley's son's classrooms for kindergarten through fifth grades immersed children in an examination of one culture at a time. This immersion cut across disciplines. When the students studied China, they learned about mathematics, literature, history, art, and science while exploring Chinese culture. The lessons focus on a single culture and the diversity within it (e.g., by class or religion) for months before moving on to focus on another culture. This allowed the students to fully explore issues of race, culture, and power in a way that was integrated into their learning experience.

⁓

Education scholar Michelle Jay calls for change, identifying that a critical antibias examination of education is "social justice work. We need to be reminded that working for social change requires commitment, perseverance, and a vision for a better society. But most important, it requires action."[70] Critical race theorists in education, like others who challenge us to focus on cultural materialism, are calling for specific actions that will make white privilege visible and create a fair classroom environment for all students, regardless of race. Revealing and openly critiquing the hidden curriculum will empower students to understand how racism affects school opportunities. "The ultimate goal of multicultural education is to move us towards the creation of concepts, paradigms, themes, and explanations that challenge mainstream knowledge, not help to keep it in place."[71]

Following his ethnographic work with white youths in neo-Nazi and Ku Klux Klan groups (conducted in the 1990s), psychologist Raphael S. Ezekiel finds himself troubled to realize he came to care about young men whose beliefs he abhors. When embarking on the research, this Jewish intellectual did not anticipate that he might make empathic connections with individuals who spout hate that directly targets him. Emerging from this empathic connection, Ezekiel wishes for nonracist alternative options for troubled, young, white men who might be attracted to the power of white supremacy groups.

He speculates regarding options that might fulfill what the young men are missing in a way that would not be destructive, and he predicts that honest classroom discussions about race might be able to steer individuals away from hate groups. Ezekiel calls for educational reform that addresses the social and academic needs of students, noting that classroom discussions of racism should acknowledge the diverse messages about race to which students are exposed outside of the classroom.

Educators should acknowledge students' personal experiences related to race and recognize that the topic of racism can be emotionally laden for students in remarkably different ways. Strong emotional reactions to open discussions of racism may include intense feelings of being misunderstood, apprehension regarding how honest sharing will be perceived, and experiences of guilt. If teachers work to build a sense of trust and to acknowledge students' sometimes intense reactions to critical discussions of race, all students may be more open to examining the destructive power of racism. Although such lessons about racism will be challenging to teach, they provide an opportunity for educators to connect with students, to help students critically analyze their own identity and emotional reactions within an important social context, and for teachers to model empathic communication. Ideally, critical lessons about racism will help students to better understand themselves and to build a sense of community across racial distinctions.[72]

Box 6.1

Empathic Interracial Communication

In chapter 3, we argue that asking another person "What are you?" when one is curious about race or ethnicity can be rude and make the other person uncomfortable. If the person asking the question is white, we argue that such a question may reveal an unconscious sense of white privilege. In chapter 6, we encourage critical discussions of race and claim that failure to critically address race may reveal an unconscious expectation that everyone should act like white people.

A person might feel pulled in different directions when trying to comply with both these arguments simultaneously, but curiosity about another person's life experiences and how those might relate to race or ethnicity can be expressed in socially sensitive ways that encourage honest, thoughtful, and open discussion. The way curiosity is phrased can greatly influence reactions. Investing a moment to formulate a question and anticipate how it might be perceived could facilitate communication.

Social psychologists Walter G. Stephan and Cookie W. Stephan identify that intergroup anxiety can lead individuals to avoid critical discussions of race. Intergroup anxiety occurs when one feels uncomfortable interacting with an individual from another social category, such as someone from a different racial or ethnic group. Intergroup anxiety can be caused by fear of appearing racist or concern about being insensitive to another person. Concerns about miscommunication may include questioning what is acceptable to share or ask in a conversation with someone from a different group.[1] Walter G. Stephan's subsequent work with Krystina Finlay reveals that an empathic approach to an intergroup situation, such as a conversation about race among individuals of different races, reduces intergroup anxiety and improves communication. *Empathy* can be applied by taking the perspective of another person or by anticipating another person's emotional reactions to aspects of the conversation.[2] Based on extensive research on intergroup communication, Stephan and Finlay offer recommendations for discussion facilitators to explicitly encourage empathy across groups and to maintain an awareness of the possible historical variables that could influence contemporary interactions among group members.

With awareness of intergroup anxiety and of the potential for empathy to improve communication, social psychologist Claude M. Steele worked with colleagues at the University of Michigan to institute interracial "living and learning" communities designed to encourage students to share their experiences at college with each other, including critical discussions of race.[3] This program and others that apply similar principles of sensitive communication of curiosity on the topic of race have been demonstrated to help all students to succeed academically and to feel welcome on college campuses.

Notes

1. Walter G. Stephan and Cookie W. Stephan, "Intergroup Anxiety," *Journal of Social Issues* 41, no. 3 (Fall 1985): 157–75.

2. Walter G. Stephan and Krystina Finlay, "The Role of Empathy in Improving Intergroup Relations," *Journal of Social Issues* 55, no. 4 (Winter 1999): 729–43.

3. Theresa Perry, Claude Steele, and Asa G. Hilliard III, *Young, Gifted, and Black: Promoting High Achievement among African-American Students* (Boston: Beacon Press, 2003), 128–30.

Discussion Questions

1. Compare and contrast having a critical conversation about race with having a racist conversation. What aspects of the conversation will cause these to be distinct from each other? Could a critical conversation about race ever be racist?

2. School choice programs can have the effect of creating greater racial segregation among students. What considerations might be important for a school choice program to be effective in reducing racial segregation? How might schools challenge families to critically examine race in the schools and to reconsider what constitutes a "good" school?

3. Would you support, oppose, or feel neutral regarding the introduction of a fraternity or sorority on your campus that is focused on attracting members of a specific racial group? Would you feel similarly or differently if such an organization focused on members of a specific ethnic group? What if it focused on members of a specific religious group? Connect your response to Tatum's explanation for why Black adolescents may choose to sit with other Black adolescents in a cafeteria.

4. Do you think discussions of potential discrimination that occur within a school will be more productive among peers from the same racial group or in an interracial group of peers? Could each be equally productive in different ways? Please explain the potential benefits and problems of each. What steps might educators take to facilitate honest and critical discussions of race and racism?

5. Note the images of people of your own racial group and images of other racial groups in the media. Reflect on how many distinct images you observe for whites, Blacks, Asians, Latina/os, American Indians, Arabs, and other groups. Do any groups seem to have very limited identities as they are portrayed in the media? Select a film or television program that you perceived as promoting a stereotype. What techniques were used to communicate the stereotype and to support it? Can media portrayals of stereotypes lead to critical thinking about race? Use specific examples from film or television to support your answer.

6. What do you think the effects would be if teachers revealed the hidden curriculum by critically analyzing with students the subtle messages about race, class, gender, and sexuality that might exist in a school? Would it be valuable to teach a course on the hidden curriculum that examines how the hidden curriculum has changed across history and how it operates today? How much resistance do you predict would occur if schools consciously attempt to eliminate white privilege from classrooms?

7. If racism is generally unexamined within a school, how much impact might one teacher have in his or her classroom if the teacher is dedicated to critically examining race? If a teacher was concerned about systemic, subtle, and unexamined racism in his or her school, what would you advise?

8. What evidence is there to support the concept of stereotype threat? What type of student is most likely to be affected by stereotype threat? What impact can an individual teacher have on stereotype threat?
9. How does race relate to socioeconomic class and funding in public schools? What might be the long-term effects of discrepant funding?
10. What would you say to someone who claims, "Education is the key to addressing bias and privilege"? What sort of education would this require? How might this be achieved? What claims might critical race theorists make about this statement?

Notes

1. Maureen T. Reddy, "Smashing the Rules of Racial Standing," in *Race in the College Classroom: Pedagogy and Politics*, eds. Bonnie TuSmith and Maureen T. Reddy (New Brunswick, N.J.: Rutgers University Press, 2002), 51–61.

2. Reddy, "Smashing the Rules."

3. George J. Sefa Dei, Nisha Karumanchery-Luik, and Leeno Luke Karumanchery, *Playing the Race Card: Exposing White Power and Privilege* (New York: Peter Lang Publishing, 2004).

4. William H. Frey, "Central City White Flight: Racial and Nonracial Causes," *American Sociological Review* 44 (September 1977): 425–48.

5. Frank Margonis and Laurence Parker, "Choice, Privatization, and Unspoken Strategies of Containment," *Educational Policy* 9, no. 4 (December 1995): 375–403.

6. Luis Urrieta Jr., "Community Identity Discourse and the Heritage Academy: Colorblind Educational Policy and White Supremacy," *International Journal of Qualitative Studies in Education* 19, no. 4 (July–August 2006): 455–76.

7. Annegret Staiger, "Whiteness as Giftedness: Racial Formation at an Urban High School," *Social Problems* 51, no. 2 (May 2004): 161–81.

8. Staiger, "Whiteness as Giftedness," 180.

9. Claude M. Steele, "A Threat in the Air: How Stereotypes Shape Intellectual Identity and Performance," in *Foundations of Critical Race Theory in Education*, eds. Edward Taylor, David Gillborn, and Gloria Ladson-Billings (New York: Routledge, 2009), 163–89.

10. Staiger, "Whiteness as Giftedness."

11. Stephen J. McNamee and Robert K. Miller Jr., *The Meritocracy Myth* (Lanham, Md.: Rowman & Littlefield, 2009), 107.

12. Jonathan Kozol, *Savage Inequalities: Children in America's Schools* (New York: Crown, 1991).

13. Eduardo Bonilla-Silva, *Racism without Racists: Color-Blind Racism and the Persistence of Racial Inequality in the United States*, 3rd ed. (Lanham, Md.: Rowman & Littlefield, 2010).

14. Sharon M. Chubbuck, "Whiteness Enacted, Whiteness Disrupted: The Complexity of Personal Congruence," *American Educational Research Journal* 41, no. 2 (Summer 2004): 301–33.

15. Gunnar Myrdal, *An American Dilemma: The Negro Problem and Modern Democracy* (New York: Harper & Brothers, 1944).

16. Kristen E. Henkel, John F. Dovidio, and Samuel L. Gaertner, "Institutional Discrimination, Individual Racism, and Hurricane Katrina," *Analyses of Social Issues and Public Policy* 6, no. 1 (December 2006): 99–124.

17. Regina D. Langhout and Cecily A. Mitchell, "Engaging Contexts: Drawing the Link between Student and Teacher Experiences of the Hidden Curriculum," *Journal of Community and Applied Psychology* 18, no. 6 (November–December 2008): 593–614.

18. David Tom and Harris Cooper, "The Effect of Student Background on Teacher Performance Attributions: Evidence for Counterdefensive Patterns and Low Expectancy Cycles," *Basic and Applied Social Psychology* 7, no. 1 (March 1986): 53–62.

19. Nora E. Hyland, "Being a Good Teacher of Black Students? White Teachers and Unintentional Racism," *Curriculum Inquiry* 35, no. 4 (Winter 2005): 429–59.

20. See also Julie Kailin, *Antiracist Education: From Theory to Practice* (Lanham, Md.: Rowman & Littlefield, 2002), 3–5.

21. Beverly E. Cross, "New Racism, Reformed Teacher Education, and the Same Ole' Oppression," *Educational Studies: Journal of the American Educational Studies Association* 38, no. 3 (December 2005): 263–74.

22. For an example of programs that are truly working to encourage white teachers to critically think about race and unintentional racism in the classroom, see Julie Landsman and Chance W. Lewis, eds., *White Teachers/Diverse Classrooms: A Guide to Building Inclusive Schools, Promoting High Expectations, and Eliminating Racism* (Sterling, Va.: Stylus, 2006).

23. For example, please see Paula Rothenberg's *Invisible Privilege: A Memoir about Race, Class and Gender* (Lawrence: University Press of Kansas, 2000), and *What's the Problem? A Brief Guide to Critical Thinking* (Worth Publishers, Inc., 2010), and eds. Ellen G. Friedman, Wendy K. Kolmar, Charley B. Flint, and Paula Rothenberg, *Creating an Inclusive College Curriculum: A Teaching Sourcebook from the New Jersey Project* (New York: Teacher's College Press, 1995).

24. Cross, "New Racism," 266.

25. Gloria Ladson-Billings and William F. Tate IV, "Toward a Critical Race Theory of Education," in *Critical Race Theory in Education: All God's Children Got a Song*, eds. Adrienne D. Dixson and Celia K. Rousseau (New York: Routledge, 2006), 11–30.

26. Kailin, *Antiracist Education*.

27. Landsman and Lewis, eds., *White Teachers/Diverse Classrooms*.

28. Beverly Daniel Tatum, *"Why Are All the Black Kids Sitting Together in the Cafeteria?": And Other Conversations about Race* (New York: Basic, 2003).

29. Barack Obama, *Dreams from My Father: A Story of Race and Inheritance* (New York: Three Rivers Press, 1995/2004).

30. Barack Obama, *Dreams from My Father*, 78.

31. U.S. Census Bureau, *2009 American Community Survey*.

32. Ali Michael of the University of Pennsylvania has successfully used The Minority Reporter www.minorityreporter.com/ to ask future teachers to critically examine this question in Hollywood films. Through academic exercises, she has future teachers critically examine whiteness in children's literature as well as under-representation of individuals of color.

33. Alison MacAdam, "Long Duck Dong: Last of the Hollywood Stereotypes?" *All Things Considered*. Aired on National Public Radio, March 2008, www.npr.org/templates/story/story.php?storyId=88591800 (January 24, 2010).

34. Arun Rath, "The Return of Harold and Kumar," *Studio 360* episode entitled "Morris, Abu Ghraib, Film Club." Aired on National Public Radio, April 2008, http://www.studio360.org/people/arun-rath/ (January 24, 2010).

35. Peter Chua, "Negotiating New Asian-American Masculinities: Attitudes and Gender Expectations," *Journal of Men's Studies* 7, no. 3 (Spring 1999): 391–413.

36. Henry A. Giroux and Anthony N. Penna, "Social Education in the Classroom: The Dynamics of the Hidden Curriculum," *Theory and Research in Social Education* 7, no. 1 (1979): 21–42.

37. Langhout and Mitchell, "Engaging Contexts," 593–614.

38. Peggy Orenstein, *Schoolgirls: Young Women, Self-Esteem, and the Confidence Gap* (New York: Anchor, 1994), 135.

39. Peggy Orenstein, *Schoolgirls*, 270.

40. Rickie Sanders, "Gender Equity in the Classroom: An Arena for Correspondence," *Women's Studies Quarterly* 28, no. 3/4 (Fall–Winter 2000): 182–93.

41. George A. Akerlof and Rachel E. Kranton, "Identity and Schooling: Some Lessons for the Economics of Education," *Journal of Economic Literature* XL (December 2002): 1167–201.

42. Langhout and Mitchell, "Engaging Contexts."

43. Langhout and Mitchell, "Engaging Contexts."

44. James W. Loewen, *Lies My Teacher Told Me: Everything Your American History Textbook Got Wrong* (New York: Touchstone, 2007), 114.

45. Claude M. Steele, *Whistling Vivaldi: And Other Clues to How Stereotypes Affect Us* (New York: Norton, 2010).

46. Steele, *Whistling Vivaldi*.

47. Claude M. Steele, "Thin Ice: 'Stereotype Threat' and Black College Students," *Atlantic Monthly* 284, no. 2 (August 1999): 44–54.

48. For a relevant study of women's performance on a mathematics exam under conditions of stereotype threat, see Laurie T. O'Brien and Christian S. Crandall, "Stereotype Threat and Arousal: Effects on Women's Math Performance," *Personality and Social Psychology Bulletin* 29, no. 6 (January 2003): 782–89.

49. Claude M. Steele, "A Threat in the Air."

50. Claude M. Steele and Joshua Aronson, "Stereotype Threat and the Intellectual Test Performance of African Americans," *Journal of Personality and Social Psychology* 69, no. 5 (November 1995): 797–811.

51. Steele and Aronson, "Stereotype Threat."

52. Joshua Aronson, Michael J. Lustina, Catherine Good, Kelli Keough, Claude M. Steele, and Joseph Brown, "When White Men Can't Do Math: Necessary and Sufficient Factors in Stereotype Threat," *Journal of Experimental Social Psychology* 35, no. 1 (January 1999): 29–46.

53. Geoffrey L. Cohen, Claude M. Steele, and Lee D. Ross, "The Mentor's Dilemma: Providing Critical Feedback across the Racial Divide," *Personality and Social Psychology Bulletin* 25, no. 10 (October 1999): 1302–18.

54. Claude M. Steele, "Thin Ice," 54.

55. Harriet E. S. Rosenthal, Richard J. Crisp, and Mein-Woei Suen, "Improving Performance Expectancies in Stereotypic Domains: Task Relevance and the Reduction of Stereotype Threat," *European Journal of Social Psychology* 37, no. 3 (May–June 2007): 586–97.

56. Claude M. Steele, "Thin Ice."

57. Kozol, *Savage Inequalities*.

58. Kozol, *Savage Inequalities*, 83.

59. Kozol, *Savage Inequalities*, 123.

60. Kozol, *Savage Inequalities*, 4.

61. Kozol, *Savage Inequalities*, 121.

62. The Education Trust, *Funding Gaps 2006*, www.edtrust.org/sites/edtrust.org/files/publications/files/FundingGap2006.pdf (August 27, 2010).

63. U.S. Census Bureau, *Public Education Finances, 2008*, 2010.

64. Ladson-Billings and Tate, "Toward a Critical Race Theory of Education," 11.

65. Kailin, *Antiracist Education*, xvii–xviii.

66. National Association for the Advancement of Colored People, "NAACP: Rosa Parks," www.naacp.org/pages/naacp-history-rosa-parks (September 28, 2010).

67. Louise Derman-Sparks and Patricia G. Ramsay, *What If All the Kids Are White? Anti-Bias Multicultural Education with Young Children and Families* (New York: Teachers College Press, 2006).

68. Landsman and Lewis, eds., *White Teachers/Diverse Classrooms*.

69. Michelle Jay, "Critical Race Theory, Multicultural Education, and the Hidden Curriculum of Hegemony," *Multicultural Perspectives* 5, no. 4 (October 2003): 3–9.

70. Jay, "Critical Race Theory," 8.

71. Jay, "Critical Race Theory," 5.

72. Raphael S. Ezekiel, "An Ethnographer Looks at Neo-Nazi and Klan Groups," *American Behavioral Scientist* 46, no. 1 (September 2002): 65–66.

CHAPTER SEVEN

~

(White) Workplaces

If you were to open a business, say a restaurant, and hire members of your family or your friends, would you consider that to be discrimination? Similarly, if you recommend your friend for an opening at your workplace, is there anything discriminatory about that? Most of us would probably say that neither of these situations could be classified as discrimination. Many people get jobs through referrals or through knowing somebody. In fact, many companies offer referral bonuses to their employees. While such situations do not immediately conform to our notions of discrimination, they are, in fact, the other side of discrimination—privilege. It is a privilege to know someone who can offer a job, make a referral, or even act as a role model for a given profession. Such privilege provides a significant advantage, particularly at the start of a person's career. Lack of such privilege is a disadvantage that makes it harder for someone to break into a profession or a career.

An important link between this privilege and discrimination is established when we look at how the privilege is distributed in the economy. Of course, not all of us are equally well connected or know people who can help us. But there are patterns that we can discuss. For example, we can look at whether some groups are more connected to better jobs than others, and therefore, are better able to perpetuate the privilege of their group. And similarly, we can also look at groups that are underrepresented in certain kinds of jobs.

One way to answer this question is to look at the data on employment in different occupations as compiled by the U.S. Census Bureau. Table 7.1 shows the major occupation groups in the economy, the average income for

Table 7.1. Employment by Occupation 2009

	Median Weekly Earnings	Employment		
		Black	Hispanic	White
Management, professional, and related occupations	$1,044	29.2	19.4	38
Service occupations	$470	25.5	25.8	16.5
Sales and office occupations	$624	25.2	21.3	24.2
Natural resources, construction, and maintenance occupations	$719	6.1	16.4	10.3
Production, transportation, and material moving occupations	$605	14.3	17.1	11.1

Source: Bureau of Labor Statistics, Labor Force Statistics from the Current Population Survey, Table 10, 39 (www.bls.gov/cps/tables.htm, retrieved August 12, 2010).

these groups, and the employment numbers in these groups. The highest-paid occupations are within the professional and managerial occupation groups. This group includes a long list of occupations, some of which will be very familiar to us. For example, chief executives of companies, accountants, human relations managers, doctors, lawyers, teachers (including professors), and engineers all belong to this group. We can compare this to the services group, which has one of the lowest average incomes. Once again, we will find familiar occupations here, such as restaurant servers, childcare workers, dental assistants, hairdressers, nursing aides, housekeepers, and janitors.

The employment numbers in these occupational groups show that race plays a role in the work experiences of people. There is a strong presence of white people in the occupation groups that pay more. The largest concentration of white people is in the professional and managerial occupations, the category with the highest average income. Thirty-eight percent of all white people work in these occupations. There are about 114 million white workers in the entire economy. So 38 percent of white workers, or about forty-three million, is a very large number. In contrast, only about 19 percent of all Hispanic people, about four million people, and about 28 percent of all Black people, again about four million, are professionals or managerial workers.

Given these numbers, it is easy to understand that when we think of managers or doctors or lawyers or professors it is most likely that we think of a white person in that role and not a person of color. In chapter 5, you were introduced to the case of Harvard University professor Henry Louis Gates, an African American. When attempting to enter his own home in a neighborhood of well-paid professionals, Gates did not have an easy time convincing a police officer that it was his house.

When we look at the lower-paid occupations, race once again plays a role. Only 16 percent of the white population works in the service occupations, which have one of the lowest average incomes. On the other hand, service occupations have a large concentration of people of color. About 25 percent of all Black people and 26 percent of all Hispanic people work in the service occupations. The largest concentration of Hispanic people is, in fact, in the service occupations.

We can now get back to the question of whether the privilege of being associated with family and friends who can give us a start professionally is equally distributed in the economy. These numbers indicate there are more white people in the better jobs in the economy. We also know that in the United States we continue to live racially segregated lives. It begins from school, where as we saw in chapter 6, school districts, particularly in the suburbs, continue to be segregated. Even if schools do have mixed populations, as author Beverly Daniel Tatum describes, it is all too common to see Black students sitting together in the cafeteria apart from the white students.[1] In her book, Tatum discusses how this segregation is quite common in our society at all levels. In schools, colleges, and workplaces, not just Black people but other people of color also group together among themselves, and white people group together among themselves.

Even in our private lives we see glimpses of this segregation. We have Black churches, Latino churches, and white churches. We have numerous television channels, shows, and movies that show mostly white people and white family experiences. Though far less in number, we also have channels, shows, and movies that are primary for a Black audience with Black actors (e.g., the shows *Girlfriends* and *Everybody Hates Chris* on the CW network, and movies by Tyler Perry). Interracial couples are still unusual, out of the norm whether in television, on film, or in real life.

As a result of this segregation in society, it is very likely that if you are white, not only is your family mostly white, but your friends are also mostly white. And if you are a person of color, then your friends and family are also predominantly people of color. Since our social lives are segregated and white people dominate better-paid occupations, it follows that if you are from a white family it is more likely that you will know a relative or a friend who is in a better-paid profession. So the privilege of knowing someone who can offer you a job or a referral, or act as a role model for better-paid occupations, is more likely to be available to you if you are white. If you are not white, the privilege is less accessible to you.

This difference in access to privilege exists in our society regardless of whether individual white people have racist opinions and prejudices or not. Due to past discrimination and the continued social segregation, white people as a group are more likely to have access to the privilege even if they are not consciously racist. Sociologists refer to this as *institutional racism*. Sociologists Nijole Benokraitis and Joe Feagin, who have written extensively on this topic, explain, "Institutional racism has been interpreted as a dynamic process whose persistence and existence does not rely on prejudicial attitudes."[2] It is instead a "cumulative" process where discrimination in one sector or time period creates patterns of privilege, or institutions, that continue to reinforce the impact of the original discrimination. This cumulative nature makes institutional racism less noticeable. Since it is not specifically attached to a particular person it is easy for individuals to not acknowledge the institution of privilege.

Employment: "Fitting In" to the Workplace

The invisibility of institutional racism is evident in the argument some people make that when hiring, employers don't see Black, white, or any other color. All they are interested in is finding the most qualified and hardest working employee who will contribute the most to the firm. But the terms *most qualified* or *hardest working* are deceptive in how straightforward they make the hiring process sound. Most of us who have applied for jobs or have been in a position to hire know that there are usually several applicants who will match the basic qualifications for the job, whether it is the college degree, the grade-point average, or the number of years of experience in a particular type of work. Therefore, it is often the case that when applying for a job or going for an interview we think about how to make ourselves "stand out" from the crowd. It is not just job seekers who want to "stand out," employers are also trying to decide who the "standout" is among the many applicants with very similar qualifications.

Economists call this part of the hiring process an *information problem*.[3] The employer is looking at several résumés with similar qualifications and has to pick one, and he or she cannot possibly know for sure who the best and hardest-working person is within the space of an interview. How hard the person works will only become fully evident once he or she is hired and has been on the job for some time. This lack of complete information about a new hire is one of the reasons why people often prefer to hire someone they know, or someone who is recommended by someone they know.

If there is no such recommendation to fall back on, at the time of hiring the employer is at best making a judgment based on the impressions the candidates are creating. The judgment is often based on two things. One, the employer can judge candidates based on how they might fit within the culture of the workplace. Most jobs in the modern workplace are based on teamwork and interactions with many others. We are no longer independent artisans making an entire object by ourselves. So the ability to work with others or fit into the culture of a workplace is an important attribute that can help us "stand out." The decision of who fits into the culture is, of course, highly subjective. Often it is the person who talks like you, has gone to similar schools as you, can make references to the same movies and television shows, enjoys similar foods, etcetera, who "fits" in. In other words, employers make up for the lack of complete information about the candidates by picking people who are most similar to them culturally. Since white people dominate higher-paid occupations, the culture to fit into is the white culture. It therefore follows that white candidates will have an easier time establishing the "fit" or the "standout" quality.

There are many examples of workplace culture being defined by white culture. When Vijaya first came to the United States from India, she was puzzled to hear that it was considered unprofessional for women to wear their hair in a braid at work. It is common for women in India to have long, braided hair at work. Vijaya soon realized that hair that was considered professional was a big challenge for women of color in the United States. "Professional" hair was straight, smooth, and unbraided, modeled after white hair. Many of Vijaya's Indian women friends in the United States worry about having "puffy," unprofessional hair and try many ways of getting smoother hair.

Vijaya also discovered that this is an even bigger issue for African American women. African American women often spend a lot of time and money straightening their naturally curly hair to conform to the ideal in order to fit in. More traditional African American hairstyles like braids or twists are considered unprofessional. In the summer of 2009, Malia Obama, the daughter of President Barack Obama, provoked a discussion about hair stereotypes when she wore her hair in twists on a trip to Italy. Describing the negative reactions to her hairstyle, journalist Catherine Saint Louis notes that African American women continue to view hair as a particular challenge.

Anyone who thought such preconceptions were outdated would have been reminded otherwise by some negative reactions to the president's 11-year-old daughter, Malia Obama, who wore her hair in twists while in Rome this summer. Commenters on the conservative blog Free Republic attacked her as unfit to represent America for stepping out unstraightened.

Saint Louis further describes the pressures of conforming to the white ideal:

> Getting "good hair" often means transforming one's tightly coiled roots. . . . Straightening hair has been perceived as a way to be more acceptable to certain relatives, as well as to the white establishment. "If your hair is relaxed, white people are relaxed," the comedian Paul Mooney, sporting an Afro, says in the documentary "Good Hair," which won a jury prize at the Sundance film festival and comes out in October. "If your hair is nappy, they're not happy."[4]

Ideas about "professional" hair at the workplace are a reflection of the overall perception of beauty in our society. This perception is very much influenced by whiteness. In the book, *The Bluest Eye*, author Toni Morrison evocatively describes the painful impression of inferiority that the unattainable white beauty standards, such as blond hair and blue eyes, create on African American children.[5] Perceptions of beauty are another important area where the impact of whiteness and white culture is pervasive.

The experience of Halley's good friend, an immigrant woman of color, at an undergraduate college illustrates more of the complexities of establishing a "fit" into the white culture of most workplaces. Soon after finishing a PhD in economics, Halley's friend was teaching at a college in a temporary, one-year position. The undergraduate economics courses at the college were filled with predominantly white students, who were also mostly male and inclined to ultimately major in business. At the end of the year, a permanent position (tenure track) opened up at the economics department, and, encouraged by other members of the department, Halley's friend applied for it. Despite fairly good teaching evaluations, a completed PhD, and a publication in a peer-reviewed journal—all three being the general requisites for a tenure-track position, she did not get the job. Instead, the department, which was all white, hired a white male who had not yet completed his PhD and had no publication record. The department members very politely explained to the denied candidate that while they were impressed with her credentials and her work at the college so far, they decided to hire someone whose research and interests were a better fit with the interests of the students of the college.

While the specific research areas of the two candidates did differ, both of them would be using the same tools of economic research, and at an undergraduate college, they would be teaching very similar courses. Moreover, the position description for the job was very broad and in fact did not specify a particular area of research.

Looking back on the experience, Halley and her friend have often discussed whether students would be better served by someone whose interests and curiosity were a close "fit" to theirs or by someone who could introduce them to new interests. This incident also shows us the difficulty of defining clearly who the most qualified person is. Halley's friend had completed a PhD and was therefore technically more qualified. The person hired by the college was yet to finish his PhD but was considered a better fit.

A study by economists Arthur Goldsmith, Darrick Hamilton, and William Darity on the wage differences between darker-skinned Black men to lighter-skinned Black men also illustrates an interesting point about "fitting in."[6] Using information from the Multi-City Study of Urban Inequality (MCSUI), a database that surveyed several households in Los Angeles, Atlanta, Boston, and Detroit, the study compared the wages of dark-skinned to light-skinned Black males to the wages of white males. The authors found that even after adjusting for all worker and job characteristics, like education, years of employment, the occupational category, firm size, etcetera, which might cause people to have different earnings, dark- and medium-skinned Black males had lower wages when compared to white men. On the other hand, using the same adjustments, lighter-skinned Black men did not have a statistically significant wage difference when compared to white men. The authors conclude that employers "display a preference for light-skinned blacks. Perhaps in many cases, they are not aware that a light-skinned black man conceives of himself as black and believe they are hiring someone who is just as white as they are themselves." In other words, a light-skinned Black person passes the "fitting in" test more easily than a darker-skinned person.

Preconceived Notions and the Interview Process

Economist Lisa Saunders and William Darity Jr. also discuss the second factor that influences employer judgment in their desire to pick the best person among equally qualified candidates. They argue that employers will tend to make decisions about individuals based on what they might know about the groups that they belong to.[7] For example, in the past employers often judged women, particularly younger women, as not being reliable or long-term workers when compared to similarly qualified men since women might leave to have children. So in addition to her own individual qualifications, a female candidate is also being judged on the basis of the perception the employer has about her group. Similarly, while evaluating a person of color, employers may often be influenced by the fact that on an average it is white people, not people of color, who are more visible in higher-paid and more prestigious occupations. A person of color with the same qualifications as a white person is less convincing because his or her group is less visible in such positions.

Economists refer to this as statistical discrimination since the statistics regarding how groups are currently doing in the job market are used to judge an individual belonging to the group. Such discrimination easily becomes a self-reinforcing cycle. If white people are more convincing in an interview since white people as a group tend to be more visible in better occupations, then more white people are hired and the link between good jobs and whiteness is perpetuated. When people of color are less convincing in interviews and less likely to be hired because as a group they are less associated with better occupations, then people of color continue to be underrepresented in such occupations. We can relate this self-reinforcing cycle to the social construction approach introduced in chapter 3. Racial groups are treated in unequal ways because of stereotypes, and this unequal treatment continues to perpetuate the differences in jobs and social power between the groups and preserve the privilege of one group (white people).

Sociologists and social psychologists also explore how the expectations of an individual who holds power in a social situation may influence perceptions of a target person.[8] In the case of interviewing, we are particularly interested in how the person making the decision about hiring may perceive an interviewee. Two types of *self-fulfilling prophecies* may lead an individual with social power (an interviewer) to perceive what seems to be clear support of his or her assumptions, even when inappropriately applying an inaccurate stereotype. Through *hypothesis confirmation*, individuals may interpret the behavior of a target person (an interviewee) in unconsciously biased ways by focusing on any information that seems to confirm the stereotype and by discounting any evidence that contradicts the stereotype.[9] Job candidates are likely to have a mixed performance in an interview. Many candidates will answer some questions very well and stumble when responding to others. If an interviewer is focused on a candidate seeming like a "good fit" based on inaccurate stereotypes, that interviewer may interpret the candidate's performance as worthy of hire by focusing on the ways the candidate performed well and discounting any weaknesses. Alternatively, the same mixed performance could be interpreted as revealing flaws if the interviewer held a stereotype that suggested that the candidate would not fit in well with the firm.

A self-fulfilling prophecy may also operate through *behavioral confirmation*.[10] Like hypothesis confirmation, the individual with social power holds an initially incorrect assumption about the target person. In the case of interviewing, the interviewer applies an inaccurate stereotype about an interviewee, assuming that she is not a good fit for a position when she is actually a strong candidate. With behavioral confirmation, the person with social power then acts in ways that are consistent with his or her inaccurate assumption. The interviewer may seem uninterested in the candidate's responses. The target person then responds to the behavior of the person with social power. The candidate's performance during the interview is likely to be affected by the unapproachable style of the interviewer. Finally, the person with social power will interpret the target person's response as evidence of the initially incorrect expectation. The interviewer will pride herself that she is a quick and accurate judge of character. She could tell the interviewee would not impress her from the moment she shook the candidate's hand.

In a classic 1974 laboratory study of the self-fulfilling prophecy as behavioral confirmation, social psychologists Carl O. Word, Mark P. Zanna, and Joel Cooper tested how subtle communication of interracial discomfort by white interviewers may harm the performance of candidates of color.[11] The researchers first asked white Princeton University students to interview high school students, purportedly to choose a member of a work team to plan a marketing campaign. Each interviewer expected to work with the selected candidate on the otherwise all-white team in a competition with other teams. Interviewers first interviewed a white candidate to give the interviewers an opportunity to experience the interview process. The researchers next observed the interviewer's behavior when interviewing a Black candidate followed by a white candidate or a white candidate followed by a Black candidate. (The interviewers were given the impression that there would be a fourth interview, so that the third interview would not be influenced by the impression that it would be the final interview.) Unbeknownst to the interviewers, these candidates had been trained by the researchers to act in consistent ways in each interview.

The researchers measured the behavior of the interviewers, finding that the white interviewers sat farther away from Black candidates than from white candidates, made more speech errors when interviewing Black candidates, and ended the interview more quickly for Black candidates. To test the effects of this style of being interviewed, in a second study white interviewers were trained to interview in the style experienced by Black candidates in the first study (sitting farther away, making more speech errors, ending the interview relatively quickly) or in the style experienced by white candidates in the first study (sitting closer, making few speech errors, investing more time in the interview). The interviews in each style were videotaped, with the camera focusing only on the interviewee, always a white, male Princeton University student. The interviewees' performances were each rated by two peer judges who did not know the purpose of the study. White interviewees who were treated like a Black candidate were judged to have performed more poorly in the interview and to have seemed more nervous compared to interviewees treated like a white candidate. The interviewees who were treated like a Black candidate also responded by sitting farther away from the interviewer. These interviewees additionally reported evaluations of the interviewer as less competent and less friendly compared to the interviewees who were treated like white candidates.

We invite you to critically evaluate this study. What do you think would occur if this study were replicated today? To what extent do you predict that white interviewers today might respond differently to candidates based on race? Is it valuable to conduct a study with university students and then try to apply that work to a setting such as the workplace?

Rational Choice Revisited: The Power of Group Knowledge

This discussion of the hiring process also illustrates the inconsistency in the belief in individualism that often permeates middle-class culture and particularly economic thinking in the United States. As we mentioned earlier, people sometimes argue that employers will be objective since it is in their benefit to hire the best workers. This kind of thinking is part of the larger theory of rational choice that we discussed in chapter 5. According to the rational choice theory, individuals make the best decisions for themselves, taking their own best interests into account. In this thinking, individuals are not influenced by or do not gain by their belonging to any groups. Individuals act completely independently and are independently responsible for their own actions. But in the case of hiring, given the lack of information and the risk involved in hiring an unknown person, it becomes natural and "rational" to hire on the basis of some group knowledge. Our actions are rarely completely objective; indeed, it is difficult to even define what "objective" is when we consider issues such as fitting in. So here, contrary to the view of individualism in the rational choice theory, the "rational" and independent individual is being influenced by and gains from subjective group information.

It is easy to recognize the influence of more immediate groups such as family and friends on our working lives. But as we start to understand family and friends in the context of the racial segregation and privilege that exists in our society, we can begin to see that groups and the power structure of groups influence individuals. Again referring back to social construction, an individual white person may not feel personally powerful in the job market, but white people as a group continue to be more dominant and this influences many decisions in the workplace, which in turn perpetuates the power of whiteness.

Unemployment

The impact of white privilege is also very visible when we look at the patterns of joblessness in the United States. To understand how many people and what kinds of people do not have jobs, the U.S. Bureau of Labor Statistics collects and reports the unemployment rate. An *unemployed* person is someone who is of working age (above sixteen years of age) and actively looking for work but cannot find a job. For example, if you graduate from college and send out your résumé to various job listings but haven't found a job yet, then you would be part of the unemployment statistic. But if you are in school and want to focus full-time on your studies and not work, then you are not "unemployed" since you are not actively looking for work. Similarly, a child who is perhaps ten years old is not "unemployed" since he or she is not of working age. Table 7.2 gives us an idea of the tremendous racial differences in the availability of employment.

In the year 2008, before the big economic crisis, only about 5 percent of white men were unemployed. In comparison, the unemployment rate for African American men was more than double that at 11 percent. So while one in eighteen white men was unemployed, in comparison one in nine African American men was unemployed. Unemployment among Hispanic men was also substantially higher than white men. Similarly, unemployment rates for African American women were almost double that of white women. Hispanic women also fared much worse than white women. In 2009, when the U.S. economy went into a deep recession, many people lost their jobs and the unemployment rates increased for everybody. Yet, the white unemployment rate continued to remain significantly below both African American and Hispanic unemployment rates. Unemployment rates for African American men in particular rose to a staggering 17.5 percent.

Table 7.2. Unemployment Rates by Gender and Race, 2008–2009

	Women			Men		
Year	Black	Hispanic	White	Black	Hispanic	White
2008	8.9	7.7	4.9	11.4	7.6	5.5
2009	12.4	11.5	7.3	17.5	12.5	9.4

Source: Bureau of Labor Statistics, Labor Force Statistics from the Current Population Survey, Table 24 (www.bls.gov/cps/tables.htm, retrieved August 12, 2010).

This major imbalance in the opportunity to work reinforces the structure of privilege and inequality. White people remain more connected to jobs and people who have jobs. People of color, particularly African Americans and Latina/os, have fewer connections to jobs and people who have jobs, and therefore, fewer opportunities to break into the mainstream, white working world. The cycle that this lack of connections perpetuates becomes disturbingly obvious when we look at the other major trend among African American men. Black men have a 32 percent chance of being in prison at some point during their lives compared to only a 6 percent chance for white men. The threat of prison looms large for Latinos as well. Hispanic men have a 17 percent chance of being in prison, more than three times the percentage for white men.

The parallels between the racial differences in unemployment and imprisonments are striking. One in ten Black men between the ages of twenty-five to twenty-nine was in prison in 2008, a figure very close to the 11 percent unemployment rate for Black men.[12] In fact, the unemployment rate does not include people in prisons. So when we combine the unemployment rate with the rate of imprisonment, close to one in five Black men do not have a job. Without opportunities in the formal world of work, African American men and Latinos have become segregated into an increasingly dangerous space. And once in that space, it becomes even harder to get back into the mainstream of work. Current laws restrict the ability of people with a record of incarceration for even minor, nonviolent offenses from applying for many kinds of employment, public housing assistance, and education loans.

Prison and sentencing reform activist Marc Mauer gives the example of an African American woman denied the opportunity to become a Census worker for the 2010 census due to a very minor record of arrest more than three decades ago. Mauer describes the case of a sixty-nine-year-old woman arrested in 1981 for theft and forgery involving a check she had found near a Dumpster and cashed. She was never formally convicted, merely placed in a diversion program. Since then she has had no arrests and no criminal record and was even hired as a Census taker in 1990. However, since she did not have court records to show that her case had been settled, she was denied employment in 2010. Mauer argues that these "collateral consequences" of arrests for even minor infractions is placing a particular burden on communities of color by restricting their abilities to integrate into the world of work even more.[13]

Law professor David Cole writes that the link between the lack of economic opportunities and incarceration rates is compelling:

For an entire cohort of young black men in America's inner cities, incarceration has become the more-likely-than-not norm, not the unthinkable exception. . . . And in part because prisons today offer inmates little or nothing in
the way of job training, education, or counseling regarding their return to
society, ex-offenders' prospects for employment, housing, and marriage upon
release drop precipitously from their already low levels before incarceration.[14]

Ironically, while the trend in incarceration has made it harder for people
of color to break into the mainstream world of work, it has also opened up a
whole new sector of work in the "corrections" industry. With about 2.3 million people (Bureau of Justice Statistics) in prisons (and jails), the United
States has the largest incarceration levels among all developed nations. The
rate of incarceration has expanded rapidly in the last thirty years. To keep
pace with this increase, the expenditure and employment related to corrections at both the federal and state level has also increased dramatically. In
2005 a little more than 760,000 people were employed for federal, state, and
local corrections operations.[15] Compared to 1982 this figure represents an
increase of more than 150 percent.

Economist Glenn C. Loury argues that this increase in imprisonment rates
and prison infrastructure has happened even as crime rates have fallen.[16]
Given this anomaly many scholars have pointed out that the explosive
growth in the prison population can be attributed to the adoption of excep-
tionally tougher prosecution and sentencing for drug-related offenses beginning with the "war on drugs" in the 1980s. As we saw in chapter 4, drug laws
have been disproportionately harsh on people of color, particularly African
Americans. As Professor Cole points out:

African-Americans have borne the brunt of this war (on drugs) . . . The average time served by African-Americans for drug crimes grew by 62 percent
between 1994 and 2003, while white drug offenders served 17 percent more
time. Though 14 percent of monthly drug users are black, roughly equal to
their proportion of the general population, they are arrested and imprisoned at
vastly disproportionate rates: 37 percent of those arrested for drug offenses are
black as well as 56 percent of those in state prisons for drug offenses. Blacks
serve almost as much time in prison for drug offenses (average of 58.7 months)
as whites do for violent crimes (average of 61.7 months). The majority (more
than sixty percent) of the incarcerated are African Americans or Latinos.

Together African Americans and Latina/os account for a majority (61
percent) of the record 2.3 million imprisoned people in the United States.[17]

When we combine these numbers with the fact that unemployment rates favor white employment over the employment of people of color, we can see a disturbing pattern. The growth in the prison system adds to the employment advantage of white people at the expense of people of color. Fittingly, Loury points out, "Mass incarceration has now become a principal vehicle for the reproduction of racial hierarchy in our society."[18]

Wages and Social Structure

The way we view different professions and the value we attach to different kinds of work has also been historically influenced in part by social structures. In the late nineteenth century and early twentieth century, for example, wages for different kinds of work were influenced in part by what is known as the male breadwinner model. As the name suggests, in this view, there was one breadwinner for the family, the male who worked outside the home and earned a wage. In this model, women did not work outside the home and did not earn a wage, but they provided essential services within the home like cooking, cleaning, and childcare. The wage earned by the male then had to be sufficient to support the entire family so that women could continue to stay at home and provide the household services uninterrupted. When women did have jobs outside the home, the payment for such jobs was not considered to be very important since it was merely extra spending money. It was not the main source of support for the family—that would come from the male wage.

This thinking was very influential in creating a separation between jobs that were perceived to be "male," particularly jobs in factories, and jobs that were perceived to be "female," which were predominantly service jobs. No matter how hard they worked, women's jobs always paid less because it was considered extra spending money. It created a pattern of systematic devaluation of work associated with women, which had long-lasting impacts. Sociologist Linda M. Blum gives the example of nurses in Denver, Colorado, who sued the city for discrimination in the 1970s when they discovered that they were being paid less than tree trimmers and sign painters. It is hard to imagine that latter group of workers were more qualified and worked harder than nurses. However, while nurses were predominantly female, tree trimmers and sign painters were predominantly male. Blum describes while ruling against the nurses' suit, "The judge in this case also was responsible for the infamous remark, 'This case is pregnant with the possibility of disrupting the entire economic system of the United States of America!'"[19] The judge was presumably referring to an economic system where female jobs are systematically undervalued in comparison to so-called male jobs.

Sociologist Paula England describes the same trend in the 1980s. The California School Employees Association discovered that school librarians and teaching assistants, mostly female, tended to be paid less than custodians and groundskeepers, who were mostly male.[20] Using data from the 1990s, England, along with economists Nancy Folbre and Michelle Budig, find that occupations that involve care work, for example, teaching, counseling, nursing, or childcare, work that tends to be associated with women, tends to pay less than other occupations with similar educational requirements.[21]

More importantly for our discussion, the male breadwinner model was also very influential in creating a separation between jobs for white men and jobs for people of color. It was, of course, not true that all women who worked outside the home were merely supplementing the male breadwinner's incomes. African American women in the United States had no choice but to work. Initially, as slaves, they had little control over their own labor. Even after the end of slavery, African American men did not have access to jobs that paid enough to support a family. In fact, the development of the breadwinner model is closely associated with the emergence of a white working-class identity, which wanted to distance itself from Black workers. As we discussed in chapters 3 and 5, historian David Roediger argues that white workers settled for a psychic wage of perceived superiority by distancing themselves from Black workers and slave labor.[22] Feminist economists Deborah Figart, Ellen Mutari, and Marilyn Power explain, "New definitions of whiteness and masculinity went hand-in-hand with the growth of men's (wage) work."[23] In this definition of masculinity, white men were providers for their families, a role that set them apart from Black slave labor. Figart, Mutari, and Power argue that due to outright racism and white workers organizing against Black labor, "For the first hundred years after slavery, relatively few African American men earned wages sufficient to support a family, a so-called breadwinner wage or family wage."[24]

As a result most African American women continued to work. According to Census data, a majority (54 percent) of Black women were engaged in "gainful employment" in 1910. In comparison only about 20 percent of white women were classified as gainfully employed. A large number (42 percent) of Black women who worked found work in the service sector; for example, working as domestic servants.[25] However, in general, since a woman's job was only considered to be an additional income, domestic work, which was considered women's work, was systematically undervalued. As a result, while

Black men had no access to breadwinner wages, Black women were also working at jobs that would not support a family.

Even today immigrant women of color continue to be crowded in devalued and often invisible service jobs. Sociologist Arlie Russell Hochschild and author Barbara Ehrenreich argue that as women, particularly white women in the United States, have had increasing successes penetrating male-dominated jobs, they have relied on immigrant women to do the domestic work they no longer have time for. Ehrenreich and Hochschild observe that about 40 percent of the legal household workers in the United States were born abroad[26] and as such poor immigrant women take on the "cast-off domestic roles of middle- and high-income women in the First World—roles that have been previously rejected, of course, by men."[27] These jobs continued to be devalued, as we described earlier, since they are "female" jobs. Moreover, as Ehrenreich and Hochschild point out, they are also subject to *racial discounting* due to the concentration of immigrant women of color who have very limited bargaining power when dealing with their richer, often white employers.

Conclusion

Sociologists Stephen J. McNamee and Robert K. Miller Jr., whose work we introduced in chapter 5, write that there is a "myth" of meritocracy in the United States (please do see chapter 6 for more on the myth of meritocracy). They claim that it is a myth that getting ahead in life in the United States is primarily based on merit. Instead they argue, "It is a myth because of the combined effects of non-merit factors such as inheritance, social and cultural advantages, unequal educational opportunity, luck and the changing structure of job opportunities, the decline of self-employment, and discrimination in all of its forms."[28]

As we have seen in this chapter, the issue of hiring and "fitting" in to the workplace, the dynamic between unemployment and incarceration, and the historic example of the male breadwinner model all point to the fact that our working lives are not neatly enveloped in a vacuum of objectivity where the "best" workers are always easily identified and get their just rewards. Neither are we as individual workers completely independent and uninfluenced by our place in the social hierarchy. The history of privilege and discrimination that continues to influence and dominate social arrangements in the United States also shapes the dynamic of work and working life, making it hard to even define what is "objective." The very nature of work is social. We work with other people, sell our products to other people, and buy from other people. Work itself, therefore, is as influenced by our current and historical social arrangements as any other aspect of our lives. Each of us individually may not feel privileged (or the lack of it), but we can learn to recognize the influence of group hierarchy on the overall system. As long as we fail to recognize this influence, the privilege (or the lack of it) is perpetuated.

Discussion Questions

1. Explore the different kinds of networks and resources that people use when searching for a job. How might these networks and resources be linked to race and privilege?
2. Different television shows and channels offer examples of our racially segregated lives in the United States. Can you think of other such examples of segregation?
3. Define institutional racism. Can you think of an example of how discrimination can be cumulative?
4. Recall the example of Halley's friend who was not hired at the college because she supposedly did not "fit in." Discuss the ways in which a professor might be (or not be) a good "fit" for the students of a particular college. Would "fitting in" involve issues such as accent and cultural background? What about the professor's knowledge of her or his subject?
5. Give examples of what you think constitutes a professional dress code. Critically evaluate what culture such a code might be derived from, and why.
6. Think of your own example regarding the possible influence of a self-fulfilling prophecy in the interview process.
7. Explain statistical discrimination. Given examples of how statistical discrimination might disadvantage people of color.
8. Describe racial trends in unemployment. Critically evaluate the links between (un)employment and incarceration rates.
9. How and why have incarceration rates changed since the "war on drugs"?
10. Explain the male breadwinner model. What impact has this model had on both white families and families of color?
11. Critically evaluate why meritocracy is a myth.

Notes

1. Beverly Daniel Tatum, *Why Are All the Black Kids Sitting Together in the Cafeteria? And Other Conversations about Race* (New York: Basic Books, 2003).

2. Nijole Benokraitis and Joe Feagin, "Institutional Racism: A Perspective in Search of Clarity and Research," in *Black/Brown/White Relations: Race Relations in the 1970s*, ed. Charles V. Willie (New Brunswick, N.J.: Transactions, Inc., 1977), 124.

3. Economist Joseph Stiglitz's research focuses on various kinds of information problems in the economy, including the information issues involved in hiring. Joseph Stiglitz, "Information and the Change in the Paradigm in Economics" (Noble Prize Lecture, December 8, 2001), http://nobelprize.org/nobel_prizes/economics/laureates/2001/stiglitz-lecture.pdf.

4. Catherine Saint Louis, "Black Hair, Still Tangled in Politics," *New York Times*, August 26, 2009.

5. Toni Morrison, *The Bluest Eye* (Holt, Rinehart and Winston, Inc., 1970).

6. Arthur H. Goldsmith, Darrick Hamilton, and William Darity Jr., "From Dark to Light: Skin Color and Wages among African Americans," *Journal of Human Resources* 42, no. 4 (2007): 701–38.

7. Lisa Saunders and William Darity Jr., "Feminist Theory and Racial Economic Inequality" in *Feminist Economics Today: Beyond Economic Man*, eds. Marianne A. Ferber and Julie A. Nelson (Chicago & London: The University of Chicago Press, 2003), 101–14.

8. Robert K. Merton, *Social Theory and Social Structure* (New York: Free Press, 1957).

9. For an excellent analysis of misjudgment based on socioeconomic class, see John M. Darley and Paget H. Gross, "A Hypothesis-Confirming Bias in Labeling Effects," *Journal of Personality and Social Psychology* 44, no. 1 (January 1983): 20–33.

10. Mark Snyder, Elizabeth D. Tanke, and Ellen Berscheid, "Social Perception and Interpersonal Behavior," *Journal of Personality and Social Psychology* 35, no. 9 (September 1977): 656–66.

11. Carl O. Word, Mark P. Zanna, and Joel Cooper, "The Nonverbal Mediation of Self-Fulfilling Prophecies in Interracial Interaction," *Journal of Experimental Social Psychology* 10, no. 2 (March 1974): 109–20.

12. "Facts about Prison and Prisoners," The Sentencing Project (citing the Bureau of Justice Statistics), www.sentencingproject.org/PublicationDetails.aspx?PublicationID=425 (June 15, 2010).

13. Marc Mauer, Testimony of Marc Mauer, Executive Director, The Sentencing Project, before the House Judiciary Subcommittee on Crime, Terrorism, and Homeland Security, United States House of Representatives (Washington, D.C.: June 9, 2010): 2, http://judiciary.house.gov/hearings/pdf/Mauer100609.pdf.

14. David Cole, "Can Our Shameful Prisons Be Reformed?," *New York Review of Books*, November 19, 2009.

15. Bureau of Justice Statistics, "2006 Expenditure and Employment Statistical Abstracts," 2008, http://bjs.ojp.usdoj.gov/index.cfm?ty=pbdetail&iid=1022 (July 15, 2010).

16. Glenn C. Loury, *Race, Incarceration, and American Values* (MIT Press, 2008).

17. "Facts about Prison and Prisoners."

18. Loury, *Race, Incarceration*, 36.

19. Linda M. Blum, *Between Feminism and Labor: The Significance of the Comparable Worth Movement* (Berkeley: University of California Press, 1991), 49.

20. Paula England, *Comparable Worth: Theories and Evidence* (New York: Aldine de Guyter, 1991), 2.

21. Paula England, Michelle Budig, and Nancy Folbre, "Wages of Virtue: The Relative Pay of Care Work," *Social Problems* 49, no. 4 (2002): 455–73.

22. David Roediger, *Wages of Whiteness: Race and the Making of the American Working Class*, Revised Edition (London: Verso, 1991).

23. Deborah Figart, Ellen Mutari, and Marilyn Power, *Living Wages, Equal Wages: Gender and Labor Market Policies in the United States* (New York: Routledge, 2002), 17.

24. Figart, Mutari, and Power, *Living Wages, Equal Wages*, 17.

25. U.S. Census Bureau, Fourteenth Census of the United States Taken in the Year 1920 Volume IV, Occupations, www2.census.gov/prod2/decennial/documents/41084484v4_TOC.pdf.

26. Barbara Ehrenreich and Arlie Russell Hochschild, *Global Woman: Nannies, Maids and Sex Workers in the New Economy* (New York: Henry Holt & Company, LLC, 2002), 16.

27. Ehrenreich and Hochschild, *Global Woman*, 3.

28. Stephen J. McNamee and Robert K. Miller Jr., "The Meritocracy Myth," *Sociation Today* 2, no. 1 (2004), www.ncsociology.org/sociationtoday/v21/merit.htm (August 16, 2010).

CHAPTER EIGHT

~

The Race of Public Policy

In the summer of 2007, on a trip within the United States close to the Mexican border, Vijaya was traveling with a group of white Americans when they approached an immigration checkpoint. Since the trip was within the United States and they had no intention of going across the border, neither Vijaya nor her friends were carrying any immigration or citizenship documents with them. The immigration officers stopped their car and asked if all of them were born in the United States. The white Americans in the car declared yes. No further proof was required from them. Vijaya responded that she was not born in the United States but had a work permit and a visa that allowed her to legally work and reside in the country. The officers wanted to know why she did not carry her papers with her and detained the group for several tense minutes while they attempted to trace Vijaya's legal status through her driver's license. Before they were allowed to proceed she was warned that she should carry her papers at all times and should not let this happen again.

Vijaya was not aware that it was necessary to carry immigrations papers all the time within the United States. She later became aware that while there is a rule requiring immigrants to carry documents with them, it is seldom enforced, particularly when there is no border crossing. What if, like her white friends, Vijaya had said she was born in the United States? Would this have been credible? After all, her friends did not need to prove that they were born in this country; they were taken at their word. And if Vijaya had indeed been an Indian American citizen, a person of Indian heritage born in

167

the United States or naturalized as a citizen, would she have been as credible as her white friends? Would a brown person's declaration of citizenship be as convincing as a white person's? In April 2010, the state of Arizona passed a controversial law that prompted similar questions regarding how to identify and separate citizens from noncitizens and would have made Vijaya's situation more dangerous.

Under the (State of Arizona) Senate Bill 1070, supposed to go into effect on July 29, 2010, failure to carry immigration documents would become a state crime. The new law makes it possible for law enforcement authorities to indefinitely detain anyone when "reasonable suspicion exists that the person is an alien who is unlawfully present in the United States"[1] and to verify their immigration status. These provisions have prompted an outcry from many civil rights groups who have questioned whether the law can be enforced without applying a racial criterion. Against whom would law enforcement have "reasonable suspicion"? Would a white person attract as much "reasonable suspicion" as a person of color? If a person of color is indeed a citizen or has all the legal documents required to be in the country but yet is not carrying the papers, perhaps on a quick run for coffee, would he or she be detained? Or would an individual be able to convince law enforcement as easily as Vijaya's friends did that they are "legal"? Because of many lawsuits pending against the bill, including one by the U.S. (federal) Department of Justice, it is uncertain whether the law will take effect.

Immigration policy in the United States has a long history of being clouded in controversial questions regarding the face of citizenship—often the white face of citizenship. There are two paths to citizenship in any country. One path is *birthright* citizenship, which usually necessitates being born in the country or born to citizens of the country. The other path is *naturalization*. Naturalization is the process by which immigrants who do not have birthright citizenship can become citizens by fulfilling certain criteria established by law. African Americans were barred from either path until 1868. As late as 1857, in a case involving Dred Scott, a former slave seeking to be declared free, the Supreme Court declared that African Americans, whether they were slaves or not, were not citizens and were not eligible for citizenship. It was only in 1868 with the passage of the Fourteenth Amendment to the Constitution, which declared *all persons* born in the United States to be citizens, that African Americans born in the United States were granted the rights to citizenship.

Naturalization has a longer history of exclusion. The first rules regarding citizenship were established under the Naturalization Act of 1790. In a nation of immigrants such as the United States, the process of naturalization is particularly important. The 1790 act limited naturalization to "free white persons" who are of "good moral character" who have resided in the United States for two years.[2] As we have seen in chapter 2, race is not biological and it is not possible to neatly demarcate biological racial categories. However, the implementation of a law that explicitly offers a privilege exclusively to white people needed to have a definition of race—a definition of who would be included and excluded from the special privilege. The naturalization law, therefore, opened up a debate about who is legally white, and in doing so, revealed the extent to which race is socially constructed. It also served to establish an image of whites as the morally superior group, those fit to be citizens. The debate around defining whiteness for the purpose of the law is evident in two prominent naturalization lawsuits in the early twentieth century.

In 1922 Takao Ozawa, a Japanese immigrant, attempted to convince the Supreme Court that he was eligible to become a naturalized citizen under the law. In his arguments, Ozawa attempted to connect being white with "good moral character." Recounting the Ozawa case, law professor Devon Carbado writes,

> Needless to say, Ozawa did not conceive of himself as an undesirable. On the contrary, he maintained that he was precisely the kind of person that America should desire: "I neither drink liquor of any kind, nor smoke, nor play cards, nor gamble nor associate with any improper persons. My honesty and industriousness are well known among my Japanese and American acquaintances and friends. . . ." From Ozawa's perspective, his "good character" and respectable mode of living rendered him a "free white" person within the meaning of the naturalization statute.[3]

The Supreme Court (and lower courts before that) did not agree with this definition of white as being merely a descriptor of moral character. Rejecting Ozawa's claim to citizenship, the Supreme Court declared that Japanese people were not of the Caucasian race and therefore not white. In referring to the Caucasian race, the court was using what was considered to be the accepted "scientific" classification of race at that time. According to this classification, heavily influenced by Johann Blumenbach's work that we discussed in chapter 2, the Japanese were of the Mongoloid race, not Caucasian, and therefore not white. But the questionable science of racial classification and the law's ambiguous use of the science to define white were soon exposed.

In 1923, just a few months after the Ozawa ruling, Bhagat Singh Thind, an Asian Indian, presented his case for naturalization before the Supreme Court. In his arguments, Thind referred to the Supreme Court's linking of white with Caucasian in the Ozawa case. By the very same Blumenbach-influenced racial classification of the time, in which Japanese were not Caucasian but Mongoloid, Asian Indians *were* classified as Caucasians. Thind therefore claimed that since he was Caucasian and the Court had ruled in the Ozawa case that being white equaled being Caucasian, he was white and so entitled to become a naturalized citizen under the law. Despite its own record of linking Caucasian with white, the Court rejected Thind's petition for naturalization. In this case the Court reversed its earlier declaration of faith in the "science" of racial classification and questioned the inclusion of Asian Indians in the Caucasian racial category. The ruling contended that Asian Indians were not what was commonly understood to be white and as such scientists had erred in including such a wide range within the Caucasian group. Law professor Ian Haney López writes, "In the Court's opinion, science had failed as an arbiter of human differences, and common knowledge was made into the touchstone of racial division."[4] The Court was in effect acknowledging that the ideology of the normative culture was more relevant for policy purposes.

Policy and Privilege

The normative culture and its ideology are the culture and ideology of the groups that are in power. When such ideology influences policy it most often advances the benefits of those groups in power. Such policies have long-lasting impacts since they establish social structures that perpetuate power. The social structures continue to confer benefits on descendants long after the original unfair laws are dismantled. Providing an example of this structural view of policy and power, journalist and journalism professor Peter Beinart writes that some people might believe there is no racism if they answer yes to the question, "Would you invite your black neighbor for dinner?" But when you think about structural racism you would ask, "Why don't you have any black neighbors?"[5] From our brief discussion of Federal Housing Authority policies in chapter 5 we know that homeownership patterns in the United States in the early twentieth century were heavily influenced by overtly racist government loan policies. Even though those explicitly racist policies no longer exist, by providing a big jump-start to white wealth accumulation, the impact of those policies continue to be felt today. People of color have far less accumulated wealth, which makes it far less likely that a "middle-class" white person will have a Black neighbor.

In this chapter we look at how key laws and policies have enabled the creation of a structure of white privilege. This structure continues to influence discussions in the public sphere. Further, unless conscious efforts are made to recognize and undo the power structures created by past policies, the legacy of white privilege will continue.

We continue with our discussion of immigration policy from this structural point of view. By assigning a particular legal definition to whiteness and by excluding people of color from citizenship, the nineteenth-century immigration policy had the obvious long-term impact of helping to establish the normative white culture in the United States. If people like Ozawa and Thind were allowed to become citizens in the early nineteenth century, there would have been much more intermixing of people and cultures and this might have translated into a different national identity and a different normative culture. Drawing on critical race theory, López writes:

> A "white" citizenry took on physical form, in part because of the demographics of migration, but also because of the laws and cases proscribing non-White naturalization and immigration. The idea of a White country, given ideological and *physical* effect by law, has provided the basis for contemporary claims regarding the European nature of the United States, where "European" serves as a not-so-subtle synonym for White. In turn, the notion of a White nation is used to justify arguments for restrictive immigration laws designed to preserve this supposed national identity.[6]

The current debate over immigration that has intensified over the Arizona law continues to echo the issue of a white identity. Supporters of the new law justify it as a law-and-order issue; a necessary response to an increase in both undocumented immigration and violence along the U.S. and Mexico border in the state of Arizona. The argument is that this would allow them to detect and deport undocumented immigrants in larger numbers in an effort to achieve "attrition through enforcement."[7] Opponents contend that the law institutionalizes the stigmatization of people who do not fit the (white) image of a citizen. Law professor Hiroshi Motomura argues,

> The rule of law clearly matters, but this is a very malleable phrase. In judging whether immigration enforcement adheres to the rule of law, it is most important to examine how laws are enforced. From this perspective, it is deeply troubling that Arizona's new law uses a vague "reasonable suspicion" standard.
> This standard gives institutional cover for selective immigration enforcement through racial and ethnic profiling. . . . Moreover, though the statute targets noncitizens who are in the U.S. unlawfully, it has an impact on U.S. citizens and lawful immigrants who will be caught in the same enforcement net, denying them the rights of other Arizonans to live their lives free from unwarranted suspicion.[8]

To understand the unfairness of citizens of color being caught in the same enforcement net as undocumented individuals in Arizona, consider the possibility of a similar law in a state like Michigan, close to the Canadian border. In response to a hypothetical increase in undocumented immigration or border violence from Canada, another predominantly white culture, could Michigan enact a law requiring the detaining of people who might arouse suspicion? What would be the basis for "reasonable suspicion" here? How would predominantly white immigrants from Canada be easily distinguished from the predominantly white citizens of Michigan? Would white citizens who live in Michigan fear being stopped and mistaken for undocumented immigrants just as much as Latina/o citizens who live in Arizona? In fact, since Canada is understood to be white much like the United States is understood to be white, such a law would not be attempted along the Canadian border in Michigan. The fact that the Latina/o immigrants and citizens in Arizona do not fit the white image of U.S. citizenship clearly makes the law more workable in Arizona than in Michigan.

The Image of Poverty and Welfare:
A Case of Mistaken Identity

The impact of viewing people of color with suspicion extends beyond this law. López argues that the Supreme Court decisions restricting naturalization to white Caucasians attached positive connotations of "moral authority, intelligence and belonging"[9] to whiteness. In contrast, by being deemed unfit for naturalization, the Court attached the opposite connotations to non-white; connotations of "degeneracy of intellect, morals, self restraint and political values."[10] Current immigration laws that raise suspicions about Latina/os have the same power to stigmatize—to create an image of who belongs and who does not.

This stigmatizing of people of color has enabled the disregard for the history of privilege in discussions about poverty and economic opportunity. As we saw in chapter 5, it is a common misperception that economic mobility is easy in the United States. In chapters 5, 6, and 7, we also explored the great inequalities in wealth, inheritance, education, and employment between white people and people of color, inequalities that can often be traced to the history of white privilege. These inequalities continue to disproportionately influence the relative immobility of people of color. Yet many believe in the economic philosophy of individualism, in which the inability of people to move up the income ladder is often blamed on the poor themselves, particularly poor people of color. This thinking is very much in evidence in the opposition to government policies that are perceived as helping economically disadvantaged people of color—policies commonly known as "welfare."

Sociologists Kenneth J. Neubeck and Noel A. Cazenave argue that the images associated with welfare are some of the most "powerful racialized cultural icons in contemporary society."[11] The image of welfare is the image of the "welfare queen" often perceived to be an African American woman living an irresponsible life of luxury with government funds obtained under the pretext of having more children. Such images of the welfare queen became dominant in the 1980s and 1990s and contributed to the discussion and enactment of a welfare reform law in 1996. The law aimed to reorganize and restrict welfare to prevent such alleged misuse of welfare. The discussions of the welfare queen image in the lead-up to the welfare reform of the 1990s advanced the stigmatization of people of color, particularly African American women, without regard to the history of discrimination that is at the root of the poverty. It also disregarded the actual statistics regarding welfare. Neubeck and Cazenave note, "While the percentage of families receiving welfare in 1996 who were African American was almost identical to that for whites (thirty-six versus thirty-seven), survey research in the first half of the 1990s revealed that many European Americans had come to view AFDC[12] as a 'black program.'"[13]

The percentage of white and Black families on welfare continues to remain close. In 2008, the latest year for which data are available, about 32 percent of the families receiving welfare were white and 34 percent were Black.[14] So there are almost as many white families receiving welfare as there are Black families. Hispanic families constituted 28 percent of the total. It is the case that given the size of the white population, people of color have a proportionately higher representation among welfare recipients. However, we have also seen that white people as a group had greater access to wealth accumulation and continue to have greater access to inheritances and employment. It is also important to understand that welfare does not afford a life of luxury for the recipients of color at the expense of white people. The average amount of cash assistance received by families in 2008 was $382.95 per month,[15] not a luxurious income by any standard. In fact, this amount would barely pay the rent in most places.

Political scientist Robert C. Lieberman also notes that opposition to assistance to poor families is a "narrow focus on a small slice of the welfare state."[16] In fact, the government provides a broad range of assistance or "welfare" to all citizens under programs such as Social Security, unemployment insurance, and Medicare. Most of these programs are not viewed as

specifically benefiting one race or another and have rarely attracted as much
negative attention as the aid to poor families. But Social Security does have
a racial history, a history of racial privilege. Social Security was part of the
New Deal policies of President Franklin D. Roosevelt, instituted as a reaction to the turmoil of the Great Depression. The Social Security Act of 1935
established the system of welfare in the United States. The act introduced
Social Security—the system of old-age insurance for workers and the unemployment insurance program. The original intention of the framers of the act
was to extend old-age security to all workers in the economy. But the idea
of broad coverage was unpopular with the white power structure. Lieberman
writes:

> Old Age Insurance threatened to create a system of payments directly from the
> federal government to citizens, which held the potential to advance the social
> and economic status of working African-Americans, regardless of their place
> in the economic hierarchy, by providing them with an independent source of
> retirement income.[17]

These perceived fears were particularly strong among white legislators
in Congress from Southern states where the majority of African Americans
lived and worked as agricultural and domestic workers. In chapter 7 we saw
how dependent African American women were on domestic work. Similarly,
explaining the dependence of African American males on agricultural work,
particularly in the South, law professor Marc Linder notes, "In the South in
1940, about one-third of all white males, but more than one-half of all black
males, were listed by the census as farmers or farm laborers."[18] Non-Black immigrants of color were also heavily engaged in agricultural work. Linder adds,
"In 1930, 26.5 percent of all farm workers ten years and older were reported
by the census to be Negro or 'other races' than white."[19] We can judge the
overrepresentation of people of color in agricultural work when we compare
this 26 percent to the fact that Black and other non-white people formed
only about 10 percent of the total population in 1930.

Given the dependence of Southern agriculture on workers of color, Linder
notes it is no wonder that Southern legislators viewed it as "a system threatened by many New Deal reforms."[20] Underpaid Black farm workers with
barely any possibility of savings rarely had the choice to retire at any age. A
social security system would have allowed a very small compensation for the
years of toil; a small but guaranteed income that might have opened up the
possibility of retirement. This possibility was extremely troubling for white
farm owners. The availability of low-wage workers might have declined

slightly as some people considered the option to retire. More importantly, it opened up the prospect of white farm owners paying into the social security funds to support the retirement plans of the Black workers.

In order to accommodate their fears that a wide-ranging social insurance program would upset the racial hierarchy by advancing the economic status of farm workers of color, the Social Security Act of 1935 excluded agricultural workers and domestic workers from receiving old-age insurance. Agricultural and domestic workers were finally included under the social security umbrella only after an amendment to the Social Security Act in 1950.

Reaffirming the Commitment to Social Justice

A discussion of the stigmatization of people of color cannot be complete without addressing the issue of affirmative action. The controversies over affirmative action policies present yet another example of the false but often effective use of negative stereotypes about people of color to disparage social justice efforts. For some white people, the phrase *affirmative action* conjures up images of people of color taking over jobs and educational opportunities from white people. The following quote from Jennifer Gratz in an article in the *New York Times* is typical, "We have a horrible history when it comes to race in this country, but that doesn't make it right to give preference to the son of a black doctor at the expense of a poor student whose parents didn't go to college."[21]

Gratz, a white student from Michigan, became a central figure in the opposition to affirmative action when she filed a lawsuit against the University of Michigan's affirmative action policy in its admission process. Wait-listed when she applied to the highly ranked public university in 1995, Gratz contended that students of color with lower academic achievements than she had gained admission because of the preference given to them under the affirmative action policy. Her suit against the university claimed that policy had discriminated against her on the basis of race and was therefore a violation of the equal protection clause in the Constitution. At the core of her arguments was the evaluation process for applications to the College of Literature, Science, and Arts. The selection process was based on a 150-point index. Applicants received points toward the total based on various criteria. The primary criterion was academic performance. Students received up to eighty points for their high school GPA, SAT, and ACT scores added to their points. Points were also awarded for a variety of nonacademic categories designed to promote a wide-ranging student body and to privilege certain categories of students. Some of those categories included being a resident of

Michigan, coming from geographic areas of the state not well represented on campus, having family members who were alumni of the university, being a scholarship athlete, and coming from a socioeconomically disadvantaged background or from an underrepresented racial and ethnic group.

With so many different nonacademic criteria receiving admission points, a student's disappointment at not getting in could have focused on the supposed unfairness of any of these categories. Four points were awarded just for the privilege of having a parent who was an alumni—a predominantly white privilege in a university where the majority of the students are and have historically been white. In the wake of the Gratz's lawsuit the *Wall Street Journal* published a report that noted that children of alumna, known as legacy applicants, often received substantial advantages at many selective universities. According to the report,

> Sons and daughters of graduates make up 10% to 15% of students at most Ivy League schools and enjoy sharply higher rates of acceptance. Harvard accepts 40% of legacy applicants, compared with an 11% overall acceptance rate. Princeton took 35% of alumni children who applied last year, and 11% of overall applicants. The University of Pennsylvania accepts 41% of legacy applicants, compared with 21% overall. At Notre Dame, about 23% of all students are children of graduates.[22]

In addition, the University of Michigan's point system reserved twenty points for a category known as "provost's discretion"—a discretion that could be activated, perhaps, for a major donor to the college. These points for privilege exist in some form at many colleges, and yet they do not generate the same level of attention as the points for those without privilege. It was, of course, the points for racial and ethnic minorities that Gratz's lawsuit challenged in court and that many white students perceived to be unfair.

Twenty points were awarded to students who were either from socioeconomically disadvantaged backgrounds or an underrepresented racial or ethnic group. Students only received a total of twenty points for one of the two categories; that is, they could not get double points for being both economically disadvantaged as well as a racial minority. Economically disadvantaged white students therefore also received the twenty points. It is important to note that the racial or ethnic minority category did not include Asian Americans since they were not *underrepresented*. The university was not providing assistance to a group of people of color when they were already relatively economically privileged. Yet it is often the misperception, as evident in Gratz's quote regarding sons of Black doctors, that affirmative action endlessly privileges people of color even when they have achieved economic success.

Social psychologist Jo-Ann Tsang, a friend of one of the authors, recalls cruel remarks from peers when she was admitted as an undergraduate student to the University of California, Berkeley, in the early 1990s. At that time, California universities were using an affirmative action system that worked to increase the number of African American, Latina/o, and Native American students. While Tsang's peers were aware that there was an affirmative action system intended to increase racial diversity at the university, it seems many were unaware that the system did not increase the probability of admission for Asian American students. Because Asian American students were not underrepresented in the California university system, their likelihood of admission did not benefit from the affirmative action program.

Tsang, a Chinese American woman, was told by white peers that she had only been admitted to the highly selective university because of affirmative action. She was targeted with microaggression on this issue, and she recalls hurt feelings despite her personal knowledge that the then-operative affirmative action program had not increased her likelihood of admission. The insults had not only been malicious but also inaccurate. (California Proposition 209, voted into law in 1996, ended all affirmative action programs in the state.)

Moreover, Tsang was valedictorian of her high school. If an individual is succeeding as a student or in the workplace, why might others question whether the person "deserves" being admitted, hired, or promoted to a prestigious position? What is communicated when someone uses affirmative action as an insult?

Enrollment patterns from the University of Michigan also easily challenge the inaccurate idea that affirmative action helps undeserving students of color take away opportunities from white students in large numbers. In 2003, when Gratz's case wound its way to the Supreme Court, the university received applications from about twenty-four thousand students for the College of Literature, Science and the Arts. A mere 1,800 applications, only about 8 percent, were from students categorized as underrepresented minorities. This led the university to point out, "It is not mathematically possible that the small numbers of minority students who apply and are admitted are 'displacing' a significant number of white students under any scenario."[23] In a well-regarded national study of admission statistics from selective universities, economist William Bowen and law professor Derek Bok found that the dismantling of race-based admissions criterion in all universities changed the probability of a white student being admitted into a selective college by very little—only from 25 percent to 26.2 percent.[24]

The same mathematical fallacy applies to the fears about jobs as well. The much higher unemployment numbers for African Americans and Latina/os we saw in chapter 7 disprove the notion that people of color are taking jobs away from white people in large numbers. In fact, affirmative action in employment does not come with a point system that affords extra points to applicants of color, and neither is it a policy focused entirely on race. Affirmative action is intended to ensure that there is no discrimination in hiring and there is wider representation of people who have been historically discriminated against. The implementation of the policy involves an analysis of whether certain groups are underutilized in various job categories. According to the Department of Labor, the government agency that monitors labor policies, "underutilized" is defined as

> having fewer minorities or women in a particular job group than would reasonably be expected by their availability. When determining availability of women and minorities, contractors consider, among other factors, the presence of minorities and women having requisite skills in an area in which the contractor can recruit.

The above definition highlights two very important aspects of affirmative action that are often misunderstood and ignored. First, the policy very specifically focuses on *qualified* candidates who have the *requisite skills*. As we explored in chapter 7, there are often several equally qualified candidates for most positions. The hiring decision often rests on imperceptible issues of cultural fit. Breaking into that culture is difficult for people from groups who are not already part of the ingroup, no matter how qualified they are. Affirmative action policy merely equalizes the chances for people from the outgroup by making sure that employers look more carefully at underrepresented groups than they otherwise might, given the natural cultural inclination. If there are no qualified women or people of color for a particular job, then there is no action under the policy. Second, affirmative action is not merely about people of color, it includes all women, including white women in the underrepresented target group. In fact, women have been the major beneficiaries of affirmative action. White women, who as a group vastly outnumber qualified people of color, have been in a better position to take advantage of the opening of opportunities that affirmative action provided.

Repeating the History of the Irish Becoming White

Affirmative action and welfare have attracted a vast amount of controversy despite the relatively short-term and limited nature of assistance that both programs provide. Attaching false and negative racial connotations to such policies has in fact provided a distraction from the more central issues regarding privilege in the United States—limited economic mobility and the increasing economic power of the already privileged. In chapter 5, we presented numbers that show that the amount of income going to those already in the richest income groups is increasing. Correspondingly, those in the poorer income groups have less access to economic resources and tend to stay poor for successive generations. To the extent that the rich are getting richer and the rest are unable to get ahead, poverty is not a race-specific problem, and it certainly cannot be attributed to the failings of people of color. The barriers to mobility can be clearly seen when we go behind the racial rhetoric of welfare and affirmative action and look at the reality of low-income jobs in the United States.

Let us consider a hypothetical case of a family, two adults and a child, currently receiving welfare assistance and trying to work their way out of the welfare system. Despite the high unemployment rates in 2009, let us suppose that one of the adults manages to get a job at a fast-food restaurant. Given the trend that almost a quarter of the hourly workers at food preparation and serving jobs are paid the minimum wage or less, it is most likely that the adult from our example would be paid the federal minimum wage of $7.25. Let us also assume that the person is lucky enough to be able to work a full forty-hour shift per week. At the rate of $7.25 a week, the person would be able to make a total of $290 a week or about $15,080 a year. Can you imagine a family of three surviving on $15,080 a year?

In fact, at that amount the family is still considered officially "poor." According to the poverty threshold established by the U.S. Census for 2009, a family of three with one child needs to make at least $17,268 in order to be *not* counted as poor. Think about expenses, including rent, food, transportation, and all other basic costs for three people with only about $1,500 a month. After all that, what would remain for savings in case of an emergency, such as someone falling sick? Certainly the family would not be able to save enough to send the child to college. And without higher education, the child will very easily repeat the cycle of low-income jobs and poverty.

One might argue that both adults in the family could work. However, as we explored in chapter 5, both parents working inevitably involves greater expenses since now the family has to pay for childcare. Average childcare expenses range from between $4,000 and $11,000 a year.[25] At minimum-wage pay, this would amount to almost the entire yearly income of one parent. Moreover, finding reliable childcare is almost as difficult as getting together the money for childcare. As we saw in chapter 7, due to its association with women's work (particularly women of color), childcare tends to be devalued and underpaid. As a result childcare workers find it very difficult to sustain themselves and have to constantly seek other kinds of employment. This leaves people seeking childcare with very limited options.

In a well-known experiment, writer Barbara Ehrenreich attempts to survive on low-wage jobs in different parts of the country in order to find out if people can indeed work their way out of assistance.[26] She quickly realizes the hopeless odds of breaking out of the cycle of poverty when she discovers that at close to minimum wage, it is unfeasible to save up money even for a security deposit for renting an apartment. This leaves the working poor with the constant threat of homelessness. For most of the people on such jobs, the impossibility of covering living expenses also means that they will not be able to invest in any kind of higher education or skills required to transition out of these jobs.

When we look at these impossible circumstances facing people with limited means, we have to confront the fallacy of the economic philosophy of individualism. How can we expect people to work their own way toward economic mobility when wages in the economy start so low that full-time work is not sufficient to cover even basic living expenses? In fact, the situation for many low-wage workers has been getting worse over the years because the minimum wage has stayed so low for so long. When the past minimum wages are converted into today's dollars, the minimum wage for most of the period from 1961–1981 was actually higher than the value of the current minimum wage of $7.25.[27] Instead of having opportunities to get ahead, the decline in the value of the minimum wage has actually pulled people back.

The minimum wage, in fact, mirrors the long-term trend of declining compensation for most of the working class in the United States. The real median incomes of all households, not just minimum-wage households, declined by 2 percent over the ten-year period 1998 to 2008.[28] The median is the midpoint, so instead of getting ahead both middle-income and minimum-wage workers are losing ground. At the same time, the cost of college, the cost of childcare, and the cost of health care have all increased very rapidly. The decline in incomes, while costs are rising even faster, is particularly devastating when we consider that the United States is the only country among western developed economies where households have to rely solely on their own incomes to cover these basic living expenses. For example, all industrialized countries except the United States provide universal access to basic health care. As a result of the declines in incomes and the increase in health care costs, about forty-six million people in the United States could not afford basic health insurance in 2008[29] and therefore had limited access to basic medical care.

Acknowledging the severe burden on working-class households, a health care reform law was adopted in March 2010. The law makes it mandatory for everybody to have health insurance by 2014. In order to achieve this mandate, various levels of monetary assistance is offered to people close to the poverty line who cannot afford to pay the health insurance premiums. The law also provides mandates for employers to offer health insurance to their employees. There are yet many unknowns about the effectiveness of this law; for example, it remains to be seen whether the assistance to people unable to afford health insurance will be enough to cover insurance costs—as these costs may continue to rise—and how much coverage the various new kinds of insurance programs will offer. This new law is just a small step against the long-term trend of declining living standards for the working class.

Of course, not all incomes and living standards have declined. As we saw in chapter 5, the income share of the richest groups in the country has been steadily increasing since the 1960s. Even during the decade from 1998 to 2008 when the median incomes declined by 2 percent, the real incomes of the richest 20 percent of the population actually increased by about the same amount (1.68 percent).[30] Interestingly, the economy was actually expanding during this period. Productivity, which refers to the amount of output the economy is making per hour of work, grew by about 2.5 percent each year from 2000 to 2007.[31] So the average worker was contributing more to the economy but receiving less compensation. Meanwhile, those who already had economic privilege were getting richer.

It is interesting that the decline in average incomes was taking place so soon after the "reorganization" of welfare (1996) and while the affirmative action lawsuit of Jennifer Gratz was winding its way to the Supreme Court (2003). Both welfare reform and the challenges to affirmative action are supposedly based on rewarding and encouraging *individual* effort. Such thinking is situated within the larger context of rational choice theory and the ideology of the trade-off between equity and efficiency as we saw in chapter 5. In this thinking, as long as individual effort is adequately rewarded, the economy will expand, and in an expanding economy everybody is better off without the need for special programs like welfare or affirmative action. But the economy *was* expanding, and workers *were* producing more than ever, and still, the average living standard for workers was actually falling, with costs rising faster than incomes.

The racial rhetoric of both affirmative action and welfare, which unjustly pictured people of color as undeserving and lazy, diverted attention from the key facts—that the U.S. economy was not rewarding hard work uniformly. Instead, the economy has been rewarding the work of those who were already quite privileged. This diversion is reminiscent of the history of Irish Americans distancing themselves from people of color despite their common class interests. Instead of organizing with people of color to seek better working conditions for all workers, the Irish and other white working-class communities chose to organize around whiteness and in the process lost bargaining power as workers. Given the history of white wealth accumulation, the rich are predominantly white. The trend of the rich getting richer ensures that this group remains mostly white. However, working-class white people do have to contend with the trend of declining middle incomes. By organizing against policies that provide limited assistance to the most disadvantaged in the economy, working-class white people like Gratz are once again organizing around whiteness rather than challenging the power structure of the rich.

Instead of attacking programs that support people of color who face the dual disadvantage of stigma and the lack of wealth accumulation, we could focus on policies and programs that challenge the unfair economic trends. For example, we could focus on a living wage policy. When students at Vanderbilt University realized that the close-to-minimum-wage earnings of longtime custodial staff (people who cleaned and maintained the university buildings) were so low that some could not even make it above the poverty line, they joined a minimum wage campaign on campus. In 2004, the student organization Living Income for Vanderbilt Employees (LIVE) joined the workers' union to demand that the university pay all its employees at least a living wage—a wage that would allow a full-time worker to meet the basic living costs in the city where they live and work. Students at many other universities, including Harvard University, have also organized around a living wage.

As discussed above, since the 1980s, changes in the minimum wage have been so infrequent and so limited that it actually lost value compared to the minimum wage of the previous decades. As we saw earlier, a minimum wage does not even get families over the very low poverty threshold. Nor does the minimum wage take into account the vastly different costs of living in different parts of the United States. The original intent of the minimum wage, first established under the Fair Labor Standards Act of 1938, was to offer a degree of protection to workers from exploitation and poverty. However, the implementation of such a protection has always run up against the economic interests of business owners. Using the philosophy of rational choice again, some economists and business owners have argued that a higher minimum wage raises costs and therefore reduces the incentives for businesses to expand. In addition, they argue that higher costs could prompt some businesses to lay off workers. From this point of view, the best protection for workers is to let businesses expand, and thus, grow the economy. In spite of significant evidence to the contrary in recent decades, they contend that such an expansion would automatically increase wages for workers.

Indeed, such arguments were used to affect a freeze on the minimum wage. From 1996 to 2006, the federal minimum wage remained at the very low level of $5.15. By 2006, due to the increase in all other costs, the real value of the minimum wage was the lowest it had been since the 1950s. At the same time, the economy *was* expanding; yet, as we have seen, the benefits did not automatically reach workers. In fact, the stagnation in the minimum wage led to a lowering of overall wages in the economy. The minimum wage sets the scale for wages in the economy. When the lower end of the scale is set so low, it is to be expected that it would impact all other wages as well. Researchers have also found no evidence that past increases in the minimum wage might have caused any businesses to lay off workers.[32]

The decline in the wages, even during periods of economic growth, compels us to reflect on the value of economic growth, when such growth does not lead to improvements in most people's lives. In various parts of the United States, such reflections have led many to advance a living wage movement. Instead of an arbitrary minimum wage that offers no protection against poverty, the living wage movement proposes a wage scale that affords people the basic necessities of life. A living wage will necessarily differ from region to region. In urban areas like New York City or Los Angeles, the cost of basic housing, food, childcare, and transportation will obviously be more expensive than in a small rural community like that of Laramie, Wyoming, or in a smaller and less affluent urban area such as the city of Albuquerque, New Mexico.

The living wage campaigners at Vanderbilt found that without any benefits a wage of $11.50 per hour would be required to meet basic living expenses in Nashville, Tennessee, the city where the university is located. Since the university offered its employees health insurance and other benefits, a living wage for university employees would be $9.50 an hour. After lengthy negotiations involving the university, the workers' union, and the student organization LIVE, the university finally agreed to implement a phased wage increase for its lowest-paid employees in 2007.

Students at many other colleges and universities have also organized around a living wage at their campuses. More importantly, beginning with Baltimore in 1994, many cities have passed living wage ordinances that require businesses with city contracts to pay their workers a living wage. The Vanderbilt students used the basic family budget calculator provided by the Economic Policy Institute. A basic budget includes the cost of housing rentals, food, transportation, childcare, and health care. We encourage you to find the living wage in your own community (see the list of living wage calculators in discussion question 11). We also encourage you to see if a discussion about living wages is currently occurring within your campus community.

A living wage is just one form of pushing back against the deteriorating economic circumstances for those without the privilege of wealth or inheritance. We could also focus on tax policies that have increasingly supported the wealthy. The federal income tax rate for the highest income group began to decline dramatically in the late 1980s. It recovered briefly in the later part of the 1990s. But beginning in 2001, even as wages for middle- and low-income workers were declining, the people in the highest income groups received a large cut in their income tax rate. The top federal income tax rate was reduced from 39.6 percent to 35 percent. Economist Paul Krugman notes, "With the exception of a brief period between 1988 and 1993, that's the lowest rate since 1932."[33] The 2001 tax cut was supposed to offer relief across the board to all income groups. However, the biggest reductions went to the top income group. In a comparison of the saving from the tax cuts, a study by the Tax Policy Institute found that the richest 20 percent of taxpayers would be able to retain an extra 3.5 percent of their income due to the tax cuts. The poorest 20 percent would only retain an additional 0.3 percent of their income.[34]

Krugman argues that an effective myth has been created that all taxes are bad and that taxes are too high in the United States. This myth asserts that high taxes discourage people from working harder and will lead to lower economic growth and lower standards of living. However, the working class has no choice but to work harder as their incomes have declined even while the economy grows. Moreover, in comparison to almost every other advanced industrial economy, the United States collects the lowest percentage of total national output in the form of taxes.[35] Yet, the myth of high taxes continues and has been used to market tax cuts for the wealthy as benefiting everyone. The reduction in the estate taxes, the taxes people pay on inheritances, is a good example of this marketing. The estate tax only applies to inheritances that are larger than a million dollars. Only 2 percent of people have inheritances larger than a million dollars. Yet Krugman contends that by renaming it a "death tax," a public perception has been created that the estate tax has a broad impact on everyone. Aided by this misperception, the 2001 tax cuts included a substantial reduction in the estate taxes for the rich.

The policy of lowering taxes on the rich while working-class households have seen declines in their living standards exacerbates inequalities in two ways. By allowing the rich to retain more money, the policy obviously supports the concentration of wealth at the top and promotes the historic cycle of inheritances and rigid class structure in the United States. At the same time, with less taxes being collected, less money is available for social support policies such as those involving health care and education that can give everyone a fair chance to move up the class ladder. The tax policies in effect have acted as a welfare or support policy for the rich to sustain their dominant position.

Conclusion

As cultural materialism helps us understand, discussions about race, privilege, and discrimination can sometimes become limited to personal experiences and anecdotes. These personal, individualistic anecdotes tend to reinforce the problematic idea that each person gets what she or he deserves. In other words, these individualistic ideas support the contemporary position of those in power. Conversely, this thinking blames the poverty of the poor on the poor.

If we personally do not see or experience discrimination, we tend to think it does not exist. Or if we personally know successful people of color then we tend to assume that the problems of race and privilege do not exist. But privilege and discrimination are both entrenched in our society through years of laws and policies that have supported the creation of an unequal economic system. Critical race theory, which we explored in chapter 4, helps us understand the importance of investigating such systemic (white) privilege built into the law.[36] In this chapter, we looked at more examples of policies that have created and continue to sustain a system of economic and social privilege for a small (mostly white) minority. Such entrenched systems can only be counteracted with policies and programs that specifically seek to reverse the past inequalities. In the concluding chapter we present a few examples of such counteractive strategies.

Discussion Questions

1. Please describe and explain how citizenship and immigration laws in the United States created a perception of whiteness as the normative culture and face of the country.
2. In this chapter, the possibility of implementing an Arizona-style immigration law along the Canadian border in Michigan is briefly discussed. Why might the implementation of such a law be different in Michigan versus Arizona?

3. What are the different kinds of welfare assistance that U.S. citizens receive from the government? Why is welfare often associated with low-income families of color?

4. We argue that white privilege influenced the history of welfare legislation in the United States. Please describe and explain our argument. Do you agree? Why or why not?

5. Describe the evidence against the misconception that affirmative action takes positions away from whites and gives them to unqualified people of color.

6. What are the trends in wages for low- and middle-income workers in the U.S. economy? Simultaneously, what has happened to the incomes of the very rich?

7. What are the reasons for the resistance to change in the minimum wage?

8. Explain why the rational choice arguments have not really worked in the case of wages in the United States.

9. Discuss how the racial rhetoric of affirmative action and welfare resembles the history of Irish Americans distancing themselves from Black people in the nineteenth century.

10. What is a living wage? Discuss some of the basic living expenses that you think should be included in a living wage.

11. Find the living wage for individuals and for diverse family sizes in your town by using the basic family budget calculator provided by the Economic Policy Institute at www.epi.org/content/budget_calculator/ and the Living Wage calculator provided by the Living Wage Project at the Pennsylvania State University at www.livingwage.geog.psu.edu/. Compare the list of basic expenses that each of these calculators include in their calculation of a living wage to your own list of basic expenses.

Notes

1. Senate Bill 1070, State of Arizona 49th Legislature Second Regular Session (2010).

2. An Act to Establish a Uniform Rule of Naturalization, 2nd Cong. (1790).

3. Devon W. Carbado, "Yellow by Law," *California Law Review* 97, no. 3 (2009): 633–92.

4. Ian F. Haney López, *White by Law: The Legal Construction of Race* (New York: New York University Press, 2006).

5. Peter Beinart, "Fix Affirmative Action Now," *Daily Beast*, July 22, 2010, www.thedailybeast.com/blogs-and-stories/2010-07-21/tea-party-naacp-race-flap-time-for-a-new-kind-of-affirmative-action/.

6. López, *White by Law*, 13.

7. Senate Bill 1070, State of Arizona 49th Legislature Second Regular Session (2010).

8. Hiroshi Motomura, "Impulsive Extremism," *Room for Debate* (blog), *New York Times*, April 26, 2010, http://roomfordebate.blogs.nytimes.com/2010/04/26/will-arizonas-immigration-law-survive/.

9. López, *White by Law*, 11.

10. López, *White by Law*, 11.

11. Kenneth J. Neubeck and Noel A. Cazenave, *Welfare Racism: Playing the Race Card Against America's Poor* (New York: Routledge, 2001).

12. Prior to the welfare reform of 1996, the "welfare" program was known as Aid for Families with Dependent Children (AFDC).

13. Neubeck and Cazenave, *Welfare Racism*, 5.

14. U.S. Department of Health and Human Services, *Characteristics and Financial Circumstances of TANF Recipients Fiscal Year 2008*, Table 8, www.acf.hhs.gov/programs/ofa/character/FY2008/indexfy08.htm (July 15, 2010).

15. U.S. Department of Health and Human Services, *Characteristics and Financial Circumstances of TANF Recipients Fiscal Year 2008*, Table 41, www.acf.hhs.gov/programs/ofa/character/FY2008/indexfy08.htm (July 15, 2010).

16. Robert C. Lieberman, *Shifting the Color Line: Race and the American Welfare State* (Cambridge, Mass.: Harvard University Press, 2001), 5.

17. Lieberman, *Color Line*, 29.

18. Marc Linder, "Farm Workers and the Fair Labor Standards Act: Racial Discrimination in the New Deal," *Texas Law Review* 65, no. 4 (1987): 1335–87, 1343.

19. Linder, "Discrimination in the New Deal," 1344.

20. Linder, "Discrimination in the New Deal," 1343.

21. Tamar Lewin, "Race Preferences Vote Splits Michigan," *New York Times*, October 31, 2006.

22. Daniel Golden, "Admission Preference of Alumni Children Draws Fire," *Wall Street Journal*, January 15, 2003.

23. "Q&A re University of Michigan Former Admissions Policies," University of Michigan, revised February 19, 2003, www.vpcomm.umich.edu/admissions/archivedocs/q&a.html.

24. William G. Bowen and Derek Bok, *The Shape of the River: Long-Term Consequences of Considering Race in College and University Admissions* (Princeton, N.J.: Princeton University Press, 1998).

25. Terrell McSweeny, "Helping Middle Class Families with Soaring Child Care Costs," Middle Class Task Force of the Vice President of the United States, www.whitehouse.gov/blog/2010/01/29/helping-middle-class-families-with-soaring-child-care-costs.

26. Barbara Ehrenreich, *Nickel and Dimed: On (Not) Getting by in America* (New York: Henry Holt and Company, LLC, 2001).

27. Kai Filion, "Minimum Wage Issue Guide," Economic Policy Institute, last modified July 21, 2009, http://epi.3cdn.net/9f5a60cec02393cbe4_a4m6b5t1v.pdf.

28. Authors' calculations using data from the U.S. Bureau of Census. U.S. Bureau of Census, Historical Income Tables, Current Population Survey Table H-6, www.census.gov/hhes/www/income/data/historical/household/index.html (August 1, 2010).

29. U.S. Census Bureau, "Income, Poverty, and Health Insurance Coverage in the United States: 2008," Current Population Reports, September 19, 2009, Table C-1, www.census.gov/prod/2009pubs/p60-236.pdf (August 5, 2010).

30. Authors' calculations using data from U.S. Bureau of Census. U.S. Bureau of Census, Historical Income Tables, Current Population Survey Table H-3, www.census.gov/hhes/www/income/data/historical/household/h03AR.xls (August 1, 2010).

31. Jared Bernstein, "Median Income Rose as Did Poverty in 2007; 2000s Have Been Extremely Weak for Living Standards of Most Households," Economic Policy Institute, last modified August 26, 2008, www.epi.org/publications/entry/webfeatures_econindicators_income_20080826/.

32. See the study by Jared Bernstein and John Schmitt on the 1996 minimum wage increase. In Bernstein and Schmitt, "Making Work Pay: The Impact of the 1996–97 Minimum Wage Increase" (Washington, D.C.: Economic Policy Institute, 1998), the authors find no systematic job losses specifically associated with the change in the minimum wage. Economists David Card and Alan Krueger conducted a well-known study of employment differences between the neighboring states of New Jersey and Pennsylvania. New Jersey introduced a state minimum wage, which was higher than the federal wage. Yet unemployment levels in New Jersey tended to be lower than the levels in Pennsylvania despite the lower wages there. For more information, please do see Card and Krueger, "Minimum Wages and Employment: A Case Study of the Fast-Food Industry in New Jersey and Pennsylvania," American Economic Review 84, no. 4 (1994): 772–93.

33. Paul Krugman, "Tax Cut Con," New York Times, September 14, 2003.

34. "A Citizens Guide for the 2008 Election and Beyond," The Tax Policy Center, www.taxpolicycenter.org/briefing-book/ (August 5, 2010).

35. The United States collects 28 percent of total output in the form of taxes. In comparison the average tax collection in all of the European Union countries is about 40 percent of total output. See the "OECD in Figures 2009" in the OECD Observer 2009 Supplement 1 for more details.

36. For a critical analysis of systemic racism as foundational to the United States, please see Joe R. Feagin, The White Racial Frame: Centuries of Racial Framing and Counter-Framing (New York: Routledge, 2010).

CHAPTER NINE

~

Looking Forward

In our conclusion, we build on the material discussed in this book and offer a few more, of the many, ideas that scholars and activists propose for moving forward in our shared challenge to racism and white privilege. We explore examples of psychological programs to confront racism and prejudice, including inspiring research on the jigsaw classroom and finding a common identity. We also argue for a concentration on policies that seek to address contemporary power imbalances that exist between the working class and poor (of color and white) and the rich, who are disproportionately white. These imbalances stem from and feed into white privilege and racism. We present these ideas and encourage our readers to imagine a world free of racism. To do so will require thinking that stretches beyond the limited conversations about race and white privilege that are the norm in most mainstream contexts today. We encourage you to explore other ideas and to come up with your own.

Whiteness is—race is—a remarkably big issue. It seeps into all aspects of our contemporary lives. In this textbook, we argue that while definitively *not* biological, *race has a social reality*. As we discussed in chapter 3, race is and continues to become "real" through social construction. Racial formations in the United States, indeed in the larger world today, come from and are bound up with a history of western imperialism. Race came into being as European powers colonized large parts of Africa, Asia, and the Americas, enslaved predominantly African peoples, and committed genocide and ethnic cleansing against many indigenous people in the Americas. Legal systems, economic structures, and social conventions were formed just as these actions were taking place. Even as social and political movements began to challenge the racial formations of the modern west, scientific racism in the form of eugenics and other pseudoscientific theories justified the oppression of people of color.[1] We use cultural materialism to inform our thinking about these theories and about other racist ways of thinking. Cultural materialism helps us to understand the links between culture and the economic lived realities of both white people and people of color (as discussed in chapters 1 and 4).

Through the twentieth century in the United States, mainstream science and the popular media continued to legitimate ideas about the inferiority of people of color. White privilege became ensconced through the socioeconomic class structure as discussed in chapter 5, residential segregation (also explored in chapter 5), unequal opportunities at all levels of education (examined in chapter 6), discriminatory hiring practices (as discussed in chapter 7), the criminal justice system (also in chapter 7), and the law (as discussed briefly in chapter 4 and more fully in chapter 8). As examined in chapters 3, 4, and 5, we claim that white people gain both a psychic wage from and a kind of property value through their whiteness.

In a society where so many suffer because of racism, everyone is harmed, albeit people of color much more than white people. We have focused our book on the harm done to people of color by the illusion of race as biological and by the social reality of whiteness. Yet white privilege harms white people, too. This happens in one form, as Nell Irvin Painter illustrates, because violence perpetuated through racism enacts psychological harm on the violent along with the violated.[2] In her powerful autobiography *Incidents in the Life of a Slave Girl*, Linda Brent details ways in which slavery debased those who owned other human beings as well as those who were enslaved.[3] Within the horrifying system of slavery, the power held by whites was often corrupting. For example, white men who owned other human beings too often sexually exploited the powerless. White women married to these men regularly denied clear evidence of this abuse or blamed enslaved women, claiming the enslaved had acted seductively. Racism can encourage people in power to act in monstrous ways and to justify these actions.

Racism also harms white people when they lose the strength in numbers to be gained by organizing across communities, labor groups, and global regions. Workers, communities, and regions are strengthened when people organize across racial and ethnic groups (in contrast to the history of Irish Americans described in chapter 3). Offering further examples of damage done to all in a racist society, Joseph L. Graves Jr. (introduced in chapter

2) notes, "Racism and discrimination lead to dysfunction in a society, even for a dominant group . . ."[4] Graves shares that racism limits contributions to society by people of color because there are fewer opportunities available to talented individuals of color with strong potential. Further, racism reduces communication across racial groups in ways that prevent understanding and promote inaccurate and stereotypic thinking. "Discrimination aggravates social problems such as poverty, delinquency, and crime" that affect all members of a society.[5] Racism disrupts interactions between people of color and law enforcement officers in ways that reduce respect for law enforcement and limit peaceful resolutions of conflicts.

White privilege and racism are justice issues. We must challenge racism and the power of white privilege because they are profoundly hurtful economically, psychologically, socially, and spiritually to all of us and most especially to people of color.

Acknowledging That Meritocracy Is a Myth

Given that beliefs in justice and a fair meritocracy are important values in the United States, acknowledging the injustice of current racism and the myth of meritocracy is highly disconcerting.[6] Social psychologist Leon Festinger identifies *cognitive dissonance*—the unpleasant experience of awareness that occurs when important beliefs are incompatible with each other.[7] (Dissonance also occurs when one becomes aware that one's actions are incongruous with one's beliefs.) Often, when an individual who has valued meritocracy discovers that the United States does not function as a meritocracy, cognitive dissonance will be experienced. The individual will be motivated to reduce the unpleasant focus on the discrepancy between important beliefs. Reducing the unpleasant awareness might be accomplished through denying the evidence that discredits meritocracy by insisting that success is justly determined in the United States. Alternatively, an individual might deny having ever believed in a system of meritocracy. Or a person could commit to working to create a fairer system, acknowledging that a meritocracy has not yet existed but striving toward the realization of a fair system.

Similarly, acknowledging the extensiveness of racism in the modern United States will generate cognitive dissonance for many whites. Most white people today in the United States want to believe that racism was a problem of the past.[8] Facing the reality of racism is likely to produce feelings of guilt and denial. It may be tempting to try to reduce the experience of cognitive dissonance by trivializing the importance of current racism. Whites may try to blame people of color for the problems of racism in an attempt to absolve themselves of personal responsibility. Beverly Daniel Tatum challenges us all to "turn the discomfort into action" by acknowledging the deep problem of racism in the United States today and working to combat it.[9] Racism is an overwhelmingly enormous problem that no reader started, yet each of us is responsible for how we address racism within our own sphere of influence. You are responsible for your actions and your reactions to those around you. How will you respond when someone who respects you makes a subtly racist remark? To what extent will you invest in civic action to challenge racism? What actions might you take to disrupt racism?

Recognizing Coded Ways of Expressing Racism

Social psychologists John F. Dovidio, Samuel L. Gaertner, and colleagues have intricately studied the ways that racism is expressed in the contemporary United States.[10] While few white Americans endorse openly prejudiced beliefs, prejudice continues to be expressed in subtle ways, often outside the perpetrator's awareness in situations in which whites can rationalize their behavior as unrelated to race.[11] In controlled studies in which individuals could explain their behavior to themselves in a way that seems unrelated to race, whites are less likely to help a person of color in need than to help an otherwise highly similar white person and are less likely to decide to hire a person of color than an equally qualified white person.[12]

Throughout their program of research on *aversive racism*, Gaertner and Dovidio have found that whites assiduously avoid actions that might be perceived as racist, demonstrating an aversion to considering themselves as racists at the same time as a desire to avoid close contact with people of color, if they can do so without seeming racist. When faced with a decision between one action that might seem racist and another action that is clearly nonracist, most whites will choose the nonracist option. For example, in one study white participants believed they were the only witness to what appeared to be an emergency situation. Through a deceptive research technique, white participants were led to believe that they were the only person communicating with a peer in a nearby room. Each participant heard a stack of chairs apparently fall on the peer. Some of these participants thought they were interacting with a Black peer, and others thought they were interacting with a white peer. Most of these participants (85 percent) quickly moved to get help for their peer. The Black victim and the white victim were helped at equal rates.[13]

Other white participants in this study believed that they were one of several individuals, each in separate rooms, who were communicating with the victim. It appeared that these other people had also witnessed the emergency event. Replicating other research on helping, the participants were less likely to try to help when others seemed equally responsible for providing assistance. Importantly, a majority of white participants who believed they were one of several witnesses tried to help a white peer (75 percent), but only a minority tried to help a Black peer (37.5 percent). Whites were "much less helpful to black than to white victims when they had a justifiable excuse not to get involved, such as the belief that one of the *other* witnesses would take responsibility for helping."[14]

When participants thought they were the only witness, the choice was clearly to seek help or to let the victim suffer. To let a Black victim suffer clearly would be racist; that racism was avoided within the study. When participants thought they were one of several witnesses, they could justify to themselves that someone else might help and could avoid seeing their failure to help as racism. From our vantage as observers of this study, we can see subtle racism revealed in the failure to help a Black peer in comparison to a white peer. Throughout the program of research by Gaertner and Dovidio, the perpetrators are not aware that their racism has been revealed, yet these studies demonstrate subtle racism through the comparison of how whites treat people of color to how whites respond to whites.

Whites also may express subtle racism through carefully selecting words that do not directly acknowledge race. As an example, a colleague in the sciences at one of our colleges was meeting prospective students and their parents at a campus visit event. The colleague, a white man from England, speaks with a distinctive accent. He was surprised when a prospective student's parent asked, "Do many of the faculty members in the sciences have strong accents?" He smiled and said, "Well, I do." The parent verbally stumbled and said, "No, not like you. I mean accents that are difficult to understand." By asking about "accents" but intending to exclude the accents of whites, this parent seems to have been asking about the race of faculty members in a coded way. She did not overtly ask, "Are many of the faculty members Asian?" Yet her question sought that information. She did not directly mention race but sought to discuss race without acknowledging it.

Acting on Awareness in the Classroom: The Jigsaw Classroom

In 1954, the Supreme Court ruled in the case of *Oliver L. Brown et al. v. the Board of Education of Topeka (KS) et al.* that racially segregated schools were inherently unequal and therefore in violation of the Fourteenth Amendment of the U.S. Constitution. Yet the public schools in many cities throughout the United States continued to be segregated in the years following the *Brown* decision.

In 1971, the public schools in Austin, Texas, were desegregated based on a court order. African American, Mexican American, and white students found themselves sharing school hallways, schoolyards, and classrooms for the first time. Because the neighborhoods in Austin were highly segregated and openly racist, the students had very little interracial contact prior to the desegregation of the schools. "Within a few weeks, longstanding, smoldering antipathy between these groups produced an atmosphere of turmoil and hostility that exploded into interethnic fistfights in corridors and schoolyards across the city."[15] The assistant superintendent of the Austin school system contacted his former professor, social psychologist Elliot Aronson. This school administrator used his power as an official to seek expertise from social scientists to combat racism. Aronson worked with colleagues first to observe the dynamics of the classroom and then to design and implement a new educational technique.

Aronson and colleagues noted that the classrooms they observed were highly competitive environments, with students vying for the teacher's attention and seeking to demonstrate superiority over peers. In social psychological research, competition has been shown to have a strong influence on feelings of prejudice.[16] In the classroom, the competition was enhanced by prevailing stereotypes, with the students quickly sorting themselves into groups of "winners" and "losers."[17] Like many other segregated towns, Austin's neighborhoods where people of color lived and the previously segregated schools for students of color were disadvantaged. Driven by these systematic disadvantages, African American and Mexican American students were quickly labeled as "losers" by their white peers.

While a competitive environment is highly common in schools in the United States, competition is not essential for the learning process. Aronson and colleagues sought to remove the competition that was exacerbating racial hostility and to create an environment in which all students would be highly motivated and encouraged to learn. To achieve these goals, they developed the *jigsaw* technique of education. In this system, students must rely on each other to learn material for an upcoming test. Students are placed in diverse learning groups of five or six individuals.[18] Each student in the learning group is responsible for teaching the other students one essential part of the content for a given lesson. For example, if groups of six students are learning about the history of the Fourteenth Amendment of the U.S. Constitution, the content would be split into six equally important components and each piece would be given to one student in the learning group. One student might be responsible for teaching the learning group about political debate regarding the amendment prior to its passage, another might be responsible for teaching recent applications of the amendment in legal decisions, etcetera.

After each student has an opportunity to read the material uniquely assigned to him or her within the learning group, the students then meet in expert groups with the students from other learning groups who have been assigned the same piece of responsibility.[19] Within these expert groups, students work cooperatively to master the material and prepare for their presentation to the learning groups. Through interacting in the learning groups, the students work cooperatively to put together the pieces of the lesson, like assembling a jigsaw puzzle.

When the jigsaw technique was first implemented in fifth-grade classrooms in Austin, some of the students who considered themselves "winners" thought they were part of an ingroup that had nothing to learn from a student in the outgroup they considered to be "losers." When a facilitator circulating around the classroom observed students being rude to a presenter, he or she simply reminded the students that they would all be responsible for knowing the presenter's material on the upcoming test. "Winners" quickly began to realize that they needed to work with the "losers."

Aronson highlights the experience of one boy whom he calls Carlos (to preserve the boy's true identity). Prior to school integration, Carlos had "attended an inadequately funded, substandard neighborhood school" at which all the students in his classroom, including himself, were Mexican American.[20] He spoke English as a second language fluently but with an accent that was ridiculed by white peers in his new, integrated school. Before the implementation of the jigsaw technique, Carlos tried to be invisible in the classroom. Within the jigsaw technique, Carlos had responsibility to learn material and teach it to his peers.

Carlos's first presentation began awkwardly. He was uncomfortable speaking in front of his peers, and they were quick to insult him. One of Aronson's research colleagues observed this and reminded all the students in the group that they were each responsible for learning what only Carlos could teach them and that the test was quickly approaching. Realizing that teasing Carlos would only harm their own performance on the test, the students in his group had to work with him to help him teach the material. In the first couple of weeks of working in that learning group, the other students became skilled at empathizing with Carlos and asking him questions about the material in a way that would help him teach clearly. The encouragement from his peers helped Carlos to feel more comfortable in the classroom, and he became a more skilled presenter.

Because Aronson and colleagues implemented the jigsaw technique in an experimental design, they are able to compare schools in which they implemented the jigsaw technique to control schools that had not yet implemented the technique. Students exposed to the jigsaw technique for eight weeks were less likely to express prejudice, felt more confident, and were more positive about school. They were less likely to be absent and more likely to interact with peers from other races in the schoolyard and in the cafeteria. Mexican American and African American students in jigsaw classrooms scored better on exams than did students from these groups in traditional classrooms, while white students performed similarly regardless of the type of classroom.

Within the jigsaw technique, no student can simply try to be invisible and quietly fail at the back of the classroom. All students who want to succeed must listen carefully and take seriously all peers in a learning group. Every student is held accountable for learning his or her piece of the lesson by all the other members of the learning group. Aronson found that students quickly began to respect all the members of their learning groups. Within eight weeks, new friendships were likely to form. Aronson wanted to make sure that students would not just assume they had been fortunate to end up in a good group. Such an assumption might allow students to perceive the members of their learning group as exceptions to otherwise valid stereotypes. Aronson required the students to interact with more of their classmates in the same way. Within the jigsaw technique, new learning groups are formed every eight weeks. This challenges students to work with different groups of diverse individuals across the school year. White students who first stereotyped Carlos, and then realized how bright he was once they really started to work with him, might be able to maintain a stereotype that Mexican American students are not as bright as white students by assuming that Carlos, and another Mexican American student in their learning group, were special cases for which the generally true stereotype did not apply. If those students are challenged to work with more bright Mexican American students eight weeks later and more after that, it will be harder and harder to maintain an incorrect stereotype.

The jigsaw technique creates a system of education that acknowledges social structures of competition and directly challenges them. Aronson and colleagues created the jigsaw technique as a response to the lessons of the hidden curriculum about race. The jigsaw technique reveals that success can be shared within a classroom rather than being an individual and competitive accomplishment. Aronson and colleagues redesigned the classroom in a way that carefully considered the individual needs of students, focusing on caring for each student rather than fostering competition between them. The technique combats racism, fosters academic success for students of color, and creates an environment in which white students continue to thrive.

Combating Racism as Aggression

Subtle racism can also be used to intentionally cause harm. *Aggression*—behavior intended to harm another individual[21]—can range from horrifying acts such as lynching to subtle, common, yet hurtful actions such as spreading rumors about a peer. (Derald Wing Sue and colleagues expand our thinking about hurtful behaviors by challenging us to consider microaggressions—addressed in chapter 5—which may or may not be intentional.) As racism has become subtler, forms of aggression that are used to express racism have also become subtle.

Relational aggression is a particularly powerful form of subtle intention to harm another. Relational aggression focuses on

> behaviors that are intended to significantly damage another [individual]'s friendships or feelings of inclusion by the peer group (e.g., angrily retaliating against a [peer] by excluding her from [a social] group; purposefully withdrawing friendship or acceptance in order to hurt or control the [target]; spreading rumors about the [target] so that peers will reject her).[22]

Because gendered social pressures limit girls from openly expressing competition or hostility,[23] relational aggression has been particularly studied among girls as the most common form of girls' aggression. Yet boys and girls, men and women can engage in behaviors intended to damage another's relationships.

Relational aggression can be used to try to connect with some peers through the technique of excluding or disparaging others.[24] For example, a white girl may seek a closer connection with another white girl by perpetuating a rumor about a Latina peer's sexuality.[25] In a situation, such as many high schools in the United States, in which spiteful gossip is normative, relational aggression by whites against individuals of color can function as a form of socially acceptable racism.[26] While this type of action is malicious against the target, the aggressor might use destructive behavior to seek to build a relationship with the person to whom she shares the gossip.

Aronson argues that the jigsaw technique disrupts an individual's comfort with engaging in subtle and overt forms of bullying because working closely and cooperatively with others builds empathy—taking the perspective of another individual in a caring way.[27] Empathy prompts a focus on the welfare of another individual[28] and is highly inconsistent with committing intentional harm. (Individuals experience cognitive dissonance when they harm a person toward whom they feel empathy.)

Following decades of research exploring contemporary racism in its subtle, often nonconscious forms, Gaertner and Dovidio began to focus on a technique for reducing prejudice by shifting individuals' perspectives. The Common Ingroup Identity Model shares principles with the jigsaw classroom but can be applied beyond the classroom by challenging individuals in any setting to focus on a shared identity.[29] This technique can be applied when individuals from different racial groups work together or live in the same community. Historic and systematic racism make it likely that individuals will perceive ingroups and outgroups based on racial categories. When people focus on a shared, superordinate identity—as members of this (racially diverse) work group or as constituents in this community—the ingroup expands to include individuals who were previously perceived as members of an outgroup. In the jigsaw classroom, this shared identity might be "our learning group," and this feeling of connection might overpower stereotypes about expected "winners" and predicted "losers." The jigsaw classroom encourages students to get to know each other as individuals in addition to sharing a common identity.

Remarkably, Gaertner, Dovidio, and collaborators have demonstrated that simply focusing on a common identity, without further interaction, reduces prejudice. In dozens of replicating studies, researchers have reduced prejudice between groups by encouraging people to focus on a shared identity. When conflicts occur across racial categories, focusing on an important common identity may facilitate open and honest discussion when individuals focus on what they share rather than how they are distinct.[30]

In collaboration with Gaertner and Dovidio, Jason A. Nier and other colleagues tested the power of a common identity to change attitudes of white female college students toward a Black female peer. In a laboratory study, the white students were either encouraged to perceive themselves as comembers of a team with a Black female peer or to perceive themselves as participating individually in the study at the same time as a Black female peer. To build a sense of being on the same team, the white participants in the study worked with the Black peer (who was actually following a script written by the researchers) and with another white woman who was also naïve (like the white female participant) to the details of the study. The three women sat at a table together while working on a task that required them to reach consensus regarding decisions about a hypothetical event. The team was given a specific team name, and all three women wore a team uniform provided by the researchers—T-shirts that advertised their university's logo.

In the other condition of the study, the researchers sought to create a sense of individuals who were simply participating in the study at the same time, rather than as members of a team. In this situation, the white participants worked individually on the same task of making decisions about the hypothetical event while sitting alone at a table. The Black woman and other white woman sat alone at other tables. There was no mention of a team name, nor did the researchers provide T-shirts. The white women who interacted as teammates with the Black peer later evaluated the Black peer notably more positively than did the white women who simply participated in the study at the same time as the Black peer. Because the Black peer followed a very similar script in each condition of the study, the content of the interaction was very similar for all the participants in the study, but the impression of a common identity was only present when participants were encouraged to perceive themselves as part of a team with the Black peer.[31]

Nier and colleagues open their research article with a powerful quote from Ralph Ellison's novel, *The Invisible Man*: "America is woven of many strands. . . . Our fate is to become one and yet many."[32] We challenge readers to consider how empathy and building a sense of common identity may be harnessed to encourage individuals to focus on meeting the needs of the members of one's (global) community.

A Policy to Challenge Systemic Racism: The Guaranteed Income

We challenge you to think critically about justice. What do you consider basic human rights? What are the minimal resources that should be available to all children in the United States? Should those minimal resources be available to all children everywhere? Should all humans, young and old, children and adults, have the right to basic nutrition, adequate shelter, and literacy education? Are these rights, or are they privileges that should be earned?

Humans today, as a global community, have the ability to relieve extreme poverty and to provide all with access to nutrition, work, shelter, a decent education, and freedom from violence. Material needs and justice in terms of these needs must be at the core of our response to racism.

As discussed in chapter 8, we deem a strong affirmative action policy across work and educational institutions to be a necessity. We advocate health care for all, along with a living wage (also discussed in chapter 8) to make a decent standard of living available to all workers. Yet beyond the living wage, one solution we find powerful is that of a *guaranteed income* for all. A guaranteed income constitutes an advance over previous existing forms of social welfare and income support.

A guaranteed income would provide a minimal economic net to keep everyone from falling into extreme poverty. It would be similar to the right to education. In the United States today, we already have a system in place guaranteeing everyone an education through the twelfth grade. For those with the financial means who want a different, perhaps better education, private schools are often available as an alternative.

On a global level, springing from the racial history of such phenomena as colonization, slavery, scientific racism, segregation, and unequal access to housing, education, and work, a small, predominantly white minority has amassed immense wealth and continues to grow in prosperity.[33] In the United States, for example, as we saw in chapter 5, the share of income going to the top 10 percent of the households has been increasing. In sharp contrast, the majority working-class and poor people (often but not always of color) have struggled economically as their income share, which was always low, has actually declined in recent years. And as we saw in chapter 8 the median income has fallen. The economic system we live with today extends and perpetuates the prosperity of the wealthy and the inequality between the prosperous and the rest. In the United States in particular, as historian Thomas Sugrue explains about our contemporary and profoundly raced inequality, "[It] emerged as the consequence of two of the most important, interrelated, and unresolved problems in American history: that capitalism generates economic inequality and that African Americans have disproportionately borne the impact of that inequality."[34]

The problems of white privilege, racism, and discrimination will not go away unless we address this racialized imbalance of power and wealth on both a national and a global level. One way to do this is to guarantee a basic standard of living for everyone through a guaranteed income.

Many conservatives, such as writer Charles Murray, coauthor of *The Bell Curve* (discussed at length in chapter 2), worry that even a minimal guaranteed income would take away people's incentive to work.[35] However, a guaranteed income merely acts as a net for all humans everywhere to have a *decent standard of living*; in other words, to live with basic access to nutritious food, adequate shelter, education, and meaningful work and other activities. A functional guaranteed income would require a commitment to "providing each and every human being with enough funding to live . . . *regardless of work.*"[36] The current economic system has created a vastly unequal playing field in which white people have benefited historically—and continue to do so today—from the economic oppression of peoples of color. Because individuals in our current economic system face enormous pressure to have an income for survival, individuals with few economic resources have often been exploited in demeaning, even dangerous, jobs for little pay. A guaranteed income would give all individuals greater choice regarding occupation. If no one accepted an exploitative job, employers would face pressure to consider how to make the work more valuable or safer.

The guaranteed income proposal is probably essential if we are ever to truly address global and national inequality. And a *fair* guaranteed income movement would act globally, seeking to guarantee all human beings, regardless of country, a basic income. We acknowledge that, for the time being, it is an idea that seems a long way off, particularly on a global level. Establishing a global guaranteed income is certainly daunting. The economic constraints of governments in the developing world and the lack of an international system of social welfare make the concept of global guaranteed income extremely challenging. So as a first step, many support the development of a guaranteed income program in the United States and Europe. Still, the guaranteed income movement *must* be an international movement to be just.

It should be noted that a limited guaranteed income program was a real possibility in the United States in the early 1970s when there was a strong movement supporting the idea. Indeed, Republican president Nixon submitted to Congress a proposal for a modest guaranteed income for all Americans. While it did not pass, Nixon's proposal was seriously considered.[37] In other words, the guaranteed income idea is not mere fantasy but stands within the outer limits of possible politics in the contemporary United States. Further, guaranteed income and other similar programs regarding income or guaranteed food have been, or are currently being, discussed in a variety of places, including the United States, South Korea, New Zealand, Norway, and India.

We argue that in order to bring about a more just society for everyone, the material conditions of all people's lives must be made fairer. By fair, we mean *more equal* but not exactly equal; inequality would still exist. A guaranteed income does not equalize wealth or earnings. Those with wealth continue to have their wealth, and those without, continue without. Those earning a large income continue earning a large income, and those earning a small income continue the same as well. Again, a guaranteed income is merely a net that stops the poor from falling too far into poverty.

The guaranteed income is an idea that has been and continues to be seriously considered.[38] And albeit far from where our world is today—politically, economically, and socially—as sociologist Ron Nerio argues, "The only way to build a better future is by imagining one and thinking about how to get there."[39]

Conclusion

Shifting our way of thinking about—and interacting in—relationships might offer one important step out of our painful history bound by racism. Perhaps it is time to think in turns of caring for each other, and the well-being of all, instead of competition and individualism. Nier and colleagues help us to see how building common identities changes our attitudes toward each other. Aronson and the jigsaw classroom offer concrete examples of how we might live our lives centered on care. The guaranteed income is an example of public policy that moves away from individual competition in a marketplace that has been and continues to be profoundly unfair to caring for all, including the most vulnerable among us.

Indeed, as we argued throughout the book, white economic privilege births most other forms of white social power. From the origins of the Modern World System to contemporary times, a relatively small, white minority has amassed immense wealth in part from the economic oppression of peoples of color. Ways of thinking about the social reality of race have evolved with the development of this (largely white) economic power. Born out of a particular economic reality, these racist ways of thinking (including the idea that race is biological) benefit those in power and harm the rest.

As we challenge and correct an unfair economic order, we can also challenge racism in its other forms in the ways we think about each other and understand our world. Social construction leaves open the possibility of reconstructing racial interaction and unjust power dynamics. Through recognition that race and therefore race relations are socially constructed, we can begin to imagine how privilege and unfair advantages could be revealed and challenged. When whiteness is clearly perceived—when we see white—whiteness can be critically evaluated.

Discussion Questions

1. What does it mean to claim that race is "real" through social construction? Explain this argument using evidence from multiple chapters of the textbook.
2. To what extent are different racial groups harmed by racism? Choose four racial groups and provide at least one example of evidence of harm for each group. (Did you choose whites as one of your groups? Why or why not?)

3. Evaluate the concept of the guaranteed income. What, if any, minimal resources would you like to see available to all individuals? Explain why you would or would not support using tax dollars to fund a guaranteed income for all.

4. How does the guaranteed income movement relate to combating racism?

5. Why might recognizing that racism is extensive in the United States generate cognitive dissonance? Describe productive and counterproductive ways that individuals might seek to reduce this cognitive dissonance.

6. Have your classroom experiences tended to be highly competitive, or did students tend to cooperate with each other? If you have had both types of experiences, please do reflect on whether and why you might learn better in one environment or the other. Thinking in terms of the jigsaw classroom, how might a cooperative learning environment reduce prejudice?

7. The jigsaw classroom is one system that can be institutionalized to focus on meeting people's needs and caring for individuals, rather than fostering competition. In what ways is the jigsaw classroom similar to or distinct from the guaranteed income in terms of addressing needs, caring, and competition?

8. After reading chapter 9, please review chapter 3. What might have happened if Irish Americans had focused on a common ingroup identity as working class with people of color?

9. Make an argument explaining why race has been such an important way of identifying individuals in U.S. history. Evaluate techniques such as the jigsaw classroom and the Common Ingroup Identity Model that suggest that humans can move beyond focusing on race.

10. Could recognizing that all humans are the same species and that race is meaningless in terms of genetics help to promote a common ingroup identity?

Notes

1. For further reading on some of the challenges to scientific racism, please do see Edwin Black, *War against the Weak: Eugenics and America's Campaign to Create a Master Race* (New York: Four Walls Eight Windows, 2003).

2. Nell Irvin Painter, "Soul Murder and Slavery: Toward a Fully Loaded Cost Accounting," in *U.S. History as Women's History: New Feminist Essays*, ed. Linda

K. Kerber, Alice Kessler-Harris, and Kathryn Kish Sklar (Chapel Hill: University of North Carolina Press, 1995), 125–46.

3. Linda Brent, *Incidents in the Life of a Slave Girl* (New York: Harcourt Brace Jovanovich, 1973).

4. Joseph L. Graves Jr., *The Emperor's New Clothes: Biological Theories of Race at the Millennium* (New Brunswick, N.J.: Rutgers University Press, 2002), 10.

5. Graves, *The Emperor's New Clothes*, 10.

6. Gunnar Myrdal, *An American Dilemma: Volume 1: The Negro Problem and Modern Democracy* (New Brunswick, N.J.: Transaction Publishers, 1944).

7. Leon Festinger, *A Theory of Cognitive Dissonance* (Stanford, Calif.: Stanford University Press, 1957).

8. Beverly Daniel Tatum, *"Why Are All the Black Kids Sitting Together in the Cafeteria?": And Other Conversations about Race* (New York: Basic, 2003).

9. Tatum, *Why Are All the Black Kids*, 99.

10. John F. Dovidio, Kerry Kawakami, Natalie Smoak, and Samuel L. Gaertner, "The Nature of Contemporary Racial Prejudice: Insights from Implicit and Explicit Measures of Attitudes," in *Attitudes: Insights from the New Implicit Measures*, eds. Richard E. Petty, Russell H. Fazio, and Pablo Briñol (New York: Psychology Press, 2009), 165–92.

11. John F. Dovidio, Samuel L. Gaertner, Kerry Kawakami, and Gordon Hodson, "Why Can't We Just Get Along?: Interpersonal Biases and Interracial Distrust," *Cultural Diversity and Ethnic Minority Psychology* 8, no. 2 (May 2002): 88–102.

12. John F. Dovidio, Samuel L. Gaertner, Jason A. Nier, Kerry Kawakami, and Gordon Hodson, "Contemporary Racial Bias: When Good People Do Bad Things," in *The Social Psychology of Good and Evil*, ed. Arthur G. Miller (New York: The Guilford Press, 2004), 141–67.

13. Samuel L. Gaertner and John F. Dovidio, "The Subtlety of White Racism, Arousal, and Helping Behavior," *Journal of Personality and Social Psychology* 35, no. 10 (October 1977): 691–707.

14. Dovidio et al., "Contemporary Racial Bias," 147.

15. Elliott Aronson, "Reducing Hostility and Building Compassion: Lessons from the Jigsaw Classroom," in *The Social Psychology of Good and Evil*, ed. Arthur G. Miller (New York: The Guilford Press, 2004), 469–88, 475.

16. Henri Tajfel and John Turner, "An Integrative Theory of Intergroup Conflict," in *The Social Psychology of Intergroup Relations*, eds. William C. Austin and Stephen Worchel (Monterey, Calif.: Brooks/Cole, 1979), 33–47.

17. Aronson, "Reducing Hostility," 478.

18. Research on diverse leadership groups used in U.S. military training has revealed that individuals who face stereotypes that they might be less likely to succeed are most successful if they are members of groups with at least one other individual who faces the same stereotype. For example, in the military setting, women fair better if placed in a group with another woman. Applying this concept to the classroom, we recommend that teachers consider issues of gender, race, and ethnic-

ity when creating jigsaw learning groups. Ideally, students who face a stereotype about performance will not be solo representatives of a stigmatized identity within a learning group. In other words, groups will be constructed to have at least two individuals of any racial or ethnic group that is relevant to stereotypes about academic success. To achieve this in classrooms, teachers may have to choose to have some groups be less diverse than others. (For example, if a classroom of twenty-five students includes four Latina/o students, the teacher should pair these children in learning groups. Some groups will have no Latina/o students while others will have two.) Because the jigsaw technique has students join new learning groups every eight weeks, ideally all students will be exposed to diversity within the classroom without any student finding himself or herself as a solo in a learning group. See Monica Biernat, Christian S. Crandall, Lissa V. Young, Diane Kobrynowicz, and Stanley M. Halpin, "All That You Can Be: Stereotyping of Self and Others in a Military Context," *Journal of Personality and Social Psychology* 75, no. 2 (August 1998): 301–17.

19. Elliot Aronson, "Jigsaw Classroom," 2010, www.jigsaw.org (August 19, 2010).

20. Aronson, "Reducing Hostility," 479.

21. Craig A. Anderson and Nicholas L. Carnagey, "Violent Evil and the General Aggression Model," in *The Social Psychology of Good and Evil*, ed. Arthur G. Miller (New York: The Guilford Press, 2004), 168–92.

22. Nicki R. Crick and Jennifer K. Grotpeter, "Relational Aggression, Gender, and Social-Psychological Adjustment," *Child Development* 66, no. 3 (June 1995): 710–22.

23. Rachel Simmons, *Odd Girl Out: The Hidden Culture of Aggression in Girls* (San Diego, Calif.: Harcourt, Inc., 2002).

24. Rosalind Wiseman, *Queen Bees & Wannabees: Helping Your Daughter Survive Cliques, Gossip, Boyfriends, and the New Realities of Girl World* (New York: Three Rivers Press, 2002).

25. Individuals seeking greater feelings of connection with a valued ingroup may be particularly likely to disparage outgroup members. See Jeffrey G. Noel, Daniel L. Wann, and Nyla R. Branscombe, "Peripheral Ingroup Membership Status and Public Negativity toward Outgroups," *Journal of Personality and Social Psychology* 68, no. 1 (January 1995): 127–37.

26. Christian S. Crandall, Amy Eshleman, and Laurie T. O'Brien, "Social Norms and the Expression and Suppression of Prejudice: The Struggle for Internalization," *Journal of Personality and Social Psychology* 82, no. 3 (March 2002): 359–78.

27. Elliot Aronson, *Nobody Left to Hate: Teaching Compassion after Columbine* (New York: W. H. Freeman and Company, 2000).

28. C. Daniel Batson, Nadia Ahmad, and E. L. Stocks, "Benefits and Liabilities of Empathy-Induced Altruism," in *The Social Psychology of Good and Evil*, ed. Arthur G. Miller (New York: The Guilford Press, 2004), 359–85.

29. Samuel L. Gaertner and John F. Dovidio, *Reducing Intergroup Bias: The Common Ingroup Identity Model* (New York: Psychology Press, 2000).

206 ~ Chapter Nine

30. See for example, Blake M. Riek, Eric W. Mania, Samuel L. Gaertner, Stacy A. McDonald, and Marika J. Lamoreaux, "Does a Common Ingroup Identity Reduce Intergroup Threat?," *Group Processes and Intergroup Relations* 13, no. 4 (July 2010): 403–23.

31. Jason A. Nier, Samuel L. Gaertner, John F. Dovidio, Brenda S. Banker, Christine M. Ward, and Mary C. Rust, "Changing Interracial Evaluations and Behavior: The Effects of a Common Group Identity," *Group Processes and Intergroup Relations* 4, no. 4 (October 2001): 299–316.

32. Ralph Ellison, *The Invisible Man*, 2nd ed. (New York: Vintage International, 1995), 577.

33. Immanuel Maurice Wallerstein, *The Modern World-System: Capitalist Agriculture and the Origins of the European World-Economy in the Sixteenth Century* (New York: Academic Press, 1974).

34. Thomas J. Sugrue, *Origins of the Urban Crisis* (Princeton, N.J.: Princeton University Press, 2005), 5.

35. Charles Murray, "The Social Scientists and the Great Experiment," *American Social Policy, 1950–1980* (New York: Basic Books, Incorporated, 1984), 147–53.

36. Stanley Aronowitz, Dawn Esposito, William DiFazio, and Margaret Yard, "The Post-Work Manifesto," in *Post-Work: The Wages of Cybernation*, eds. by Stanley Aronowitz and Jonathan Cutler (New York: Routledge, 1998), 65.

37. Daniel Patrick Moynihan, *The Politics of a Guaranteed Income: The Nixon Administration and the Family Assistance Plan* (New York: Random House, 1973).

38. For further reading on the guaranteed income, please do see Lynn Chancer's "Benefitting from Pragmatic Vision, Part I: The Case for Guaranteed Income in Principle," in *Post-Work: The Wages of Cybernation*, eds. by Stanley Aronowitz and Jonathan Cutler (New York: Routledge, 1998), 81–128. For more information on the conservative challenge to the guaranteed income, please do see Charles Murray, "The Social Scientists and the Great Experiment," 147–53. Murray lays out conservative thought on the guaranteed income in this essay, critiquing the guaranteed income movement in the United States.

39. Ron Nerio, personal communication, August 12, 2010.

Bibliography

Act to Establish a Uniform Rule of Naturalization, 2nd Cong. (1790).

Adams, Glenn, Laurie T. O'Brien, and Jessica C. Nelson. "Perceptions of Racism in Hurricane Katrina: A Liberation Psychology Analysis." *Analyses of Social Issues and Public Policy* 6, no. 1 (December 2006): 215–35.

Akerlof, George A., and Rachel E. Kranton, "Identity and Schooling: Some Lessons for the Economics of Education." *Journal of Economic Literature* XL (December 2002): 1167–201.

Allen, Theodore W. "On Roediger's *Wages of Whiteness*." *Cultural Logic* 4, no. 2 (Spring 2001).

American Anthropological Association. "American Anthropological Association Statement on 'Race.'" www.aaanet.org/stmts/racepp.htm, 1998 (July 1, 2010).

American Anthropological Association. "Race: Are We So Different?" *American Anthropological Association* (June 17, 2010).

American Association of Physical Anthropologists. "AAPA Statement on Biological Aspects of Race." *American Journal of Physical Anthropology* 101, no. 4 (December 1996): 569–70.

Andersen, Margaret L., and Patricia Hill Collins. *Race, Class and Gender: An Anthology.* 7th ed. Belmont, Calif.: Wadsworth Cengage Learning, 2010.

Anderson, Craig A., and Nicholas L. Carnagey. "Violent Evil and the General Aggression Model." In *The Social Psychology of Good and Evil*, edited by Arthur G. Miller, 168–69. New York: The Guilford Press, 2004.

Armelagos, George J., and Alan H. Goodman. "Race, Racism, and Anthropology." In *Building a New Biocultural Synthesis: Political-Economic Perspectives on Human*

Biology, edited by Alan H. Goodman and Thomas L. Leatherman, 359–77, 371. Ann Arbor: The University of Michigan Press, 1998.

Aronowitz, Stanley, Dawn Esposito, William DiFazio, and Margaret Yard. "The Post-Work Manifesto." In *Post-Work: The Wages of Cybernation*, edited by Stanley Aronowitz and Jonathan Cutler. New York: Routledge, 1998.

Aronson, Elliot. "Jigsaw Classroom." www.jigsaw.org, 2010 (August 19, 2010).

Aronson, Elliot. "Reducing Hostility and Building Compassion: Lessons from the Jigsaw Classroom." In *The Social Psychology of Good and Evil*, edited by Arthur G. Miller, 469–88. New York: The Guilford Press, 2004.

Aronson, Elliot. *Nobody Left to Hate: Teaching Compassion after Columbine*. New York: W. H. Freeman and Company, 2000.

Aronson, Joshua, Michael J. Lustina, Catherine Good, Kelli Keough, Claude M. Steele, and Joseph Brown. "When White Men Can't Do Math: Necessary and Sufficient Factors in Stereotype Threat." *Journal of Experimental Social Psychology* 35, no. 1 (January 1999): 29–46.

Bates, Timothy. *Race, Self-Employment, and Upward Mobility: An Illusive American Dream*. Washington, D.C.: Woodrow Wilson Center Press. Baltimore: Johns Hopkins University Press, 1997.

Batson, C. Daniel, Nadia Ahmad, and E. L. Stocks. "Benefits and Liabilities of Empathy-Induced Altruism." In *The Social Psychology of Good and Evil*, edited by Arthur G. Miller, 359–385. New York: The Guilford Press, 2004.

Beinart, Peter. "Fix Affirmative Action Now." *Daily Beast*, www.thedailybeast.com/blogs-and-stories/2010-07-21/tea-party-naacp-race-flap-time-for-a-new-kind-of-affirmative-action (July 22, 2010).

Bell, Derrick. *Race, Racism, and American Law*. 6th ed. New York: Aspen Publishers, 2008.

Bell, Derrick. "Epilogue." In *When Race Becomes Real: Black and White Writers Confront Their Personal Histories*, edited by Bernestine Singley, 327–28. Chicago: Lawrence Hill Books, 2002.

Bell, Derrick. *Confronting Authority: Reflections on an Ardent Protester*. Boston: Beacon Press, 1996.

Benokraitis, Nijole, and Joe Feagin. "Institutional Racism: A Perspective in Search of Clarity and Research." In *Black/Brown/White Relations: Race Relations in the 1970s*, edited by Charles V. Willie. New Brunswick, N.J.: Transactions, Inc., 1977.

Bernstein, Douglas A., Louis A. Penner, Alison Clarke-Stewart, and Edward J. Roy. *Psychology*. 6th ed. Stamford, Conn.: Cengage, 2008.

Bernstein, Jared. "Median Income Rose as Did Poverty in 2007; 2000s Have Been Extremely Weak for Living Standards of Most Households." Economic Policy Institute, www.epi.org/publications/entry/webfeatures_econindicators_income_20080826 (last modified August 26, 2008).

Bernstein, Jared, and John Schmitt. "Making Work Pay: The Impact of the 1996–97 Minimum Wage Increase." Washington, D.C.: Economic Policy Institute (1998).

Bidol, Pat A., and Richard C. Weber. *Developing New Perspectives on Race: An Innovative Multi-Media Social Studies Curriculum in Race Relations for the Secondary Level*. Detroit, Mich.: New Detroit, 1970.

Biernat, Monica, Christian S. Crandall, Lissa V. Young, Diane Kobrynowicz, and Stanley M. Halpin. "All That You Can Be: Stereotyping of Self and Others in a Military Context." *Journal of Personality and Social Psychology* 75, no. 2 (August 1998): 301–17.

Black, Edwin. *War against the Weak: Eugenics and America's Campaign to Create a Master Race*. New York: Four Walls Eight Windows, 2003.

Blum, Linda M. *Between Feminism and Labor: The Significance of the Comparable Worth Movement*. Berkeley: University of California Press, 1991.

Bonilla-Silva, Eduardo. *Racism without Racists: Color-Blind Racism and the Persistence of Racial Inequality in the United States*. 3rd ed. Lanham, Md.: Rowman & Littlefield, 2010.

Bonilla-Silva, Eduardo. "Rethinking Racism: Toward a Structural Interpretation." *American Sociological Review* 62, no. 3 (June 1997): 465–80.

Bowen, William G., and Derek Bok, *The Shape of the River: Long-Term Consequences of Considering Race in College and University Admissions*. Princeton, N.J.: Princeton University Press, 1998.

Bradbury, Katherine, and Jane Katz. "Trends in U.S. Family Income Mobility 1967–2004." *Federal Reserve Bank of Boston Working Paper Series*, www.bosfrb.org/economic/wp/wp2009/wp0907.pdf (September 10, 2009): No. 09-7.

Branscombe, Nyla R., Michael T. Schmitt, and Kristin Schiffhauer. "Racial Attitudes in Response to Thoughts of White Privilege." *European Journal of Social Psychology* 37, no. 2 (March–April 2007): 203–15.

Brent, Linda. *Incidents in the Life of a Slave Girl*. New York: Harcourt Brace Jovanovich, 1973.

Brooks, David. "The Formerly Middle Class." *New York Times* (November 17, 2009).

Brown, Ryan A., and George J. Armelagos. "Apportionment of Racial Diversity: A Review." *Evolutionary Anthropology* 10, no. 1 (February 2001): 34–40.

Brunsma, David L., and Kerry Ann Rockquemore. "What Does 'Black' Mean? Exploring the Epistemological Stranglehold of Racial Categorization." *Critical Sociology* 28, number 1/2 (2002).

Bryant, Bunyan I., and Paul Mohai. *Race and the Incidence of Environmental Hazards: A Time for Discourse*. Boulder, Colo.: Westview Press, 1992.

Bucks, Brian, Arthur Kennickell, Traci Mach, and Kevin Moore. "Changes in U.S. Family Finances from 2004 to 2007: Evidence from the Survey of Consumer Finances." *Federal Reserve Bulletin* 95 (February 2009): A1–A56.

Bullard, Robert D. *Dumping in Dixie: Race, Class, and Environmental Quality*. 3rd ed. Boulder, Colo.: Westview Press, 2000.

Bureau of Justice Statistics. "2006 Expenditure and Employment Statistical Abstracts." http://bjs.ojp.usdoj.gov/index.cfm?ty=pbdetail&iid=1022, 2008 (July 15, 2010).

Carbado, Devon W. "Yellow by Law." *California Law Review* 97, no. 3 (2009): 633–92.

Card, David, and Alan B. Krueger. "Minimum Wages and Employment: A Case Study of the Fast-Food Industry in New Jersey and Pennsylvania." *American Economic Review* 84, no. 4 (1994): 772–93.

Carlson, Elof Axel. *The Unfit: A History of a Bad Idea*. Woodbury, N.Y.: Cold Spring Harbor Laboratory Press, 2001.

Chancer, Lynn. "Benefitting from Pragmatic Vision, Part I: The Case for Guaranteed Income in Principle." In *Post-Work: The Wages of Cybernation*, edited by Stanley Aronowitz and Jonathan Cutler, 81–128. New York: Routledge, 1998.

Chavis Jr., Benjamin F., *Toxic Wastes and Race in the United States: A National Report on the Racial and Socio-Economic Characteristics of Communities with Hazardous Waste Sites*. New York: The United Church of Christ Commission for Racial Justice, 1987.

Christianson, Scott. "Bad Seed or Bad Science: The Story of the Notorious Jukes Family." *New York Times*, www.nytimes.com/2003/02/08/arts/08JUKE.html, February 8, 2003 (June 29, 2010).

Chua, Peter. "Negotiating New Asian-American Masculinities: Attitudes and Gender Expectations." *Journal of Men's Studies* 7, no. 3 (Spring 1999): 391–413.

Chubbuck, Sharon M. "Whiteness Enacted, Whiteness Disrupted: The Complexity of Personal Congruence." *American Educational Research Journal* 41, no. 2 (Summer 2004): 301–33.

Cialdini, Robert B. "Crafting Normative Messages to Protect the Environment." *Current Directions in Psychological Science* 12, no. 4 (August 2003): 105–09.

Clough, Patricia Ticineto. *The End(s) of Ethnography: From Realism to Social Criticism*. New York: Peter Lang Publishing, Inc., 1998.

Coffey, Michael, and Terry Golway. *The Irish in America*. New York: Hyperion, 1997.

Cohen, Geoffrey L., Claude M. Steele, and Lee D. Ross. "The Mentor's Dilemma: Providing Critical Feedback across the Racial Divide." *Personality and Social Psychology Bulletin* 25, no. 10 (October 1999): 1302–18.

Cole, David. "Can Our Shameful Prisons Be Reformed?" *New York Review of Books* (November 19, 2009).

Comas-Díaz, Lillian. "Hispanics, Latinos, or Americanos: The Evolution of Identity." *Cultural Diversity and Ethnic Minority Psychology* 7, no. 2 (May 2001): 115–20.

Corak, Miles. "Do Poor Children Become Poor Adults? Lessons from a Cross Country Comparison of Generational Earnings Mobility." IZA Discussion Paper, no. 1993 (Bonn: Institute for the Study of Labor, 2006).

Cox, Oliver Cromwell. *Caste, Class, and Race: A Study in Social Dynamics*. New York: Monthly Review Press, 1948.

Cozby, Paul C. *Methods in Behavioral Research*. 10th ed. New York: McGraw-Hill, 2009.

Crandall, Christian S., and Amy Eshleman. "A Justification-Suppression Model of the Expression and Experience of Prejudice." *Psychological Bulletin* 129, no. 3 (May 2003), 414–46.

Crandall, Christian S., Amy Eshleman, and Laurie T. O'Brien. "Social Norms and the Expression and Suppression of Prejudice: The Struggle for Internalization." *Journal of Personality and Social Psychology* 82, no. 3 (March 2002): 359–78.

Crenshaw, Kimberle. "Mapping the Margins: Intersectionality, Identity Politics, and Violence against Women of Color." In *Foundations of Critical Race Theory in Education*, edited by Edward Taylor, David Gillborn, and Gloria Ladson-Billings. New York: Routledge, 2009.

Crick, Nicki R., and Jennifer K. Grotpeter. "Relational Aggression, Gender, and Social-Psychological Adjustment." *Child Development* 66, no. 3 (June 1995): 710–22.

Cross, Beverly E. "New Racism, Reformed Teacher Education, and the Same Ole' Oppression." *Educational Studies: Journal of the American Educational Studies Association* 38, no. 3 (December 2005): 263–74.

Darity, William. "Stratification Economics: The Role of Intergroup Inequality." *Journal of Economics and Finance* 29, no. 2 (July 2005): 144–53.

Darley, John M., and Paget H. Gross. "A Hypothesis-Confirming Bias in Labeling Effects." *Journal of Personality and Social Psychology* 44, no. 1 (January 1983): 20–33.

DeCuir-Gunby, Jessica T. "'Proving Your Skin Is White, You Can Have Everything': Race, Racial Identity, and Property Rights in Whiteness in the Supreme Court Case of Josephine DeCuir," in *Critical Race Theory in Education: All God's Children Got a Song*, eds. Adrienne D. Dixson and Celia K. Rousseau, 89–111, 93–94. New York: Routledge, 2006.

Dei, George J. Sefa, Nisha Karumanchery-Luik, and Leeno Luke Karumanchery, *Playing the Race Card: Exposing White Power and Privilege*. New York: Peter Lang Publishing, 2004.

Derman-Sparks, Louise, and Patricia G. Ramsay. *What If All the Kids Are White? Anti-Bias Multicultural Education with Young Children and Families*. New York: Teachers College Press, 2006.

Dickie, Jane. "The Unconscious Devil Within." *Church Herald: The Magazine of the Reformed Church in America* 46, no. 3 (March 1989): 12–15, 51.

Dixson, Adrienne D., and Celia K. Rousseau, eds. *Critical Race Theory in Education: All God's Children Got a Song*. New York: Routledge, 2006.

Dovidio, John F., Samuel L. Gaertner, Kerry Kawakami, and Gordon Hodson. "Why Can't We Just Get Along?: Interpersonal Biases and Interracial Distrust." *Cultural Diversity and Ethnic Minority Psychology* 8, no. 2 (May 2002): 88–102.

Dovidio, John F., Samuel L. Gaertner, Jason A. Nier, Kerry Kawakami, and Gordon Hodson. "Contemporary Racial Bias: When Good People Do Bad Things." In *The Social Psychology of Good and Evil*, edited by Arthur G. Miller, 141–67. New York: The Guilford Press, 2004.

Dovidio, John F., Kerry Kawakami, Natalie Smoak, and Samuel L. Gaertner. "The Nature of Contemporary Racial Prejudice: Insights from Implicit and Explicit Measures of Attitudes." In *Attitudes: Insights from the New Implicit Measures*, edited by Richard E. Petty, Russell H. Fazio, and Pablo Briñol, 165–19. New York: Psychology Press, 2009.

Du Bois, W. E. B. *Black Reconstruction in the United States*. New York: Harcourt, Brace and Company, 1935.

Education Trust. *Funding Gaps 2006*. www.edtrust.org/sites/edtrust.org/files/publications/files/FundingGap2006.pdf (August 27, 2010).

Ehrenreich, Barbara. *Nickel and Dimed: On (Not) Getting by in America*. New York: Henry Holt and Company, LLC, 2001.

Ehrenreich, Barbara, and Arlie Russell Hochschild. *Global Woman: Nannies, Maids and Sex Workers in the New Economy*. New York: Henry Holt & Company, LLC, 2002.

Ellison, Ralph. *The Invisible Man*. 2nd ed. New York: Vintage International, 1995.

England, Paula. "Separative and Soluble Selves." In *Feminist Economics Today*, edited by Marianne A. Ferber and Julie A. Nelson, 35–59. Chicago: University of Chicago Press, 2003.

England, Paula. *Comparable Worth: Theories and Evidence*. New York: Aldine de Guyter, 1991.

England, Paula, Michelle Budig, and Nancy Folbre. "Wages of Virtue: The Relative Pay of Care Work." *Social Problems* 49, no. 4 (2002): 455–73.

Estabrook, Arthur H. *The Jukes in 1915*. Washington, D.C.: Carnegie Institution of Washington, 1916.

Ewen, Stuart, and Elizabeth Ewen. *Typecasting: On the Arts and Sciences of Human Inequality*. New York: Seven Stories Press, 2006.

Ezekiel, Raphael S. "An Ethnographer Looks at Neo-Nazi and Klan Groups." *American Behavioral Scientist* 46, no. 1 (September 2002): 51–71.

Feagin, Joe R. *The White Racial Frame: Centuries of Racial Framing and Counter-Framing*. New York: Routledge, 2010.

Feagin, Joe R., Hernán Vera, and Pinar Batur. *White Racism*. 2nd ed. New York: Routledge, 2001.

Fein, Steven, and Steven J. Spencer. "Prejudice as Self-Image Maintenance: Affirming the Self through Derogating Others." *Journal of Personality and Social Psychology* 73, no. 1 (July 1997): 31–44.

Festinger, Leon. *A Theory of Cognitive Dissonance*. Stanford, Calif.: Stanford University Press, 1957.

Figart, Deborah, Ellen Mutari, and Marilyn Power. *Living Wages, Equal Wages: Gender and Labor Market Policies in the United States*. New York: Routledge, 2002.

Kai Filion, "Minimum Wage Issue Guide," Economic Policy Institute, last modified July 21, 2009, http://epi.3cdn.net/9f5a60cec02393cbe4_a4m6b5t1v.pdf.

Fischer, Claude S., Michael Hout, Martin Sanchez Jankowski, Samuel R. Lucas, Ann Swidler, and Kim Voss. *Inequality by Design: Cracking the Bell Curve Myth*. Princeton, N.J.: Princeton University Press, 1996.

Flagg, Barbara J. "'Was Blind But Now I See': White Race Consciousness and the Requirement of Discriminatory Intent." *Michigan Law Review* 91 (March 1993): 953–1017.

Flagg, Fannie. *Welcome to the World, Baby Girl!* New York: Ballantine Books, 1998.

Freeden, Michael. "Is Nationalism a Distinct Ideology?" *Political Studies* 46, no. 4 (September 1998): 748–65.

"French Plan to Break Taboo on Ethnic Data Causes Uproar." *Guardian* (March 23, 2009).

Frey, William H. "Central City White Flight: Racial and Nonracial Causes." *American Sociological Review* 44 (September 1977): 425–48.

Friedman, Ellen G., Wendy K. Kolmar, Charley B. Flint, and Paula Rothenberg, eds. *Creating an Inclusive College Curriculum: A Teaching Sourcebook from the New Jersey Project.* New York: Teacher's College Press, 1995.

Gaertner, Samuel L., and John F. Dovidio. *Reducing Intergroup Bias: The Common Ingroup Identity Model.* New York: Psychology Press, 2000.

Gallagher, Charles A. "White Reconstruction in the University," in *Privilege: A Reader*, eds. Michael S. Kimmel and Abby L. Ferber, 299–318. Boulder, Colo.: Westview Press, 2003.

Giroux, Henry A., and Anthony N. Penna. "Social Education in the Classroom: The Dynamics of the Hidden Curriculum." *Theory and Research in Social Education* 7, no. 1 (1979): 21–42.

Goffman, Erving. *Stigma: Notes on the Management of Spoiled Identity.* Englewood Cliffs, N.J.: Prentice-Hall, Inc., 1963.

Golden, Daniel. "Admission Preferences Given to Alumni Children Draws Fire." *Wall Street Journal* (January 15, 2003).

Goldsmith, Arthur H., Darrick Hamilton, and William Darity Jr. "From Dark to Light: Skin Color and Wages among African Americans." *Journal of Human Resources* 42, no. 4 (2007): 701–38.

Goodman, Alan H. "Why Genes Don't Count (for Racial Differences in Health)." *American Journal of Public Health* 90, no. 11 (November 2000): 1699–1700.

Gould, Stephen Jay. *The Mismeasure of Man.* New York: W. W. Norton & Company, 1996.

Graves Jr., Joseph L. *The Emperor's New Clothes: Biological Theories of Race at the Millennium.* New Brunswick, N.J.: Rutgers University Press, 2002.

Gravlee, Clarence C. "How Race Becomes Biology: Embodiment of Social Inequality." *American Journal of Physical Anthropology* 139, no. 1 (February 2009): 47–57.

Gravlee, Clarence C., H. Russell Bernard, and William R. Leonard. "Boas's Changes in Bodily Form: The Immigrant Study, Cranial Plasticity, and Boas's Physical Anthropology." *American Anthropologist* 105, no. 2 (June 2003): 326–32.

Guthrie, Robert V. *Even the Rat Was White: A Historical View of Psychology.* 2nd ed. Boston: Pearson, 2004.

Halley, Jean. *Boundaries of Touch: Parenting and Adult-Child Intimacy.* Champaign, Ill.: University of Illinois Press, 2007.

Halley, Jean. "Book Review of *Inequality by Design: Cracking the Bell Curve Myth.*" *Theoretical Criminology* 2, no. 1(1998), 135–38.

Haskins, Ron, Julia Issacs, and Isabel Sawhill. *Getting Ahead or Losing Ground: Economic Mobility in America.* Washington, D.C.: Brookings Institution Press, 2008.

Helms, Janet E. "Racial Identity and Racial Socialization as Aspects of Adolescents' Identity Development," in *Handbook of Applied Developmental Science: Promoting Positive Child, Adolescent, and Family Development through Research, Policies, and Programs, Volume 1,* eds. Richard M. Lerner, Francine Jacobs, and Donald Wertlieb, 143–63. Thousand Oaks, Calif.: Sage Publications, Inc., 2003.

Helms, Janet E. "An Update of Helms's White and People of Color Racial Identity Models," in *Handbook of Multicultural Counseling,* eds. Joseph G. Ponterotto, J. Manuel Casas, Lisa A. Suzuki, and Charlene M. Alexander, 181–98. Thousand Oaks, Calif.: Sage Publications, Inc., 1995.

Henkel, Kristen E., John F. Dovidio, and Samuel L. Gaertner. "Institutional Discrimination, Individual Racism, and Hurricane Katrina." *Analyses of Social Issues and Public Policy* 6, no. 1 (December 2006): 99–124.

Hernandez, Tanya Kateri. "'Multiracial' Discourse: Racial Classifications in an Era of Color-Blind Jurisprudence." *Maryland Law Review* 57 (1998): 97.

Herrnstein, Richard J., and Charles Murray. *The Bell Curve: Intelligence and Class Structure in American Life.* New York: Simon & Schuster, 1994.

Hockenbury, Don H., and Sandra E. Hockenbury. *Psychology.* New York: Worth, 2008.

Hyland, Nora E. "Being a Good Teacher of Black Students? White Teachers and Unintentional Racism." *Curriculum Inquiry* 35, no. 4 (Winter 2005): 429–59.

Ignatiev, Noel. *How the Irish Became White.* New York: Routledge, 1995.

Jäntti, Markus, Bernt Bratsberg, Knut Roed, Oddbjörn Raaum, Robin Naylor, Eva Osterbacka, Anders Bjorklund, and Tor Eriksson. "American Exceptionalism in a New Light: A Comparison of Intergenerational Earnings Mobility in the Nordic Countries, the United Kingdom and the United States." IZA Discussion Paper no. 1938, Bonn: Institute for the Study of Labor (2006).

Jay, Michelle. "Critical Race Theory, Multicultural Education, and the Hidden Curriculum of Hegemony." *Multicultural Perspectives* 5, no. 4 (October 2003): 3–9.

Jensen, Robert. *The Heart of Whiteness: Confronting Race, Racism, and White Privilege.* San Francisco, Calif.: City Lights, 2005.

Jost, John T. "Negative Illusions: Conceptual Clarification and Psychological Evidence Concerning False Consciousness." *Political Psychology* 16, no. 2 (June 1995): 397–424.

Jost, John T., and Mahzarin R. Banaji. "The Role of Stereotyping in System-Justification and the Production of False Consciousness." *British Journal of Social Psychology* 33, no. 1 (March 1994): 1–27.

Jost, John T., Mahzarin R. Banaji, and Brian A. Nosek. "A Decade of System Justification Theory: Accumulated Evidence of Conscious and Unconscious Bolstering of the Status Quo." *Political Psychology* 25, no. 6 (December 2004): 881–920.

Jost, John T., Yifat Kivetz, Monica Rubini, Grazia Guermandi, and Cristina Mosso. "System-Justifying Functions of Complementary Regional and Ethnic Stereotypes:

Cross-National Evidence." *Social Justice Research* 18, no. 3 (September 2005): 305–33.

Kailin, Julie. *Antiracist Education: From Theory to Practice.* Lanham, Md.: Rowman & Littlefield, 2002.

Kellogg, Alex P. "Detroit's Food Banks Strain to Serve Middle Class." *Wall Street Journal* (July 10, 2009).

Kennedy, Randall. *Nigger: The Strange Career of a Troublesome Word.* New York: Vintage Books, 2003.

Kimmel, Michael S. *The Gendered Society.* 2nd ed. New York: Oxford University Press, 2004.

Kornbluh, Karen, and Jared Bernstein. "Running Faster to Stay in Place." Work and Family Program Research Paper, New America Foundation, www.newamerica.net/publications/policy/running_faster_to_stay_in_place (June 2005).

Kozol, Jonathan. *Savage Inequalities: Children in America's Schools.* New York: Crown, 1991.

Krugman, Paul. "Tax Cut Con." *New York Times* (September 14, 2003).

Kunda, Ziva, Paul G. Davies, Barbara D. Adams, and Steven J. Spencer, "The Dynamic Time Course of Stereotype Activation: Activation, Dissipation, and Resurrection." *Journal of Personality and Social Psychology* 82, no. 3 (March 2002): 283–99.

Ladson-Billings, Gloria, and William F. Tate IV. "Toward a Critical Race Theory of Education." In *Critical Race Theory in Education: All God's Children Got a Song,* edited by Adrienne D. Dixson and Celia K. Rousseau, 11–30. New York: Routledge, 2006.

LaFond, Deborah M. "What Is the Race, Class, Gender Lens?" *Global Citizenship through a Race, Class, Gender Lens,* www.albany.edu/~dlafonde/Global/whatisrgc.htm, 2010 (July 13, 2010).

Landsman, Julie, and Chance W. Lewis, eds. *White Teachers/Diverse Classrooms: A Guide to Building Inclusive Schools, Promoting High Expectations, and Eliminating Racism.* Sterling, Va.: Stylus, 2006.

Langhout, Regina D., and Cecily A. Mitchell. "Engaging Contexts: Drawing the Link between Student and Teacher Experiences of the Hidden Curriculum." *Journal of Community and Applied Psychology* 18, no. 6 (November–December 2008): 593–614.

Larsen, Clark Spencer. *Our Origins: Discovering Physical Anthropology.* New York: W. W. Norton & Company, 2008.

Lauderdale, Diane S. "Birth Outcomes for Arabic-Named Women in California before and after September 11." *Demography* 43, no. 1 (February 2006): 185–201.

Lazzare, Jane. *Beyond the Whiteness of Whiteness: Memoir of a White Mother of Black Sons.* Durham, N.C.: Duke University Press, 1996.

Leonardo, Zeus. "The Color of Supremacy: Beyond the Discourse of 'White Privilege.'" In *Foundations of Critical Race Theory in Education,* edited by Edward Taylor, David Gillborn, and Gloria Ladson-Billings, 261–76. New York: Routledge, 2009.

Lewin, Tamar. "Race Preferences Vote Splits Michigan." *New York Times* (October 31, 2006).

Lewontin, R. C. "Apportionment of Human Diversity." *Evolutionary Biology* 6 (1972): 381–98.

Lieberman, Robert C. *Shifting the Color Line: Race and the American Welfare State.* Cambridge, Mass.: Harvard University Press, 2001.

Linder, Marc. "Farm Workers and the Fair Labor Standards Act: Racial Discrimination in the New Deal." *Texas Law Review* 65, no. 4 (1987): 1335–87.

Lipsitz, George. *Possessive Investments in Whiteness: How White People Profit from Identity Politics.* Philadelphia: Temple University Press, 2006.

Lite, Jordan. "Please Ask Me Who, Not 'What,' I Am." *Newsweek.* www.newsweek.com/id/78724/page/1 (July 16, 2001).

Littlefield, Alice, Leonard Lieberman, and Larry T. Reynolds. "Redefining Race: The Potential Demise of a Concept in Physical Anthropology." *Current Anthropology* 23, no. 6 (December 1982): 641–55.

Loewen, James W. *Lies My Teacher Told Me: Everything Your American History Textbook Got Wrong.* New York: Touchstone, 2007.

López, Ian F. Haney. *White by Law: The Legal Construction of Race.* New York: New York University Press, 1996.

Lorde, Audre. *Sister Outside: Essays and Speeches.* Freedom, Calif.: The Crossing Press, 1984.

Lorde, Audre. "An Open Letter to Mary Daly." In *This Bridge Called My Back: Writings by Radical Women of Color*, edited by Cherrie Moraga and Gloria Anzaldua, 94–97. Latham, N.Y.: Kitchen Table: Women of Color Press, 1981/1983.

Lorde, Audre. "The Master's Tools Will Never Dismantle the Master's House." In *This Bridge Called My Back: Writings by Radical Women of Color*, edited by Cherrie Moraga and Gloria Anzaldua, 98–101. Latham, N.Y.: Kitchen Table: Women of Color Press, 1981/1983.

Loury, Glenn C. *Race, Incarceration, and American Values.* Cambridge: Massachusetts Institute of Technology Press, 2008.

Lynd, Robert S., and Helen Merrell Lynd. *Middletown: A Study in Modern American Culture.* Orlando, Fla.: Harcourt Brace Jovanovich, Publishers, 1929/1957.

MacAdam, Alison. "Long Duck Dong: Last of the Hollywood Stereotypes?" *All Things Considered.* Aired on National Public Radio, www.npr.org/templates/story/story.php?storyId=88591800, March 2008 (January 24, 2010).

Mace, William H., and Edwin P. Tanner. *The Story of Old Europe and Young America.* New York: Rand McNally & Company, 1915, 142–45.

Main Justice: Politics, Policy and the Law. www.mainjustice.com/2010/03/17/senate-passes-crack-cocaine-sentencing-bill (June 30, 2010).

Margolis, Maxine L. *True to Her Nature: Changing Advice to American Women.* Prospect Heights, Ill.: Waveland Press, Inc., 2000.

Margonis, Frank, and Laurence Parker. "Choice, Privatization, and Unspoken Strategies of Containment." *Educational Policy* 9, no. 4 (December 1995): 375–403.

Massey, Douglas, and Nancy Denton. *American Apartheid: Segregation and the Making of the Underclass.* Cambridge, Mass.: Harvard University Press, 1993.

Massumi, Brian. "Requiem for Our Prospective Dead (Toward a Participatory Critique of Capitalist Power)." In *Deleuze and Guattari: New Mappings in Politics, Philosophy, and Culture,* edited by Eleanor Kaufman and Kevin Jon Heller, 40–64. Minneapolis: University of Minnesota Press, 1998.

Mauer, Marc. "Testimony of Marc Mauer, Executive Director, The Sentencing Project, before the House Judiciary Subcommittee on Crime, Terrorism and Homeland Security." U.S. House of Representatives, Washington, D.C., http://judiciary. house.gov/hearings/pdf/Mauer100609.pdf (June 9, 2010): 2.

McCall, Leslie. "The Complexity of Intersectionality." *Signs: Journal of Women in Culture and Society* (2005), 1772–1800.

McIntosh, Peggy. "White Privilege: Unpacking the Invisible Knapsack." In *Race, Class, & Gender: An Anthology,* 6th ed., edited by Margaret L. Andersen and Patricia Hill Collins, 98–102. Belmont, Calif.: Wadsworth, 2007.

McIntyre, Lisa J. *The Practical Skeptic: Core Concepts in Sociology.* Boston: McGraw-Hill, 2008.

McNamee, Stephen J., and Robert K. Miller Jr. *The Meritocracy Myth.* Lanham, Md.: Rowman & Littlefield, 2009.

McNamee, Stephen J., and Robert K. Miller Jr. "The Meritocracy Myth." *Sociation Today* 2, no. 1. www.ncsociology.org/sociationtoday/v21/merit.htm, 2004 (July 15, 2010).

McSweeny, Terrell. "Helping Middle Class Families with Soaring Child Care Costs." The Middle Class Task Force of the Vice President of the United States, www. whitehouse.gov/blog/2010/01/29/helping-middle-class-families-with-soaring-child-care-costs.

Merton, Robert K. *Social Theory and Social Structure.* New York: Free Press, 1957.

Mickelson, Roslyn Arlin, and Stephen Samuel Smith. "Can Education Eliminate Race, Class, and Gender Inequality?" In *Race, Class and Gender: An Anthology,* 7th ed., edited by Margaret L. Andersen and Patricia Hill Collins, 407–15. Belmont, Calif.: Wadsworth Cengage Learning, 2010.

Mills, C. Wright. *The Sociological Imagination.* Oxford: Oxford University Press, 1959.

Minnesota State University Mankato Museum. (June 18, 2010).

Morrison, Toni. *The Bluest Eye.* Holt, Rinehart and Winston, Inc., 1970.

Motomura, Hiroshi. "Impulsive Extremism." *Room for Debate* (blog). *New York Times.* http://roomfordebate.blogs.nytimes.com/2010/04/26/will-arizonas-immigration-law-survive (April 26, 2010).

Murray, Charles. *Losing Ground: American Social Policy, 1950–1980.* New York: Basic Books, Inc., 1984, 147–53.

Myers, David. *Psychology.* 9th ed. New York: Worth Publishers, 2010.

Myrdal, Gunnar. *An American Dilemma: The Negro Problem and Modern Democracy.* New York: Harper & Brothers, 1944.

Myser, Catherine. "Differences from Somewhere: The Normativity of Whiteness in Bioethics in the United States." *American Journal of Bioethics* 3, no. 2 (Spring 2003): 1–11.

National Association for the Advancement of Colored People, "NAACP: Rosa Parks," www.naacp.org/pages/naacp-history-rosa-parks (September 28, 2010).

Nerio, Ron. "The Factories Have Gone: A Memoir." Unpublished manuscript, last modified September 12, 2010. Microsoft Word file.

Neubeck, Kenneth J., and Noel A. Cazenave. *Welfare Racism: Playing the Race Card Against America's Poor*. New York: Routledge, 2001.

Nier, Jason A., Samuel L. Gaertner, John F. Dovidio, Brenda S. Banker, Christine M. Ward, and Mary C. Rust. "Changing Interracial Evaluations and Behavior: The Effects of a Common Group Identity." *Group Processes and Intergroup Relations* 4, no. 4 (October 2001): 299–316.

Noel, Jeffrey G., Daniel L. Wann, and Nyla R. Branscombe. "Peripheral Ingroup Membership Status and Public Negativity toward Outgroups." *Journal of Personality and Social Psychology* 68, no. 1 (January 1995): 127–37.

Obama, Barack. *Dreams from My Father: A Story of Race and Inheritance*. New York: Three Rivers Press, 1995/2004.

O'Brien, Laurie T., Alison Blodorn, AnGelica Alsbrooks, Reesa Dube, Glenn Adams, and Jessica C. Nelson. "Understanding White Americans' Perceptions of Racism in Hurricane Katrina-Related Events." *Group Processes & Intergroup Relations* 12, no. 4 (July 2009): 431–44.

O'Brien, Laurie T., and Christian S. Crandall. "Stereotype Threat and Arousal: Effects on Women's Math Performance." *Personality and Social Psychology Bulletin* 29, no. 6 (January 2003): 782–9.

O'Brien, Laurie T., Christian S. Crandall, April Horstman-Reser, Ruth Warner, AnGelica Alsbrooks, and Alison Blodorn. "But I'm No Bigot: How Prejudiced White Americans Maintain Unprejudiced Self-Images." *Journal of Applied Social Psychology* 40, no. 4 (April 2010): 917–46.

"OECD in Figures 2009." *OECD Observer*, Supplement 1 (2009).

Okun, Arthur. *Equality and Efficiency: The Big Tradeoff*. Washington, D.C.: The Brookings Institution Press, 1975.

Omi, Michael, and Howard Winant. *Racial Formation in the United States: From the 1960s to the 1990s*. 2nd ed. New York: Routledge, 1994.

Operario, Don, and Susan T. Fiske, "Racism Equals Power Plus Prejudice: A Social Psychological Equation for Racial Oppression." In *Confronting Racism: The Problem and the Response*, edited by Jennifer Lynn Eberhardt and Susan T. Fiske. Thousand Oaks, Calif.: Sage Publications, Inc., 1998.

Oppenheimer, David B. "Why France Needs to Collect Data on Racial Identity—In a French Way." *Hastings International and Comparative Law Review* (2008): 31(2).

Orenstein, Peggy. *Schoolgirls: Young Women, Self-Esteem, and the Confidence Gap*. New York: Anchor, 1994.

Painter, Nell Irvin. *The History of White People.* New York: W. W. Norton & Company, 2010.

Painter, Nell Irvin. "Soul Murder and Slavery: Toward a Fully Loaded Cost Accounting." In *U.S. History as Women's History: New Feminist Essays,* edited by Linda K. Kerber, Alice Kessler-Harris, and Kathryn Kish Sklar, 125–46. Chapel Hill: University of North Carolina Press, 1995.

Penner, Louis A., John F. Dovidio, Donald Edmondson, Rhonda K. Dailey, Tsveti Markova, Terrance L. Albrecht, and Samuel L. Gaertner. "The Experience of Discrimination and Black-White Health Disparities in Medical Care." *Journal of Black Psychology* 35, no. 2 (May 2009): 180–203.

Perry, Theresa, Claude Steele, and Asa G. Hilliard III. *Young, Gifted, and Black: Promoting High Achievement among African-American Students.* Boston: Beacon Press, 2003.

Pettigrew, Thomas F. "Normative Theory in Intergroup Relations: Explaining Both Harmony and Conflict." *Psychology & Developing Societies* 3, no. 1 (March 1991): 3–16.

Public Broadcasting Corporation. "1776: Birth of 'Caucasian.'" *Race: The Power of an Illusion.* www.pbs.org/race/003_RaceTimeline/003_01-timeline.htm, 2003 (June 30, 2010).

Public Broadcasting Corporation. "1887: Jim Crow Segregation Begins." *Race: The Power of an Illusion.* www.pbs.org/race/003_RaceTimeline/003_01-timeline.htm, 2003 (June 30, 2010).

"Questions and Answers Regarding University of Michigan Former Admissions Policies." University of Michigan, Revised, www.vpcomm.umich.edu/admissions/archivedocs/q&a.html (February 19, 2003).

Race, Ethnicity, and Genetics Working Group. "The Use of Racial, Ethnic, and Ancestral Categories in Human Genetics Research." *American Journal of Human Genetics* 77, no. 4 (October 2005): 519–32.

Rath, Arun. "The Return of Harold and Kumar." *Studio 360* episode entitled "Morris, Abu Ghraib, Film Club." Aired on National Public Radio, www.studio360.org/2008/apr/25/the-return-of-harold-and-kumar/, April 2008 (January 24, 2010).

Reddy, Maureen T. "Smashing the Rules of Racial Standing." In *Race in the College Classroom: Pedagogy and Politics,* edited by Bonnie TuSmith and Maureen T. Reddy, 51–61. New Brunswick, N.J.: Rutgers University Press, 2002.

Riek, Blake M., Eric W. Mania, Samuel L. Gaertner, Stacy A. McDonald, and Marika J. Lamoreaux. "Does a Common Ingroup Identity Reduce Intergroup Threat?," *Group Processes and Intergroup Relations* 13, no. 4 (July 2010): 403–23.

Rodgers, Tom. "Native American Poverty: A Challenge Too Often Ignored." Spotlight on Poverty and Opportunity, www.spotlightonpoverty.org/ExclusiveCommentary.aspx?id=0fe5c04e-fdbf-4718-980c-0373ba823da7 (June 11, 2010).

Rodriguez, Gregory. "The Dark Side of White." *Los Angeles Times* (December 28, 2009).

Roediger, David R. *The Wages of Whiteness: Race and the Making of the American Working Class*. Revised ed. London: Verso, 1991.

Rosenthal, Harriet E. S., Richard J. Crisp, and Mein-Woei Suen. "Improving Performance Expectancies in Stereotypic Domains: Task Relevance and the Reduction of Stereotype Threat." *European Journal of Social Psychology* 37, no. 3 (May–June 2007): 586–97.

Rothenberg, Paula. *What's the Problem? A Brief Guide to Critical Thinking*. New York: Worth Publishers, Inc., 2010.

Rothenberg, Paula. *Invisible Privilege: A Memoir about Race, Class and Gender*. Lawrence: University Press of Kansas, 2000.

Saez, Emmanuel. "Striking It Richer: The Evolution of Top Incomes in the United States." http://elsa.berkeley.edu/~saez/saez-UStopincomes-2008.pdf (August 15, 2009).

Saint Louis, Catherine. "Black Hair, Still Tangled in Politics." *New York Times* (August 26, 2009).

Sanders, Rickie. "Gender Equity in the Classroom: An Arena for Correspondence." *Women's Studies Quarterly* 28, no. 3/4 (Fall–Winter 2000): 182–93.

Saunders, Lisa, and William Darity Jr. "Feminist Theory and Racial Economic Inequality." In *Feminist Economics Today*, edited by Marianne A. Ferber and Julie A. Nelson, 101–14. Chicago & London: The University of Chicago Press, 2003.

Senate Bill 1070. State of Arizona Forty-ninth Legislature Second Regular Session (2010).

Sentencing Project: Research and Advocacy for Reform. www.sentencingproject.org/template/page.cfm?id=128 (May 30, 2010).

Shapiro, Thomas M. "The Hidden Cost of Being African American." In *Race, Class and Gender: An Anthology*, 7th ed., edited by Margaret L. Andersen and Patricia Hill Collins. 129–36. Belmont, Calif.: Wadsworth Cengage Learning, 2010.

Shapiro, Thomas. *Hidden Cost of Being African American: How Wealth Perpetuates Inequality*. New York: Oxford University Press, 2004.

Shaughnessy, John, Eugene Zechmeister, and Jeanne Zechmeister. *Research Methods in Psychology*. 8th ed. New York: McGraw-Hill, 2008.

Simmons, Rachel. *Odd Girl Out: The Hidden Culture of Aggression in Girls*. San Diego, Calif.: Harcourt, Inc., 2002.

Snyder, Mark, Elizabeth D. Tanke, and Ellen Berscheid. "Social Perception and Interpersonal Behavior." *Journal of Personality and Social Psychology* 35, no. 9 (September 1977): 656–66.

Staiger, Annegret. "Whiteness as Giftedness: Racial Formation at an Urban High School." *Social Problems* 51, no. 2 (May 2004): 161–81.

Steele, Claude M. *Whistling Vivaldi: And Other Clues to How Stereotypes Affect Us*. New York: Norton, 2010.

Steele, Claude M. "A Threat in the Air: How Stereotypes Shape Intellectual Identity and Performance." In *Foundations of Critical Race Theory in Education*, edited by

Edward Taylor, David Gillborn, and Gloria Ladson-Billings, 163–89. New York: Routledge, 2009.

Steele, Claude M. "Thin Ice: 'Stereotype Threat' and Black College Students." *Atlantic Monthly* 284, no. 2 (August 1999): 44–54.

Steele, Claude M., and Joshua Aronson. "Stereotype Threat and the Intellectual Test Performance of African Americans." *Journal of Personality and Social Psychology* 69, no. 5 (November 1995): 797–811.

Steinem, Gloria. "Women Are Never Front-Runners." *New York Times* (January 8, 2008).

Stephan, Walter G., and Cookie W. Stephan. "Intergroup Anxiety." *Journal of Social Issues* 41, no. 3 (Fall 1985): 157–75.

Stiglitz, Joseph. "Information and the Change in the Paradigm in Economics." Noble Prize Lecture, http://nobelprize.org/nobel_prizes/economics/laureates/2001/stiglitz-lecture.pdf (December 8, 2001).

Strassman, Diana. "Not a Free Market: The Rhetoric of Disciplinary Authority in Economics." In *Beyond Economic Man*, edited by Marianne A. Ferber and Julie A. Nelson. Chicago: University of Chicago Press, 1993.

Sue, Derald Wing. *Microaggressions in Everyday Life: Race, Gender, and Sexual Orientation*. Hoboken, N.J.: John Wiley & Sons, Inc., 2010.

Sugrue, Thomas J. *Origins of the Urban Crisis*. Princeton, N.J.: Princeton University Press, 2005.

Sumner, William Graham. *Folkways*. New York: Ginn, 1906.

Tajfel, Henri. "Experiments in Intergroup Discrimination." *Scientific American* 225, no. 5 (May 1970): 96–102.

Tajfel, Henri, and John C. Turner. "The Social Identity Theory of Intergroup Behavior." *Psychology of Intergroup Relations* 7 (1986): 7–24.

Tajfel, Henri, and John Turner. "An Integrative Theory of Intergroup Conflict." In *The Social Psychology of Intergroup Relations*, edited by William C. Austin and Stephen Worchel, 33–47. Monterey, Calif.: Brooks/Cole, 1979.

Tapper, Melbourne. *In the Blood: Sickle Cell Anemia and the Politics of Race*. Philadelphia: University of Pennsylvania Press, 1998.

Tatum, Beverly Daniel. *"Why Are All the Black Kids Sitting Together in the Cafeteria?": And Other Conversations about Race*. New York: Basic, 2003.

Tax Policy Center. "A Citizens' Guide for the 2008 Election and Beyond." www.taxpolicycenter.org/briefing-book (August 5, 2010).

Taylor, Edward, David Gillborn, and Gloria Ladson-Billings, eds. *Foundations of Critical Race Theory in Education*. New York: Routledge, 2009.

Tom, David, and Harris Cooper. "The Effect of Student Background on Teacher Performance Attributions: Evidence for Counterdefensive Patterns and Low Expectancy Cycles." *Basic and Applied Social Psychology* 7, no. 1 (March 1986): 53–62.

Underwriting Manual. Washington, D.C.: Federal Housing Administration, 1938.

United States Census Bureau, *2009 American Community Survey*.

United States Census Bureau, *2008 American Community Survey.*

United States Census Bureau, *2007 American Community Survey.*

United States Census Bureau. Historical Income Tables, Current Population Survey Table H-3, www.census.gov/hhes/www/income/data/historical/household/h03AR.xls (August 1, 2010).

United States Census Bureau. "Income, Poverty, and Health Insurance Coverage in the United States: 2008." Current Population Reports, www.census.gov/prod/2009pubs/p60-236.pdf, August 5, 2010 (September 19, 2009): Table C-1.

United States Census Bureau. "Occupations." *Fourteenth Census of the United States Taken in the Year 1920.* Volume IV. www2.census.gov/prod2/decennial/documents/41084484v4_TOC.pdf.

United States Census Bureau. *Public Education Finances, 2008* (2010).

United States Constitution. Article One, Section Two. Modified by the Fourteenth Amendment, Section Two, www.usconstitution.net (June 11, 2010).

United States Department of Health and Human Services. *Characteristics and Financial Circumstances of TANF Recipients Fiscal Year 2008*, Tables 8 and 41. www.acf.hhs.gov/programs/ofa/character/FY2008/indexfy08.htm (July 15, 2010).

United States Holocaust Memorial Museum. "Jewish Population of Europe in 1933: Population Data by Country." *Holocaust Encyclopedia.* www.ushmm.org/wlc/en/article.php?ModuleId=10005161#RelatedArticles, 2010 (June 22, 2010).

Urrieta Jr., Luis. "Community Identity Discourse and the Heritage Academy: Colorblind Educational Policy and White Supremacy." *International Journal of Qualitative Studies in Education* 19, no. 4 (July–August 2006): 455–76.

Wallerstein, Immanuel Maurice. *The Modern World-System: Capitalist Agriculture and the Origins of the European World-Economy in the Sixteenth Century.* New York: Academic Press, 1974.

Whitley, Bernard E., and Mary E. Kite. *The Psychology of Prejudice and Discrimination.* 2nd ed. Belmont, Calif.: Wadsworth, 2009.

Williams, Gregory Howard. *Life on the Color Line: The True Story of a White Boy Who Discovered He Was Black.* New York: Plume, 1995.

Williams, Raymond. *Marxism and Literature.* Oxford: Oxford University Press, 1977.

Wilson, Dawn K., Karen A. Kirtland, Barbara E. Ainsworth, and Cheryl L. Addy. "Socioeconomic Status and Perceptions of Access and Safety for Physical Activity." *Annals of Behavioral Medicine* 28, no. 1 (August 2004): 20–28.

Wise, Tim. *White Like Me: Reflections on Race from a Privileged Son.* Brooklyn, N.Y.: Soft Skull Press, 2005.

Wiseman, Rosalind. *Queen Bees & Wannabees: Helping Your Daughter Survive Cliques, Gossip, Boyfriends, and the New Realities of Girl World.* New York: Three Rivers Press, 2002.

Word, Carl O., Mark P. Zanna, and Joel Cooper. "The Nonverbal Mediation of Self-Fulfilling Prophecies in Interracial Interaction." *Journal of Experimental Social Psychology* 10, no. 2 (March 1974): 109–20.

Zenk, Shannon N., Amy J. Schulz, Teretha Hollis-Neely, Richard T. Campbell, Nellie Holmes, Gloria Watkins, Robin Nwankwo, and Angela Odoms-Young. "Fruit and Vegetable Intake in African Americans: Income and Store Characteristics." *American Journal of Preventive Medicine* 29, no. 1 (July 2005): 1–9.

Zuckerman, Marvin. "Some Dubious Premises in Research and Theory on Racial Differences: Scientific, Social, and Ethical Issues." *American Psychologist* 45, no. 12 (December 1990): 1297–303.

Index

232 ～ Index

PSID. *See* Panel Study of Income
Dynamics

Raaum, Oddbjörn, 106
race: American Anthropological
Association on, 31; Armelagos
on, 7; based on physical traits, 25;
biological roots of, 33–35; biology
influencing, 44–46; Blumenbach
distinguishing between, 25; Bonilla-
Silva on, 7; choosing, 83; Darwin
on, 63; defined, 6–7, 83, 94;
disagreements over distinctions of,
63; distribution on television, 125;
ethnicity distinguished from, 7;
Goodman on, 7, 35; Graves on, 34;
Ignatiev on, 60–61; incarceration
and, 158; Irish, 71; Lewontin
classifying, 30–31; nature based
theories of, 26–27; origins of,
61; Painter on, 7; physical traits
defining, 33–34; power and, 64;
ranking, 28; Rodriguez on, 83;
social construction of, 62–67; social
movements and, 82; unemployment
by, *157*; United States Census
defining, 83–84; welfare and, 173;
Zuckerman on, 33
Race: The Power of an Illusion, 25
racial identity development, 16
racism, 12–14, 100, 122; as
aggression, 197–99; aversive,
192–93; avoiding discussion of,
139; Batur on, 12; Benokraitis
on, 150; coded expressions of,
192–93; conceptualizing, 13; critical
antiracism education, 123; denying
modern importance of, 191–92;
and economic system, 92; Ezekiel
on, 12; Feagin on, 12; fear of,
121–22; in France, 94; Graves on,
190–91; harms everyone, 190–91;
intentional, 12; intersectionality

and, 86; misconceptions about,
12; and power, 93; Reddy on,
118; responsibility to address,
192; stereotype threat created by,
133; science and, 26, 44, 190; and
status, 73; subtle, 124, 137, 193,
197; Tatum on, 13, 66–67, 192;
unintentional, 67, 143n22, 121;
Vera on, 12; white teachers and,
143n22
racism, institutional, 12, 150, 170;
Feagin on, 150; health disparities
and, 45; invisibility of, 128, 150;
landfills and, 45
Rath, Arun, 125–26
rational choice theory, 109, 112, 113,
156–57, 181, 182
recidivism, 44
Reddy, Maureen T., 118
redlining neighborhoods, 110
religion, 3, 36, 81, *See also* Catholic
Church
replication, 30, 31–32, 129, 193, 198
Rodgers, Tom, 82
Rodriguez, Gregory, 83
Roed, Knut, 106
Roediger, David R., 73, 74, 97n17,
100–101, 161
Roosevelt, Franklin D., 174
Ross, Lee D., 132
Rothenberg, Paula, 122–23

Saez, Emmanuel, 107
Saint Louis, Catherine, 151–52
Sami people, 30, 50n19
sampling, 30, 45
Saunders, Lisa, 153
*Savage Inequalities: Children in America's
Schools* (Kozol, Jonathan), 121,
134–36
SCF. *See* Survey of Consumer Finance
school: choice decisions, 119; funding,
134–36; legacy applicants, 176;

~

About the Authors

Jean Halley is an associate professor of sociology at Wagner College. Her book, *Boundaries of Touch: Parenting and Adult-Child Intimacy* (2007) is a cultural studies, social history of adult-child touch and parenting in the white, middle-class United States. Halley has numerous other publications, including four articles involving the study of whiteness in the journal *Qualitative Inquiry*. She assisted Patricia Ticineto Clough in editing and has an essay in *The Affective Turn: Theorizing the Social* (2007), and she is currently completing her next book, *The Parallel Lives of Women and Cows: Meat Markets*, a mix of memoir and social history of cattle ranching and the U.S. beef industry (Palgrave Macmillan, forthcoming 2012). Halley holds a PhD in sociology from the Graduate Center of the City University of New York and a master's degree in theology from Harvard University.

Amy Eshleman, an associate professor of psychology at Wagner College, regularly teaches courses on race, class, gender, and sexuality, in which she shares her research on expressions of prejudice with students. She holds a PhD from the University of Kansas.

Ramya Vijaya is an associate professor of economics at Richard Stockton College of New Jersey. At Stockton, besides courses in economics, she also teaches interdisciplinary courses on gender, inequality, and diversity issues. Her research is in the area of labor markets, globalization, and feminist political economy. She has published multiple articles on the impact of globalization on labor and on feminist perspectives in economics. Vijaya holds a PhD in economics from American University.